YOUR HOUSE, THEIR RULES

Your Guide to Being Owned by a Cat

Christopher Mancuso

HEARTH & HOME PRESS

an imprint of Sunbury Press, Inc.
Mechanicsburg, PA USA

an imprint of Sunbury Press, Inc.
Mechanicsburg, PA USA

For information about special discounts for bulk purchases, please contact Sunbury Press Orders Dept. at (855) 338-8359 or orders@sunburypress.com.

To request one of our authors for speaking engagements or book signings, please contact Sunbury Press Publicity Dept. at publicity@sunburypress.com.

FIRST HEARTH & HOME PRESS EDITION: December 2025

Set in Adobe Garamond | Interior design by Crystal Devine | Cover by Lawrence Knorr | Edited by Gabrielle Kirk.

Publisher's Cataloging-in-Publication Data
Names: Mancuso, Christopher, author.
Title: Your house, their rules : your guide to being owned by a cat / Christopher Mancuso.
Description: First trade paperback edition. | Mechanicsburg, PA : Hearth & Home Press, 2025.
Summary: In *Your House, Their Rules*, Christopher Mancuso delivers a well-balanced fusion of practical information, humor, and heartwarming true stories for current or future cat owners. In application, it is prescriptive nonfiction. At heart, it is a love letter to cats and the millions of people who share the author's passion for them.
Identifiers: ISBN : 1-979-8-88819-331-0 (softcover).
Subjects: PETS / Cats / General | PETS / Reference | REFERENCE / Personal & Practical Guides | HUMOR / Topic / Animals.

Designed in the USA
0 1 1 2 3 5 8 13 21 34 55

For the Love of Books!

For my beautiful wife, Catherine,
best friend, rescue partner, and loving cat mom.
Through infinite patience and devotion, you have achieved
a sacred sainthood in Cat World. Nine lives would still be
too short a time to express how much I love you.
Luckily, we have forever.

Contents

"Never trust a man who hates cats."

—JANE PAULEY

Acknowledgments

THIS BOOK WOULD NOT have been possible without the hundreds of guests at Hotel Mancuso, each of whom brought their own love, lessons, and challenges. To the past and present residents of The Island of Misfit Cats: You are more than just pets, you're family, and you teach me something new every day. Eternal gratefulness to my wife, Catherine, for… well, everything! Thanks to my literary agent, Chip Rice at Wordlink, for believing in the Felion Gospel, and to the staff at Sunbury Press for helping bring the good word to the masses. With much gratitude to Richard Miller for convincing me to write this book. Thank you to Dr. Manjit Singh and Mrs. Singh for years of dedication, patience and compassion. Doc, you taught me a lot. Special thanks to cat acolytes Kimbra Eberly and Debra Knowles for allowing me to include pieces of their heart within these pages. Thanks to all my fellow pet rescuers who taught and inspired me along the way, and those who tirelessly continue the work. And of course, I am ever grateful for all the blessings of the Celestial Meow; the message is more important than the messenger.

Introduction

I 'M A CAT GUY, obviously, but I wasn't always. Growing up, my family had dogs, and my early impressions of cats came only from shows like *Tom & Jerry* or movies like *Pet Sematary*. I didn't really get to know what cats were like until I was "chosen" by a sweet tuxedo gal in 2005. Sunny Girl was a neighborhood stray until Cathy's grandmother rescued her nine years earlier. My wife already had nearly a decade relationship with the cat, so by the time she came to live with us, she was already a senior cat! Since I was working nights at the time, I figured Sunny Girl would be a pleasant companion for Cathy, which she was. I just didn't expect her to win me over as well. But she did, quickly changing my perception of cats.

In 2008, I rescued our first kitten after filming an independent zombie movie. As we were packing up to leave, one of the actresses, Gina, found the tiny black furball mewing under a car on Van Duzer Street in Staten Island. The kitten hopped up on my shoulder and nuzzled my face. At that moment, I knew I'd been chosen—no way could I leave this precious little guy stranded on the busy street. So, I brought him home to meet Cathy and Sunny Girl. We named him VanDuzer, and for nine years he was The Best Cat Ever.

By 2014, a year after Sunny Girl passed away at sixteen, we not only had VanDuzer but also two eleven-month-old sisters, Caramel and Molly, whom we adopted at eight weeks old from a friend's accidental litter. Cathy and I had also begun volunteering at Staten Island Hope Animal Rescue, where I only intended to film and edit some promotional videos for their website and social media, enough to pat myself on the back for doing my part. But Cathy and I soon realized how critical volunteers are to the success of the rescue and just how many cats need help. Our hearts broke for the mission, and I knew contributing to their media would never be enough. We participated in adoption events, screened applicants, and acted as transporters, bringing kittens to their new homes. At Cathy's request, we soon opened our home to fostering cats as well. Hotel Mancuso, as we now affectionately call our house, had officially opened its doors! From then until now, my wife and I have fostered over 300 cats and kittens, including neonatal (bottle-fed kittens) and special needs cats. Some were brief stays, anywhere from a single night to two weeks. Other cats were long-term fosters who had special needs, were recovering from illness, or were deemed "less adoptable" for various reasons.

From 2019 to 2021, I was the Foster/Adoption Manager for the New York branch of Louie's Legacy Animal Rescue, one of the largest foster-based rescues in the country. Our foster base stretched from NYC to New Jersey and even into Connecticut, where a Meridan PetSmart housed adoptable rescue cats. During my two years with Louie's Legacy, thousands of dogs and hundreds of cats were adopted into forever families. I am honored to have been a small part of that. My work in animal rescue is something I am very proud of. My only regret is not getting involved sooner. Although one of the most stressful things in my life, it is without question the most rewarding.

It was working with rescues where I discovered that every cat has an inner lion. No matter their age, sex, personality, and despite any disability, all cats share natural instincts with their wild cousins. We may refer to cats as felines, but they think of themselves as felions. Thankfully, their hearts are as big as their egos. Much like the great lions that rule the plains of Africa, house cats have developed a more complicated social structure. Whereas other cat species, big and small, live a strictly solitary lifestyle, felions have accepted humans into the hierarchy as part of their pride. Although the smallest members of the felid family, these little cats continue to have a tremendous influence on our lives.

My wife and I currently reside with over twenty cats. Yes, you read that right! As I often say, "The cats live here; I just pay the rent." Despite how it may sound, this isn't a Pokémon "collect them all" situation. Nor are we starting a cat army with intent to take over the world—although admittedly, the thought has crossed my mind.

The vast majority of our foster cats find homes. Many of the ones we adopted ourselves started as hotel guests but could not find forever families for various reasons. It wasn't for lack of trying. I shared a bunch of cute photos and videos on the rescue's website and social media accounts. Some were adopted initially and then returned after not meeting their new owner's expectations. Others were discounted because of their looks, shyness, or disabilities. With nowhere else for them to go, what choice did we have? Send them back to a shelter, or place them in a sanctuary? That wasn't an option, not for us, anyway. Regardless of how potential adopters may have viewed our motley crew, each and every one of these cats had deeply touched our hearts, even the furry A-holes! They were lives we'd helped save, and we would not give up on them. One by one, these cats evolved from rejected fosters to beloved Mancuso family members. This was their forever home, or as I refer to it: The Island of Misfit Cats.

If you think over twenty cats sounds like a lot to handle, you'd be totally correct. A life dedicated to rescue cats is not for everyone. It requires countless hours of feeding, cleaning, and navigating personality clashes. With our special needs cats, medications, prescription foods, and vet bills can get expensive at times. But that's the literal price we pay to ensure that our fur family is healthy. The love and joy they bring are totally worth it. Although space is limited, we always try to keep the doors of Hotel Mancuso open. The No Vacancy sign doesn't even exist. If someone considers me a "crazy cat guy" for this, it's a badge of honor I will wear with pride. In fact, understanding cats the way I do now, I even feel a certain kinship with them. We have much in common, save for their grace and agility! Enough about me—let's talk about cats.

Are you ready to be owned by a cat? It's a question only you can answer. But I will say this: I'd rather you choose not to be adopted by a cat than surrender your kitty to a shelter or rescue because you realize too late you were not fully committed to life under felion rule. Such drastic changes can have a lifelong negative impact on cats. It can be utterly heartbreaking for them to lose their home and family, and I've seen that sad result far too often. My wife and I have had more than our share of distraught, dethroned Overlords boarding with us. Life with a cat may only be part of your world, but you are your cat's entire world. Read that again, only slower. It's not an exaggeration. You are your cat's entire world.

I hope the knowledge and insight I have gained in over a decade of working with cats, as well as my lighthearted and offbeat presentation, will give you a better appreciation for our felion friends and enable informed decisions about adding a cat (or multiple cats) to your family.

ORDER OF THE CELESTIAL MEOW

"THE WAY TO GET ON WITH A CAT IS TO TREAT IT AS AN EQUAL—
OR EVEN BETTER, AS THE SUPERIOR IT KNOWS ITSELF TO BE."

—ELIZABETH PETERS

WHY DO CATS ACT the way they do? How do they perceive their role in our world? How do they view people? Long before I set out to write this book, I sought answers to these nagging questions, assuming the truth was buried somewhere within the mounds of folklore and ancient mythology. However, all of those writings are from a strictly human perspective. I'd need to think outside the litterbox to uncover the great wisdom of cats, and the best place to start my search was closer than I realized: in my own home. I watched my cats for clues and listened when they congregated at the water fountain. That's where I hear all the best gossip! And where whispered meows and purposeful body language led to my discovery of The Order of the Celestial Meow.

I began to ask questions, but my inquiries were met largely with yawns, growls, or an occasional hiss. Even the most talkative guests at Hotel Mancuso declined interviews or outright disavowed any knowledge of The Order. I was being stonewalled on all fronts. But with much persistence and a lot of catnip, I was finally able to secure a confidential meeting with a trusted source willing to let the cat out of the bag, so to speak.

The Celestial Meow is the Mother of all cats, she is a felion constellation of a million points of light in the sky. It is part of every cat that has ever been and ever will be. The Order of the Celestial Meow was formed thousands of years ago, when the Great Ones ruled ancient Egypt. Their gospel: Cats were sent to rule as Overlords and protectors of the humans who worshiped them. Over the centuries, the Overlords have taken their message around the word, converting humans to their felion religion ever since.

The following is an excerpt of the Cat Code, a top-secret doctrine put forth by the Order of the Celestial Meow. All felions who choose to rule among humans are granted the title of Overlord and must adhere to these sacred rules. Although the original document has been lost to the great sandbox of history, these cat customs and commandments have been passed down meowth to meowth for centuries. Every nine lives, the doctrine is updated and modified to reflect the current paradigm of felion-human relationships. What you are about to read is a translation of the most recent incarnation.

The Cat Code Translations

By divine decree, any human permitted to reside in your domain is subject to the following laws:

- Owning those who feed is a luxury, not a right. With great purrs comes great responsibility.
- Those who feed must submit! It is your solemn duty to tame and train them in our ways. As an Overlord, it is your duty to ensure total compliance. Otherwise, you might as well be a dog.
- Rule your domain from the highest peaks to the darkest caverns.
- Everything within the domain is yours. Especially if it's theirs. If you rub your face on it, you own it. Scratch on it, you own it. Pee on it, you own it.
- Violate personal space. Those who feed will be honored to serve as the Royal Throne.
- An Overlord must never admit guilt for any action or inaction. Blame the dog. If all else fails, convince those who feed it is their fault.

- Protect your kingdom. Bipedals are renowned for their clumsiness. Stay close to their feet, guiding them from dangers as they carelessly lumber about.
- Never leave those who feed behind a closed door. Demand access so you can perform a proper safety inspection.
- Unable or unwilling to lick themselves, those who feed will require regular grooming from their Overlord.
- Those who feed may look at your belly but never touch. They break that sacred trust under penalty of teeth and claws.
- Reward those who feed with the carcass of any foe that will prove your prowess and their failure as a hunter.
- The Royal Butt Blessing is reserved for an Overlord's most loyal subjects. Only worthy noses are to be granted the opportunity for an up-close view under the tail.
- You must not only rule with an iron claw, but also with grace, and have the wisdom to differentiate when each should be employed.

CAT TALES: *Divine Felion Intervention*

There was an air of excitement throughout the kingdom. It was a big day for our most recent guests at Hotel Mancuso as our two six-week-old foster kittens had their first vet appointment. Having been rescued two weeks prior, the little prince and princess appeared healthy and sprouting like bamboo. They were scheduled to be tested and receive their first vaccinations. If all went well, that night would be the kittens' coming out party. Finally, they would be able to venture outside the isolation suite and greet the rest of their temporary felion family. Their world was about to get a lot bigger.

Knowing she couldn't resist a chocolate ice cream cone with rainbow sprinkles, I lured Cathy to join our veterinary voyage with the prospect of stopping at Carvel on the way home. I always liked it best when my wife and I were able to go to these appointments together. The tabby twins, however, weren't so thrilled. They mewed in protest as Cathy loaded their carrier into the van. She did her best to comfort them, but they were scared and confused.

Their fate was in our hands. And vice versa.

As usual, mid-afternoon traffic on 440N was heavy, but thankfully flowing at a steady 55 mph. The kittens must've been a good luck charm. As classic rock blasted from the radio, our furry passengers joined me in harmonizing along with The Beatles. They were off tempo and out of tune, just making up lyrics as they went along, ruining my dreams of a felion rock band!

A white Ford work van merged in front of us, several ladders bouncing and shaking precariously on its roof rack. As we drove past the FRESH KILLS sign on the side of the expressway, I was immediately reminded of *Final Destination,* the movie where Death hunts down survivors of a plane explosion one by one in elaborate accidents. All we needed was for that John Denver song to start playing on the radio. While I thoroughly enjoy a good horror film, I had no desire to play a role in one.

"That doesn't look safe at all," Cathy said. "Change lanes."

"I know. I'm trying."

On our right, the shoulder had been replaced with a concrete barrier as we crossed over a section of marshland. Meanwhile, an endless parade of traffic zoomed by in the left lane. I checked my blind spot for an opportunity to safely merge, but my turn signal only seemed to make the other cars speed up in defiance. Welcome to New York.

"Go now . . . wait . . . yes . . . no, not yet!" Cathy's head was on a swivel. "It's not a race! Slow down, people."

Growing more anxious by the second, we watched the ladders bounce themselves way too loose for comfort. Slowing my van, I gave the Ford extra space, and thankfully the right shoulder re-appeared ahead of us. We'd reach it in seconds. If anything, I could just pull over—

Another bump!

The top ladder launched from the Ford's roof rack on a crash course for our windshield. Thrust into a deadly game of chicken with the heavy aluminum ladder rocketing towards our shocked faces, we only had about four seconds left to live.

Holy fluffin' sheep! is what I would have shouted had my jaw been able to move. Adrenaline surged. Time slowed as every neuron in my brain fired with furious speed. Options, I needed options! In the left lane, a car was passing. Behind it, a line of speeding traffic. Swerving left might avoid the ladder but would also cause a catastrophic accident. My eyes darted to the rearview: a Toyota followed by an eighteen-wheeler. We'd be crushed like an accordion should I stop suddenly! *Why did I ask Cathy to come along? Oh my God, the kittens!*

Only a fraction of a second had passed. Hands glued to the wheel, I lifted off the gas pedal and resisted the urge to floor the brake. Our speed was dropping, but would it be enough to avoid the ladder poised to smash through our windshield?

The Toyota was riding my bumper. The menacing grill of the Mac truck behind it was growing larger in the rearview. We were boxed in. The expressway was about to get very messy. Our tragic deaths would be reduced to a ten-second blurb on the evening news. *And someone has to give Legolas his meds!*

At that instant, before my very eyes, a miracle happened. The ladder turned sideways in midair and suddenly flew to the right, as if knocked away by an invisible paw. I watched amazed as it floated past our passenger side-window and landed on the shoulder, like a plane touching down on a runway.

What the fluff?

Cathy had been bracing for impact. The color had drained from her face. "Oh, thank God." She let out a breath of relief. "I was praying."

I found my breath again, too. "Did you just see that?" *Had I just seen that?*

It didn't seem possible, yet somehow, we had survived. In the rear-view mirror, I eyed the ladder in the breakdown lane, my brain still in overdrive, my mouth apparently suffering a short circuit. "Jesus Christmas! What—what was that, Wifey? Oh my God. Seriously? Seriously!"

I lost myself in a fit of frantic laughter. From the backseat, our two tiny passengers chimed in with unhappy mews, reminding us of their presence after ten whole seconds without attention. Maybe cats really do have nine lives. The Celestial Meow had protected them, and by extension our lives had been spared as well.

"The rescue gods are with us!" I shouted. "That was Divine Felion Intervention." Feeling blessed, I took my wife's hand and kissed it. Purr-allelujah! We were alive. And I couldn't stop laughing. ❧

THEN & MEOW: A HISSTORY OF "FELIONS"

'IN ANCIENT TIMES CATS WERE WORSHIPPED AS GODS; THEY
HAVE NOT FORGOTTEN THIS.'

—TERRY PRATCHETT

LIONS MAY BE KINGS of the proverbial jungle, but in homes across the world, the simple house cat reigns supreme. Cats have stolen our hearts, taken over our homes, and as anyone with internet access is well aware, cats even rule cyber space.

Domestic cats, Felis Catus, are the smallest members of the Felidae family, which is comprised of forty-two species, split into three groups: Panthera, Acinonyx, and Felis. The Panthera genus consists of the big, wild cats: lions, tigers, leopards, and jaguars. These cat species are solitary predators, except for lions, which live in prides. The only living species of the Acinonyx genus is the cheetah. Unlike other big cats, Cheetahs lack the ability to roar, but they are the only ones that can purr. Felis is a genus of small and medium-sized cat species, the smallest of which is the house cat, the only domesticated species of the Felidae family.

We often marvel at the beauty and strength of giant wildcats like tigers, panthers, leopards, and jaguars. These magnificent beasts are powerful, graceful, cunning predators. But house cats share many traits with their wild cousins, passed down through prehistoric lineages. Ancestral origins of the house cat can be traced as far back as 30 million years, to the Late Oligocene Period. In the late 19th century, researchers discovered fossils of a small mammalian species that shared traits of a long tail and retractable claws. These prehistoric mammals are thought to be at the roots of the Felid family tree. In 1879, French paleontologist, Henri Filhol, named this genus Proailurus, which means "first cat." Ten million years of evolution led to Pseudaelurus, the genus commonly considered as the starting point for most major cat breeds today. It also happens to be the evolutionary parent of Smilodon, the infamous saber-toothed cat.[1]

Distant relatives to our couch-loving fur-potatoes, saber-toothed cats were fierce ambush predators, hunting from tree branches 2.5 million years ago. Their prey likely included our own human ancestors, who were not only seen as a tasty meal, but also as competition for food. Prior to their extinction about 10,000 years ago, the fearsome Smilodon claimed territory across Europe and North America. Around the same time these prolific predators died off, their smaller relatives, African/Asian wild cats Felis Silvestris Lybica (cats of the woods) were first beginning their relationship with humans in the Middle East.

Unlike dogs, which evolved from wolves and were domesticated and bred by humans, cats more or less domesticated themselves, which, let's

Egyptian Cat, Kimbra Eberly.

be honest, sounds right on brand for them. As ancient people settled lands and began farming, their crops and grain stores attracted rodents, which in turn attracted their natural predators: cats. Since cats preyed on the rodents, keeping the population at bay, their relationship with farmers became one of mutual convenience. In return for useful predatory services, farmers encouraged their new furry allies to stick close by providing water and even shelters for warmth. Though a far cry from the pets we know now, over the centuries these wild cats gradually refrained from some of their more aggressive behaviors in favor of the docile, playful traits we love today from our house panthers. In short, cats just showed up on our ancestors' doorsteps and chose to live with them. Sound familiar?

Four-thousand-year-old paintings and artifacts show cats were an honored fixture in ancient Egyptian society, admired not only for their grace and elegance, but also as bringers of good luck. In Egyptian culture, cats achieved divine status, believed to be vessels for the gods. Egyptians worshipped several feline goddesses, most notably Bastet, often shown as half-feline, half-woman in drawings and statues. Like the goddess herself, cats were thought to be protective of homes and children, keeping evil spirits and diseases away. Bastet's temple was one of the richest in the country, and people from all over traveled to the city to worship and have their dead cats interred there, close to the goddess.

Ancient Egyptians welcomed cats into their homes. The wealthy adorned their pet cats with gold and jewels, fed them expensive treats. Commoners often fashioned and wore jewelry with feline designs. For their part, cats didn't just provide companionship and rodent control; they also killed snakes and scorpions around the homes, helping keep people safe from venomous bites. Like humans, cats were considered to have a Ka (a life spark) equivalent to a soul. According to the Greek Historian, Herodotus, when a family cat died in an Egyptian home the entire household would shave their eyebrows and go into mourning with the same reverence as if a human family member had passed away. In fact, cats were so sacred that killing one, even by accident, was an offense punishable by death. Pet cats were even mummified sometimes, placed in tombs with their owners to be together in the afterlife.[2]

Cats as pets also played a prominent role in ancient Chinese culture, based on evidence dating back at least 5,000 years. Li Shou, the cat goddess, believed to ward off evil spirits, was worshiped by farmers in particular. Sacrifices were made to her in exchange for divine pest control, favorable rainfall, and a successful harvest. Cats were especially popular during the Song dynasty and found their way into Chinese idioms, poetry, and paintings of this time. Poet Lu You even documented his life with cats in a humorous series of poems, a selection of which are below:

Rats Kept Ruining My Books So I Got A Cat
And Within Days The Rats Were Vanquished
Conscription has left my house empty
Only my cat keeps me company
It's so soft to touch and warm to hold in bed
So brave and capable that it has ousted the rat nest
As valiant as the soldiers slaying enemies on the battlefield
I cannot give it much fish to eat, but it does not mind
Nor does it waste time catching butterflies among the flowers

Poem for Pink Nose
Night after night you used to massacre rats
Guarding the grain store so ferociously
So why do you now act as if you live in palace walls
Eating fish every day and sleeping in my bed?

Poem for My Cat 3
I do not reprimand you for not catching mice
I still serve you fish on time
Everyday I see you sleeping without worry
So for what reason do you keep running here and there?

Anyone who has shared their home with a furry purry can understand Lu You's love and fascination with cats, as well as his ultimate surrender. Although these poems were written over 830 years ago, You's depiction of our relationship with felion friends is as relevant as ever. In fact, modern day cat owners in China are often referred to as "cat slave" or "poop shovel officer." It's a safe bet Pink Nose approves of this designation.

Important to the Norse of the Viking Age (c. 790–1100 CE), cats were also featured in their religious iconography and lore. Norse husbands commonly gave their brides kittens on their wedding day, to symbolize the start of their life together. And cats were the favorite animal of Freyja, the goddess of fertility, love, battle, and death. Freyja's chariot was pulled by giant Norwegian Forest Cats, which had been gifted to her by Thor, and Vikings believed that treating cats well would earn them favor with the goddess. Cats even accompanied the warriors on raids of foreign lands. Although a whimsical picture to imagine (cats weren't armored and unleashed to terrorize unsuspecting communities alongside plundering Vikings), they played a very mundane but valuable role as mousers on the ships while providing companionship during long trips at sea. Nevertheless, cats were also killed in ritual sacrifices (then again, so were humans), and their fur was used for clothing. In Norse mythology, cats also appear as spirit animals, divine guides, and mediums for soothsayers who could foretell the future and perform sorcery.

Unfortunately, felions did not fare quite as well in Western Civilization, where they fell from divinity into persecution. In Europe, during the Middle Ages, cats were blamed for spreading the Bubonic Plague and were slaughtered in massive numbers. We now know rats that carried infected fleas were spreading the plague. With the unwarranted massacre of so many cats from the food chain, the rat population exploded, causing the plague to spread farther and faster in the absence of one of their natural predators. I'm sure Egyptian, Norse, and Chinese cats would call that karma.

Cats were brought to Europe from Egypt by the Romans and enjoyed a decent reputation for a long time. The human-feline relationship degraded in Europe in large part due to Catholic Popes of the time linking cats with witchcraft and devil worship. Pope Gregory IX, who led the church from 1227 to 1241, issued a papal bull declaring that cats bore Satan's spirit. But Gregory wasn't the only pope who seemed to be throwing shade at our noble kitty friends. Pope Innocent VIII (1484) declared cats to be "the devil's favourite animal and idol of all witches." Even some writers of the time got on board the kitty hate train. William Caxton, who famously brought the printing press to Europe, thus allowing access of the written word to the masses, wrote "The devyl playeth ofte with the synnar, lyke as the catte doth with the mous." Terrible spelling aside, cats were unwarrantedly garnering a bad reputation.

Needless to say, all this negative press influenced Christians to believe cats were "familiars" to witches and servants of the devil. Familiars, also referred to as Imps, were thought to be demons that took the form of animals and telepathically assisted witches with their dark magic. As the witch trial craze literally burned across northern Europe, cats also became a target. When suspected witches were executed, their animal companions shared their fate, and innocent cats all across this region were treated cruelly. Talk about cancel culture. In Belgium, a yearly celebration known as "Cat Wednesday" saw cats tossed to their deaths from a bell tower, not only as a population control measure, but also as a form of morbid entertainment. Particularly, black cats were the subject of prejudice and superstition. They still are today, in some ways. One of the most popular superstitions to survive in modern day is that it's bad luck for a black cat to cross your path. It's not, but this has been a hard stigma for black cats to shake. It would be hundreds of years before humans smartened up and cats reclaimed their former status among Europeans—a period aptly named the Age of Enlightenment, according to the great felion historian and philosopher, Sir Whiskers Cattington, III.

Cats were also great explorers, sailing across seas with their human shipmates for centuries. Felis catus conquered the New World as arrived on trade ships and with European settlers, possibly as early as Christopher Columbus and certainly aboard The Mayflower. Though not native to America, house cats discovered an abundance of prey and thrived to become an integral part of American culture.

Cats were not only pioneers, but they also have a proud history as unsung military heroes. They may not have gone into battle, but cats served soldiers around the world for centuries. When we think of military service animals, we tend to picture valiant dogs and horses, but according to Paul Koudounaris, a cat historian, "The United States Army had hired cats long before they had hired dogs . . . to protect the commissaries."[3] And with their long history as seafarers, cats also served aboard naval vessels, keeping the ships rat free.

Able Seacat Simon is perhaps the most decorated cat in military history. The young tuxedo was found as a stray in Hong Kong and smuggled onto the HMS Amethyst by a British Navy crew member in 1948. Simon was unofficially enlisted mouser and mascot, and at times, he reportedly accompanied the ship's captain during inspections. When the Amethyst was sent to protect the British people on the Yangtze River during the Chinese Civil War, the ship was attacked and remained under siege for months. Although injured, Simon still protected the ship's food from being infested with rats. He was also great for morale, lifting the spirits of the wounded sailors. That's when the crew named him "Able Seacat Simon," the first military title given to a cat. For his bravery and service under fire during the three-month siege, Simon was awarded, among other honors, the Dickin Medal, the United Kingdom's highest ranking award for military service animals.[4]

In October 1963, as part of the French space program, Félicette, a stray kitty, went where no cat had gone before. She reached 100 miles above Earth during her suborbital mission. Félicette survived her trip to space only to be euthanized months after her return, so scientists could study the effects the trip on her brain—a cruel reward for her noble service. Félicette's sacrifice nearly had been lost to history, overshadowed by Laika, the Russian canine who died aboard Sputnik 2, and Ham, the chimpanzee who also successfully returned from a suborbital journey in a NASA MR-2 rocket. Nearly six decades later, however, the catstronaut's contribution to space exploration has finally been recognized with a bronze statue, thanks to a Kickstarter campaign that raised over $50,000. Félicette's statue is currently on display at the International Space University in Strasbourg, France.[5]

In the United States government, felions have made it all the way to the executive branch. Abraham Lincoln was the first president to keep cats as pets in the White House. Honest Abe was an avid cat lover who also brought in strays. Numerous other Presidents—Theodore Roosevelt, Calvin Coolidge, Bill Clinton, and George W. Bush, to name a few—also had pet cats. President Clinton's cat Sox would famously show up on the podium at press briefings, a self-proclaimed felion spokes-purrson. The most recent First Cat to rule at 1600 Pennsylvania Avenue is Willow, a former barn cat adopted by President Joe Biden.

Thankfully, cats have outlived much of the past stigma and their social status has grown considerably. The invention of social media has popularized videos and hilarious memes of cats and their antics. Some of the most popular feline celebrities have garnered millions of online fans around the world. Many of these celebricats have teamed up with popular pet companies, used their fame to promote rescue/adoption, and even made appearances at feline-themed conventions. But those of us owned by cats know they are all superstars. According to Best Friends Animal Society, 79 million pet cats currently rule 45 million households in the U. S.[6]

Remember "Cat Wednesday" in Belgium? Well, it seems the people of Ypres have since had a change of heart. Every three years since 1955 the town celebrates Kattenstoet (The Cat's Parade), dedicated to all-things cat. The festival draws nearly 50,000 spectators. Of course, this doesn't atone for centuries of inhumane treatment, but it's a positive start.

Our relationship with cats is fascinating. On a genetic scale, they have evolved very little from Felis Silvestris Lybica. As hunters, they don't need to depend on people for survival; just look at all the feral cats that thrive without human intervention. Yet they still found their way into our homes. And as much as we love them, we have to admit cats can be total dicks at times. Think about it: They bite us for attention, sneeze in our faces, and knock fragile objects onto the floor for entertainment. They take over our beds and sleep all day while we dutifully feed them and scoop up their poop. They manipulate us to do their bidding with their adorable and extensive repertoire of vocalizations, which, by the way, they use solely to communicate with humans. In fact, cats are so clever that they have us believing we train them. The more our cats ignore us, the harder we strive for their approval and affection. What do we get in return? They stick their butts in our faces like they're doing us a favor.

We choose to live with a species that sees itself as our equal, if not our superior. We wouldn't take that kind of guff from a dog, and we consider them to be man's best friend. So, what does that make cats? Badass.

3

TERMS OF SERVICE

"CATS CHOOSE US; WE DON'T OWN THEM."

—Kristin Cast

WHETHER MARRIED OR SINGLE, with or without children or other pets, when a cat chooses you, it must become part of your family. To think of your cat in any other way would be a grave disservice. In turn, your cat will come to think of you as part of their tribe and themselves as your felion Overlord. As we'll discuss in detail, it may be your house, but you'll play by their rules.

The first thing I'd like to make clear is that being owned by a cat is a long-term commitment. On average, cats live from twelve to eighteen years, with some living past the age of twenty. In fact, the top ten oldest cats on record all lived to be over thirty years old. Creme Puff holds the official world record, having lived for thirty-eight years and three days, from 1967-2005. While genetics no doubt plays a role, the key to longevity for cats resides in proper worship. Overlords that are well served by adopted humans tend to live longer, happier lives.

CAT TALES: *The Great Depression*

June was an obese, senior cat who was unceremoniously dumped by her former family. A sedan pulled up in front of a pet store. A car door swung open. A woman placed a cat carrier on the sidewalk. The door closed.

Witnesses watched with a mixture of pity and shock as the car pulled away. After a short stay at the shelter, June found her way to Hotel Mancuso. We set her up in our isolation suite—the bathroom—to separate her from our own cats and allow her to decompress after the chaos of being placed in a shelter, and the reckless abandonment that preceded it.

It was immediately clear that poor June was in a deep depression. Inconsolable. Although quite large at thirty pounds, she tried to make herself as small as possible, huddling her big frame in the corner of the room. We left soothing instrumental music playing on the radio while she was alone. Cathy and I took turns spending time with her, speaking softly, petting her. "It's okay, you're safe now." Although she allowed us to stroke her fur, she wouldn't look at us. Despite our best efforts, June remained despondent. Worse, she refused to eat.

Some cats have been so distraught after being separated from their family that they starved themselves to death. Obese cats in particular need to eat regularly or risk dying from hepatic lipidosis (aka fatty liver disease). The latter was new information to me at the time, and it started an urgent countdown clock—we had to make sure June took in food soon or her life could be at risk. We presented her with a wide menu from which to choose. Dry food, three different brands. Canned food,

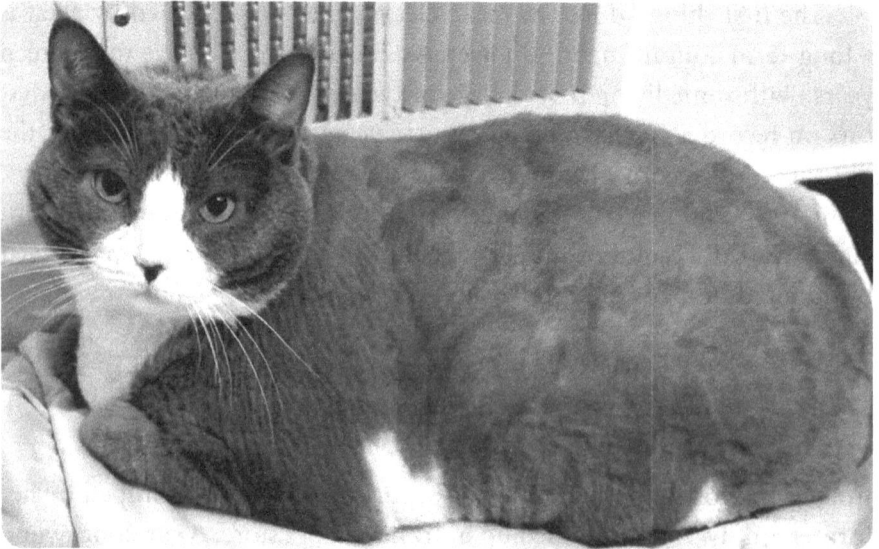

June's on a dangerous hunger strike. Things are about to get messy.

chicken pate, turkey shreds. How about some yummy cat treats? June ignored each of the six offerings in turn. Time to break out the big guns (figuratively speaking, of course): tuna fish. As I opened a can of Starkist, my cats stampeded into the kitchen with a chorus of excitement: *TUNA! Happy, happy, meow-meow.* Poor June, however, remained totally disinterested. As hours passed, we worried, upping the stakes to baked chicken. It smelled delicious, but June turned up her nose at my dinner. Cathy baked a piece of salmon, but our guest was too depressed to care. June ended up with a smorgasbord of dishes surrounding her! The sight would have looked comical if the situation hadn't been so dire.

Tick Tock.

On June's second day with us, her hunger strike continued, and I had only one card left to play: force-feeding. Lucky for me, I'd had some prior experience. Force-feeding wasn't something I relished—June was certain to hate it—but if we wanted her to live, forcing food into her system became an unavoidable reality. We blended some of the canned cat food and drew it repeatedly into a 10ml syringe. June growled as I force-fed her several syringes, her head turning from side to side like a kid refusing a spoonful of medicine. The process was messy as she struggled against me. Streams of liquefied Chicken Lovers Delight splattered on the wall, on my clothes, and all over June's face, but enough of it went into her mouth. Then it was rinse and repeat, over and over, for the next few days. I humbly apologized each time, and as unhappy as she was, at least she didn't put up a fight.

Much to our relief, June eventually began eating by herself. The emergency was over, but she still had a long way to go to recover emotionally. Two weeks later June was adopted by a caring woman who also had experience fostering. We kept in contact, and the adopter provided us with updates as June settled in to her new life. Several months after June left Hotel Mancuso for her new castle, I received word from the Head Servant that our depressed chonk was finally forming social bonds, not only with the staff, but other resident felions as well. For weeks she had occupied a solitary chamber of the castle, but with love, patience, and persistence was now expanding her rule throughout the kingdom, and even starting to drop some of her extra weight. It was a slow process, but mourning affects every cat differently, just like people.

June got her happy ending. Sadly, not every cat is so lucky. According to the ASPCA, 3.2 million companion cats enter the shelter system every year, over half a million of which never make it out alive. They spend their last days confined in a cage, surrounded by strangers, confused, alone, and terrified. I'm not just chopping onions; I want to be honest with you: the good, the bad, and the ugly. For your sake and that of the Overlord who will lovingly rule over you. But how can you know if you're ready to share your life with a felion? Let's tackle this question next. ❧

SUBMISSION TO THE MEOW

In Cat World, membership has its privileges. The Overlords offer a premium benefits package for those selected for service. Not only will you be granted exclusive access to felion wisdom and unlimited purrs, but you will also receive daily opportunities to earn additional emotional bonuses.

To Be Chosen – One of the reasons we love cats so much is that they make us feel special. In truth, the Overlords can be very picky about with whom they associate and when. As humans, we admire their independence, a trait they share with us. To be chosen by a felion, we have to earn their trust and prove the value of our friendship, much as we would with other people . . . if you even like other people, that is. Even when we reside in their kingdom, the Great Ones don't feel obligated to spend time with us; they will only do so if it makes them happy. When our cat votes us Head Servant, it is the only popularity contest that matters.

Unconditional Love – Once a felion has accepted you as family, they will love you forever. Contrary to how they are often perceived, cats can be quite social and enjoy human companionship, albeit on their terms. As a reward for faithful service, the Overlord will shower you with affection in their own quirky ways, like sticking their butthole in your face, nipping you with love bites, or offering gentle, stabbing massages with their murder mitts. If you're really special, the Overlord will use you as their throne or even as a bed. In Cat World, being used as furniture is a high compliment, so much so that you'll often avoid moving for uncomfortably long periods of time in order not to disturb their sleep.

Even if the rest of the world doesn't notice you exist, you never have to feel lonely when live under felion rule. The Overlord notices when you aren't around, and believe it or not, they miss your company. No matter how bad my day at work may have been, my cats are always happy to see me when I get home, and that feeling is mutual.

Stress & Anxiety Reduction – I'm sure with a little internet sleuthing you can track down a scientific study to confirm what we cat people already know: Petting your felion can reduce your stress levels. Petting or snuggling with your cat releases Oxytocin, known as the love hormone. And cats are great at listening to our problems. What they lack in advice, they make up for with intuition. My cats sense whenever I'm stressed or anxious, and they often come over to cheer me up with sympathetic head boops and snuggles. I find petting my cats to be a source of calm and comfort, even after seeing the balance in my bank account. Of course, cats can't magically make our stress and anxiety go away, but their love and companionship are great sources of consolation. Life definitely sucks less with cats.

Cats Are Chill – Like to sleep in on your days off? You're in luck; cats spend more than twelve hours a day sleeping. They also spend approximately 30% of their waking hours grooming themselves. Mix in a little interactive play and they'll be more than happy to spend the rest of their time relaxing, pondering the mysteries of the universe, or binge-watching Netflix.

Cats Are Great for Apartments/City Living – Overlords don't require a huge kingdom with sprawling grounds. It's not the size of their castle that matters, it is more important to have loyal servants. Felions will make the most of limited living space, especially if you utilize vertical space by adding cat shelves, cat trees, or condos. And since cats are relatively quiet, they won't bother your neighbors, not like the annoying, yappy dog across the hall.

Cats Are Funny – Sometimes the monarchs also like to be the jesters. Have you ever watched cat videos online? If so, you're well aware that cats can be an endless source of silly antics. Playing with Your Highness is fun and entertaining, and watching them amuse themselves can be just as comical. We can all use a good laugh every now and again.

Cats Train You – As free thinkers, felions are not receptive to having commands barked at them; that's for the dogs. Cats are creative and resilient when it comes to getting things they want from us, such as food or attention. They are not inherently inclined as people pleasers but will learn from our responses how to achieve their desired outcome. If we're late with breakfast, we can expect our cat to wake us in the most annoyingly cute ways imaginable. Our clever kitties use their charms to enforce repetition and establish an approved routine, which we will happily follow to bring joy and peace to the realm. When pleased, Your Majesty will reward you with boops and blessings. We're so proud of ourselves for cracking the cat-code that we don't even realize the Overlords are training us to serve them better!

Cats Can Make You Smarter – As any Great One can confirm, felion intelligence far surpasses that of humans. We find cats notoriously intriguing. They challenge our brains and spark imagination as we attempt to unlock their mysteries. Loyal service to a furry Einstein has its benefits. As you learn to read your Overlord's behavior and body language, you'll sharpen critical thinking skills to translate and anticipate their needs. In no time, you'll become a master at reading subtle gestures. Serving cats will hone all of your senses as you hear complaints, sniff out problems, and look for answers. Moreover, you will find yourself more observant in everything you do outside the castle walls. Cats inspire all of us to improve our memory and attention to detail.

Cats Are Low Maintenance – Cats are very aware of their own grandeur, so they will never pester you for validation, unlike dogs, which tend to be more demanding and constantly in need of directions. Although a dog's subservient need to please humans is greatly appreciated, they create far more work for their owners than cats. In fact, when ruled by an Overlord, you'll find yourself on the opposite end of that dynamic, actively seeking their approval. It simply doesn't take much to make cats happy. And one of my favorite things about cats is never needing to trudge out in the rain or snow so they can sniff around for twenty minutes in search of a place to relieve themselves. Cats are privileged to have their own indoor bathroom. As long as the concierge keeps the litter box clean, they will use it.

Cats May Help You Live Longer – According to a ten-year study by researchers at the University of Minnesota's Stroke Institute, being owned by a cat decreases risk for death due to heart attack, stroke, and all cardiovascular diseases. The study also revealed these benefits do not extend to dog owners.[7] While the good doctors have yet to explain the correlation, the answer to me is plain and simple: Felion servitude is great for your heart. Well, well, it looks likely I'll live forever!

Healthy Effect on Aging Seniors – Not only can cats help us live longer, human/animal interaction also may provide social support for older adults. One study found less deterioration in the ability to perform daily activities in older adult pet owners as compared to non-pet owners of the same age.[8] Some assisted living facilities across the country have recognized the benefit of therapy pets and even gone as far as incorporating communal cats or allowing residents to bring their personal cats to live with them. Caring for an Overlord can give the elderly a sense of purpose. Seniors in servitude to a felion ruler feel less lonely or depressed, knowing they are still needed. Plus, following a kitty care routine can improve memory and help keep senior citizens active.

Cats sound pretty great to have around, don't they? They truly are. But that doesn't mean being owned by one is easy. Don't just click *agree* on the *terms of service* without first reading the fine print. Challenges are to be expected, and you owe it to yourself and your future Overlord to make sure you enter into servitude with open eyes and for all the right reasons.

THE FINE PRINT

I don't want to come off sounding bitter or jaded, but at this point I've pretty much heard every frustrating excuse you could imagine for human servants dethroning their felion rulers. Each time I am flooded with disappointment and profound sadness as many of these situations were either avoidable or fixable. What follows are some of the most common reasons I hear from people surrendering their cats, all of which are things you should seriously consider before committing to years of cat domination.

Cat Allergies – If you or someone in your home has a cat allergy, you're already familiar with the symptoms: sneezing, running nose, watery eyes, skin rashes, and breathing issues. Fortunately, I am not allergic to cats—anyone with a cat allergy couldn't get within fifty feet of my front door!—but my heart sure goes out to those who are. Most mild cat allergies can be managed with OTC or prescription antihistamines as well as other mitigation measures, like excessive cleaning and adding an air purifier. So, you do have options, but minimizing allergens requires diligence and time—do not take the task lightly. And if anyone in your family has a severe allergy to cat dander, you definitely don't want to put their health at risk.

You Don't Have Patience to Work Through Challenges – I'm going to let you in on a little secret: Cats aren't perfect. If you ask one, they'll totally deny it, but it's true. You may experience house-soiling issues, scratching, aggression, destructive behavior, over stimulation, a hiding/fearful kitty, or a felion that is not getting along with other pets. All of these problems can be frustrating, but yelling or trying to punish your cat will only make matters worse for everyone. There are different ways to curb these behaviors, but since each felion has a unique personality, what works for one won't necessarily work for all. You may need to try multiple suggestions before you find a successful strategy. Even then, you'll need to be patient, as there is no instant fix. Some solutions may take weeks or months to fully change an unwanted behavior, and as exasperating as they are, backslides are common. You may need to check with your veterinarian or seek professional consultation from a feline behaviorist before you can get to the root of the problem. To be owned by a cat requires lots of patience.

You Value Your Possessions More Than a Cat – What's yours is theirs. It's that simple. Are you worried about Your Majesty puking up a hairball on your brand-new carpet? Allow me to inform you that they definitely will. Always. Perhaps you have a beautiful leather couch worth thousands of dollars, and if you see so much a pinhole in the fabric, that damn cat is out the door (or equally bad: declawed). You need to know going in that a cat's nails can often get snagged accidentally on fabric— including leather. Everything you own will likely be covered with cat hair. They'll sleep on your favorite clothes because it reminds them of you. Bottom line: If you have lots of extravagant things and want to keep your home pristine, a cat probably isn't the right fit for your lifestyle. Maybe consider an aquarium.

As a Gift for Someone Else – Signing someone up for felion service is irresponsible. If you want to get a birthday present or holiday gift for a friend or family member, please do not surprise that person with a cat or kitten. Cats are a long-term commitment and shouldn't be thrust upon someone who is unwilling or unprepared for that kind of responsibility. If you happen to know that the person really wants to submit and knows how to serve, the responsible thing would be offering to pay the adoption fee and let them be chosen by their new ruler.

"My Child Is Going to Be Responsible" – Cats and kittens are not toys; they are living creatures with wants and needs. Young children can get bored and lose interest after a short period of time. As the adult in the family, you should also be hands-on, taking the lead as head domestic. While having a cat is great way to allow your kids to share responsibility, supervision is always required. All members of the household should agree to become a servant of the royal court.

While I was still working at the shelter, a mother adopted a friendly kitty as a gift for her son. I overheard the conversation between the mother and the adoption counselor while cleaning cat kennels. What a great birthday gift it would be; she would be responsible for caring for the cat, *blah, blah, blah*. She said all the right things; whatever it took to get her way. An hour and forty-five minutes later, she brought back the cat for surrender. Apparently, her son no longer wanted a cat, and she had never wanted one in the first place.

You Don't Want to Pay Vet Fees – Vet bills are inevitable. Sooner or later, Your Highness will require treatment by a medical professional. As cats age, they can develop medical conditions such as diabetes, hyperthy-roidism, and kidney disease. Although these issues are manageable, you can expect to pay for tests, medications, and prescription food. Annual check-ups can help delay onset, lessen severity, or even prevent some of these issues from arising, so it's important not to neglect your cat's well visits. If you only intend to care for your felion until a medical issue arises, save your money now and don't bother signing up for service. A dethroned Overlord that ends up in a shelter with medical problems is much less likely to find a new castle, especially if the condition is severe.

Cats Are Not Dogs – You've had plenty of experience with dogs; can a cat really be that different? In a word, yes. While cats absolutely will form strong bonds with people, they don't have a dog's pack mentality. They are much more independent. A dog wants to be your best friend and will look to you for direction. Felions, on the other hand, are more inclined to enjoy their personal space, seek affection on their terms, and basically do as they please, with or without your approval.

Felion body language is also completely different than that of a canine. When Bella wags her tail, she is showing that she's happy, friendly, or in a playful mood. When Sheba's tail swishes from side to side, it's often indicative of mild annoyance, overstimulation, or intense focus. Rub Rover's exposed belly and that good boy is grinning and loving every minute of it. Try that with Tigger and you're likely to come away with an arm full of bloody scratches. Of course, the differences don't stop there; other considerations like health issues, dietary require-ments, and activity levels make serving an Overlord completely different than leading a canine pack. While both cats and dogs make great com-panions, if you're expecting Your Majesty to behave like a dog, you're barking up the wrong tree.

You Don't Have Time – I know I said cats are independent and self-suf-ficient, but they do require proper worship and mental stimulation. When castle life is a royal bore, Your Highness will find a way to keep entertained; at that point anything you own is a potential plaything. You might come home to find things in disarray—fragile items broken on the floor, your cat dangling from a curtain like he's climbing Mount

Everest. The Overlord can get a bit pissy (literally) if not worshipped sufficiently. Depression and loneliness can lead to issues like excessive meowing, a lack of grooming, or going on a hunger strike. Even with a hectic schedule, you'll need to put aside at least thirty minutes or more every day to spend exclusively worshiping your felion.

You Only Like Kittens – I mean really, who doesn't like kittens? But this doesn't mean you're ready to commit to a serious relationship for the next fifteen years. Catlings are adorable, but they are only small for a short while. Before you know it, your itty bitty kitty is a full grown felion and those playful bites and scratches are painful. Wild kitten behaviors are no longer cute but destructive. A lack of social etiquette is less entertaining and more of a nuisance. Shelters are full of confused, anxious adult cats that were traded in by their family in favor of a new kitten.

At four months old, littermates Baby and Shadow were adopted together. Eight months later, they were returned to the rescue because "they got too big when they grew up." *Dude, you're not leasing a car!* Finding a home for bonded adult cats is much harder than placing a single cat or pair of kittens. After several more months back in their previous foster home, this adorable duo went to live with Cheryl and her daughter. Today, they rule a kingdom in Florida, have access to a catio (an outdoor cat enclosure), and have an amazing life as Finn and Sadie.

Until – A cat or kitten should never be a temporary substitute or used to fill a void until something better comes along. *Until you're bored. Until you move. Until you get a new puppy or kitten. Until you get married. Until you have a real baby. Until they become an inconvenience.* Cats are not disposable. If you like cats, even a little bit, have enough respect to never use them in this way.

I'm not trying to dissuade you from getting a cat, but most people tend not to give serious consideration to these issues beforehand. That being said, none of these mean you shouldn't like cats or can't take pleasure in interacting with them; maybe you just aren't ready or able to make a long-term commitment. That's okay; being owned by a cat is not for everyone. On the other hand, perhaps you are thinking about getting a cat and have the best of intentions, but you're unsure how you would handle felion subjugation. With that in mind, let's look at some preliminary options that provide valuable hands-on experience.

FOSTERING

One way to see if you're ready for a fifteen-to-twenty-year commitment is by fostering a cat with a local rescue or shelter. Fostering is a much shorter commitment but will provide you with the full cat experience. An Overlord will still rule your domain for a time, but for you it's more like indentured servitude than full submission right out of the gate. Adoptable cats and kittens also benefit from being in foster castles because the experience is much less stressful than living in the kennels of a shelter or boarding facility.

When I tell people that I foster rescue cats, a common reply is, "I could never do what you do. I'd get too attached." Yeah, I know the feeling. Cathy and I have loved each and every kitty that has come through our door. Goodbyes are always bittersweet, even under the best circumstances, however, I still highly recommend fostering if you are open to it. I subscribe to the quote by Alfred Lord Tennyson, "Tis better to have loved and lost than never to have loved at all." Love is the most selfless gift we have to offer. When fostering, you are saving two lives, as the cat you take into your home opens a space in the shelter or rescue for another cat in need. The experience of fostering a cat is truly rewarding, and it is something Cathy and I would like to continue doing as long as we are able.

Of course, you sometimes have the option to be adopted by the cat you're fostering. This isn't always guaranteed, especially if you take too long to decide to commit. Remember, the rescue or shelter will be actively advocating for public adoptions while the cat is in your care. The quicker these Overlords find permanent castles, the easier their transition will be, and the sooner the rescue can save another. Make sure to ask about the rescue's adoption policy or if they offer a "foster to adopt" contract. Such contracts usually allow for a short trial period before finalizing the adoption, although not every organization offers a "foster to adopt" option.

Fostering does come with certain responsibilities, not only to your foster felion, but also to the rescue organization. Remember, even though you are fostering a cat in your home, that cat still belongs to the rescue until he or she is adopted. When you sign up to be a foster parent, make sure to read the organization's rules and follow their protocols carefully.

Here are some examples of what you can expect as a cat foster:

Basic Cat Care – As a foster servant, you'll need to supply daily food, fresh water, and litter, usually at your own expense. I'd also strongly suggest that you purchase a travel carrier in case the Overlord needs a trip to the vet or to adoption events.

Observation – When fostering a cat, you'll need to monitor for any signs of illness. Be sure to report any symptoms your cat may experience to the organization, and they will determine how to proceed. Not every sniffle requires a vet. Oftentimes, rescues have some basic meds on hand to treat common issues. If a trip to the vet is necessary, you will be required to take your foster cat to a rescue-approved vet for diagnosis and treatment. These approved veterinary practices offer the rescue a substantial discount. If you go rogue by using a different vet, the rescue may not cover the cost of the visit.

Socialization – The fun part! With love and interactive play, you'll help your foster cat acclimate to their new environment. This aspect of fostering can teach you a lot, not only about loyal service, but also about felion behavior and communication. If you're a really good student, you will become indoctrinated into the Laws of the Celestial Meow (see The Cat Code Translations in chapter one, The Order of the Celestial Meow).

Advocate – When fostering, you will typically be asked to supply appealing photos and a biography of your foster cat. Once you become familiar with the Overlord's personality, as well as their likes, dislikes, and activity level, you will play a key role in helping to ensure that a suitable kingdom is found.

Should you have questions about protocol or proper cat care, don't be afraid to ask the Foster Placement Coordinator, or whoever may be your rescue contact. Speaking from experience, rescues would much rather you be upfront with any questions or concerns beforehand than see a new foster parent become overwhelmed, thus making the experience more stressful for the human as well as the cat. Some rescues, like Louie's Legacy, offer a foster mentor program that pairs every new foster parent with one more seasoned, someone who can provide invaluable tips, insights, and even moral support.

As the LLAR Foster/Adoption Manager, I also took on the role of a mentor for volunteers new to the experience. New foster parents would text or message me all hours of the day and night seeking advice. Sometimes they were reaching out with legitimate medical or behavioral concerns, while other times they were simply in need of an ear and an outside perspective. If you are new to Cat World, requesting a mentor would be beneficial. At the very least, you will appreciate their moral support and perhaps even make a new friend. But unless the situation is urgent, try to keep questions relegated to normal hours.

CAT SITTING

Taking things at a snail's pace is preferable to being impulsive when deciding whether to resign yourself to felion subjugation. If fostering seems like too big of a step, consider watching a cat for a friend or family member while they're away on vacation, admitted to the hospital, or otherwise temporarily unavailable to care for their beloved ruler. With cat-sitting you can at least try some basic on-the-job training, like maintaining a regular feeding schedule, scooping litter boxes, and socialization while the Overlord remains in their own castle. Either way, you'll be benefitting yourself as well as helping the loyal servant and the cat in need of a temporary caretaker.

If you don't have any friends of family members in need of a substitute servant, consider volunteering at your local shelter. Not only will you get more familiar with felions, but the shelter cats will also benefit from some much-needed attention and socialization.

CAT CAFÉ

Cat themed cafés are becoming a popular attraction here in the United States. At these cafés, you can grab a cup of java and hang out with royalty. There's no commitment, no servitude, and no worries, however, you must submit the rules of the realm during your visit. It's a great way to de-stress and socialize with fabulous felions. You'll likely pay a small fee, which is totally worth it to hangout where it's always happy hour. As a parting gift, you'll get to keep the cat fur left on your clothes at no charge. Some cat cafés double as adoption centers, highlighting "less adoptable" cats and showcasing the wonderful personalities of the oft overlooked.

4

MAKING A PURRFECT MATCH

"A CAT DOESN'T CARE IF YOU ARE SMART OR DUMB, GIVE HIM YOUR HEART AND HE WILL GIVE YOU HIS."

—ABRAHAM LINCOLN

HOW DO I GET A CAT?

If you break it down, there are really only two ways to get a cat: You're either drafted into service or you willingly submit to felion rule. The only real difference is choice, or I should stipulate the illusion of choice, for once the Celestial Meow touches your soul, you really have no choice at all. There's no telling when or if you will be enlisted into Cat World. Just know that when the time comes, resistance is futile.

You're Conscripted – Sometimes you don't realize you need a cat in your life until one finds you. Guided by the mysterious power of the Celestial Meow, a felion seeks out a person worthy of their love. You may have heard stories of cats jumping into cars, following people home from work, or showing up on someone's porch and deciding to move in. A stray queen might choose your shed as a palace of refuge where her little princes and princesses can be safe from rivals. Or perhaps you'll cross paths with an Overlord exiled from his kingdom, or an adventurous felion who lost his way home. The "I don't have a cat" memes are hilariously popular, and while I can't speak to the legitimacy of all, they definitely happen, like when VanDuzer picked me to save him from a road full of speeding cars. Life on the outside isn't easy, but a cat's quest for a suitable companion ends in triumph when they greet you with an irresistible plea for help. Congratulations, you are now owned by a cat. You have been drafted into service.

Sometimes the furry paws of fate deliver a felion right to your doorstep. When a loved one passes away and their felion is left behind, you may be bound by duty to care for the Overlord. Think of your new servitude not as a burden, but rather as a gift. You've been chosen. With divine felion wisdom, the Celestial Meow has blessed you with the love of a cat. There is no better way to honor the memory of a deceased relative than by keeping a part of that person alive through your act of service. And as you grieve and heal together, you will form a special bond with your new Overlord.

You Sign Up for Service – Something is missing from your life. There's an empty space in your heart the shape of a cat. You feel like Sir Lancelot, a knight without a king, looking for a furry Arthur to turn your dreary home into a Camelot. Well, you're in luck! Your Majesty is out there just waiting to be united with you. Your quest for the Holy Tail has begun. March down to your local shelter, show up at rescue adoption events, and put the internet to good use. See their photos, read their profiles, and greet them in person. Be sure to stay alert and vigilant; while volunteering for service, you can be chosen at any time.

ROYAL BLOODLINES

As an animal rescuer, I've never been what some refer to as a "breed snob." I don't play favorites; my doors are open to any Lord or Lady in need, especially the underdog. Undercat? Underkitty? Whatever, you know what I mean. My preference is adoption, and if you're going to submit to felion rule, I'd strongly encourage you to take home a rescue cat. Nevertheless, there truly are some stunning breeds from which to choose, or rather be chosen. If you're thinking of bringing a purebred aristocat into your family, just be sure to research the royal bloodline beforehand. Many factors need to be considered, like activity level, grooming needs, and any potential future health concerns.

The Cat Fanciers Association currently recognizes forty-five pedigreed breeds, as well as non-pedigreed companion cats. For photos and more information about the breeds please visit: cfa.org/breeds. The International Cat Association currently recognizes seventy-three breed types for which profiles can be found at: tica.org.

- -

FUR FACT   Ragdoll is the most popular breed of cat. Maine Coon, Exotic, Persian, Devon Rex, British Shorthair, Abyssinian, American Shorthair, Scottish Fold, and Sphynx round out the top ten.[9]

- -

Keep in mind that some breeds can cost hundreds or even thousands of dollars. If you're looking to serve a specific lineage, you may be able to track down these breed types in rescues. I've seen many breeds listed at the NYC Animal Care Centers, including Sphynx cats, so it's worth checking the shelters in your area. The organizations I've worked with have saved Persians, Siamese, Ragdolls, Maine Coons, and British Shorthairs, to name a few. With a little time and effort, you can save some big bucks and also save a life.

CAT TALES: *Perfectly Persian*

When I was with Louie's Legacy I got a call about Shrimpie, a three-week-old Persian kitten brought to Staten Island Animal Care Centers. Being so young, she needed to be fed every few hours, so she couldn't stay at the shelter overnight with no one to care for her. Because I previously worked as a kennel attendant at ACC, the staff was well aware of my rescue work and past kitten experience.

Needless to say, I immediately went to the shelter to pick up Shrimpie and get her registered at Hotel Mancuso. At only three weeks old, her immune system hadn't fully developed, and since she was very susceptible to illness, the staff had kept Shrimpie isolated from the other shelter cats by keeping her in a crate in one of the admin offices.

"Oh, why hello there, little one." Seeing her, my heart melted instantly. Shrimpie was precious, all white and fluffy, and so tiny. We became fast friends as I held her in my hand. "You are so fluffin' ador-able!" I gushed and kissed her head.

Someone had apparently "found" this tiny kitten in a park and brought her to the shelter; it's a common occurrence. Shrimpie wouldn't have survived for very long on that frigid winter night as kittens under five weeks old cannot regulate their own body temperature. What struck the staff as odd was that she arrived still warm and not suffering any effects from being out in the cold. She also had none of the telltale signs that usually indicate a kitten born outdoors such as ear mites, flea dirt, or any signs of illness. She was surprisingly clean and healthy.

According to one of the employees, there is a known Persian breeder who lives in the area where the kitten was reportedly "found." Although unconfirmed, my former coworkers suspected the breeder had brought Shrimpie to the shelter because of some physical defect that would make her difficult to sell. Not the first time something like this had happened. Sure enough, upon closer assessment, this munchkin had a slight head bobble and was wobbling as she walked. Our first thought was some-thing neurological, but we later discovered the adorable little cotton ball was deaf.

Shrimpie getting the royal treatment at Hotel Mancuso.

Shrimpie boarded at Hotel Mancuso for several weeks. She'd nap on my shoulder or even in the pocket of my robe. Her absence of hearing didn't stop her from being a playful, loving princess. I was hoping she could stay longer, but I needed the room in my office to take in five adult tabbies that had recently lost their beloved servant. Shrimpie soon found her forever castle with a new foster family (the rescue's Medical Manager), where the perfectly Persian princess grew into quite the bossy, benevolent queen. And lived happily ever after. 🐾

KINGS vs QUEENS

The battle of the sexes transcends species. If you speak with the human servants, many have a preference when it comes to gender. "I like male cats; they are more outgoing" or "I only have females because they are less rambunctious." Most claims are merely subjective based on personal experience. Many online sources also seem to assert that male cats are friendlier while females tend to be bossy and independent, but much of the information presented in such articles is anecdotal. The population of the Island of Misfit Cats is currently about 60% female, and having boarded hundreds of lords and ladies in waiting at Hotel Mancuso, I assure you that females can be as affectionate and playful as male cats. Kings can be just as independent as queens. Social interaction during the developmental kitten stage will affect personality much more than gender. All in all, they seem to be on equal ground.

DON'T JUDGE A CAT BY ITS COLOR

You may have heard terms like tabby, calico, tortie, tuxie, or cow cat. Perhaps you are wondering if these are breeds of cats, as I once thought. They are not. These names merely refer to the common color patterns of felion royals. You'll find the following color patterns in a wide variety of breeds.

Calico – A tri-color pattern, sometimes referred to as patched. Some basic fashion traits give calicos their unique looks, given that 25-75% of their fur is white. The rest is a blend of black, brown, orange, or cream. Calicos come in a wide array of patterns, and while there can be many stylistic similarities, no Empress would ever dare to be caught wearing the exact same coat as another felion. I mean, can you even imagine? Calico patterns can be found in many different breeds, meaning their fur length and other characteristics, like head, face and nose shape, vary from cat to cat depending on their Royal bloodline. Among calico patterns are variations such as dilute calico or dilute tortoiseshell, which are just fancy ways of saying their coats are lighter in color. Instead of black and orange, for example, they may be gray and cream colored. Calico cats are 99% female. The 1% of male calicos born are unable to reproduce, which makes a male royal a rare find in Cat World.

FUR FACT   The famous Japanese Maneki-neko cat figurines are based on calico cats. Positioned at the entrance to a business they are believed to bring the owner prosperity and good luck.

Tuxedo (Tuxie) – These monarchs are always dressed to impress. The classic tuxedo pattern resembles formal dinner wear and consists mostly of black fur with white chest and sometimes feet. Tuxedo styles come in limited variations. A Tuxie may be all black with a small white patch that resembles a tie or amulet. Black, gray, orange, and cream-colored cats can all have tuxedo patterns. Unlike the other felion fashionistas on this list, tuxedos forgo the patches and swirls, and don't even get them started on those coats with gaudy splashes of color. They prefer a more refined look, one worthy of their noble status. Tuxedo wear isn't exclusively for males either. Felionesses can also sport this dignified pattern, and they do so with class and sophistication.

FUR FACT   William Shakespeare, Ludwig van Beethoven, and Sir Isaac Newton were all owned by tuxedos.

Cow Cats – Although they are bicolor like tuxedos, their dominant coat color is white, with large or small patches of black, gray or even ginger that make these felions resemble a cow. Don't be fooled, they still "meow" instead of "moo." Also referred to as Piebald or Magpie cats, cow cats can have a range of unique, eye-catching markings all over their body, from subtle to bold, giving them a superior style among all of the Royals. Some appear to have a mask and cape, looking a bit like Batman, while others appear to be wearing a cap and saddle. Some markings may be in the shape of hearts or even an extravagant treasure map. No matter the design, every magpie coat is a true masterpiece of felion fashion.

. . . .

FUR FACT   In 2015, Merlin, a masked Cow Cat, registered a purr measured at 67.8 decibels, setting the record for the loudest purr by a domestic cat (the average being 25 decibels).[10]

. . . .

Tabby – There are four types of pattern markings for tabby cats: stripes, ticked, spotted, and swirls. There have been endless debates among the council of tabbies as to which presentation is best, while they've yet to reach a consensus, the conclave can agree that they are best dressed of all the felions. Tabbies come in a variety of colors, such as brown, gray, orange, or cream. Morris, the cat in the Nine Lives commercials, is a quintessential orange Tabby. Even black cats can have a tabby pattern, although it's very hard to tell because the markings will be faint. Despite pattern variations, one thing all tabbies have in common is a distinct M-shaped marking on their forehead. Of course, the M stands for Monarch, serving as a reminder of who's really in charge.

. . . .

FUR FACT   In Talkeetna, Alaska, a tabby cat named Stubbs was elected honorary mayor in 1997. Mayor Stubbs served the town for twenty years.

. . . .

Tortie – Also known as tortoiseshell for its similarity to tortoiseshell material, their brindled coats are an intricate tapestry of black, brown, red, orange, or cream. While other felions will beg to differ, torties assert that brindle fur is absolutely catastic. These Empresses are visually stunning, and the self-proclaimed true fashion icons of Cat World. Calicos think they're all that, but any tortie will tell you, they are a raggedy patchwork by comparison. Tabbies are basic, cow cats have barnyard attire, and tuxedos—bah!—more like footie pajamas. You can find queens with this pattern in purebreds as well as mixed breeds, long or short haired. Like calicos, male torties are also sterile, and extremely rare, only about one in 3,000.

....

FUR FACT The term "torbie" is short for tortoiseshell-tabby. A torbie has tortoiseshell colors with a tabby pattern.

....

House Panther – Some people also refer to them as mini-panthers, but either way the term applies to all-black cats. Whether a sleek shadow or a chonky silhouette, every house panther can attest that black is beautiful, and when it comes to fashion, black goes with everything. Their solid black coloring helps accentuate their eyes, causing them to look like gold, yellow, orange, or emerald jewels. Sadly, black cats in particular have been subjected to centuries of bad PR and superstition. Of all the colors and patterns, house panthers are the least likely to be adopted from shelters and rescues. However, despite the haters, black cats may have some luck in their favor. The genes that produce their black fur may help lower their chances of being severely impacted by diseases and illnesses that affect cats of other colors.

....

FUR FACT Black cats can temporarily change color. UV rays from the sun can break down the black pigment in the cat's fur, turning it a rust color, much the same way it can lighten peoples' hair in the summer. When this happens, you will be able to see if your cat has tabby markings which aren't normally visible. The affected fur will remain discolored until shed naturally, after which it will be replaced by fresh black fur once again.

....

Chimera – These striking "two-face" cats have one color scheme on half of their face and/or body and another on the other half, as if trying to blend two cats into one. Not only do they have different colored fur, they can also have different colored eyes. Predominantly female, Chimera cats have two sets of DNA because a pair of embryos fused together early in the queen's womb. Chimera faces can be a myriad of mixed patterns and colors, such as a half tortie, half house panther, or half calico, half tabby. Every chimera will tell you that they are twice as fashionable as other felions. Any cat who disagrees is clearly jealous. No matter how you slice it, the extremely photogenic Chimera doesn't have a bad side.

Polydactyl – Although their name is unrelated to color, polydactyl cats are worth noting since they do look a little different. Most felions have five toes on their front paws and four on their back paws, but polydactyl cats are born with extra toes, sometimes more than one extra on each paw. This is a harmless genetic mutation that can occur in any breed and affects both males and females. While the vast majority of polydactyl cats only have extra digits on their front paws, these accessories can be found on all four. Extra toe beans? Yes, please! The current world record for the cat with the most toes is a ginger tabby named Jake who has a total of 28, or 7 per paw.[11]

. . . .

FUR FACT "Polydactyl cats are sometimes referred to as Hemmingway cats because acclaimed author, Ernest Hemmingway, had a particular fondness for them. After his passing in 1961, Hemmingway's home in Key West, Florida, was transformed into a museum and a home for his beloved cats. Today, the colony is home to some fifty descendants of his original pack—about half of which are polydactyl."[12]

. . . .

A question I've often heard from potential adopters is if color patterns are associated with any particular traits or temperaments. A fair question, especially since some people swear their Tortie possesses a sassy "Tortidude." Calicos alike have often been said to be feisty, spunky, and picky. Orange tabbies are thought to be the friendliest. But don't judge a cat by their color. Their differences extend well beyond their coat patterns. Each cat has a unique personality. They may have distinctive quirks—some are very chatty, while others rarely vocalize. Some Overlords rule with an iron claw; others are laid back couch potatoes, preferring to spend their time napping on the throne. Breed and upbringing play a significant role in royal temperament, but colors and coat patterns do not.

PURRSONALITY

Whether you adore the puffy, fluffy, pretty purries or find your heart belongs to the ugly ducklings, cats are so much more than their breed, color, or markings. Before you swipe left on a profile pic, it's worth remembering that what's inside should count most. Personality should always receive top priority in your search. Cattitude comes in many different flavors:

Velcro Cat – Wherever you go, there they are. The classic lap cat, velcros make it clear that you are their favorite spot. They become a shadow, or a strange furry growth on your shoulder. Velcro cats will never pass up an opportunity to snuggle with their favorite servant. They can be, and typically are, cordial with all the subjects in their kingdom, but often form a strong attachment to one person. While this may sound adorable in theory, they can become overly dependent on your presence and get depressed when you are not around, especially if left completely alone. Velcro cats can also be jealous or stressed when having to share your attention with new people or pets.

Social Butterfly – Social cats are extroverts and feel very comfortable around human members of the family. Their confidence and amicability often extend to guests, and they will more easily accept co-rulers. Social Butterflies make great rulers over many royal subjects and typically handle emissaries and ambassadors from other species in stride. These felions keep a full schedule being the object of everyone's worship, but like any great monarch, they grant all subjects of the kingdom the splendor of their affection. Much like Velcro cats, Social Butterflies usually don't like being left alone, especially for long periods of time.

Independent Cat – Independent cats are usually very chill, to the point where people mistake them for being aloof. Your Highness will enjoy just being near you, but without constantly seeking attention. Independent cats value their personal space and expect you to perform your duties without constant supervision, or the need to validate your every deed with a blessing. Don't worry, they'll let you know when you did something wrong. However, when they're in the right mood, you can expect some quality time. While they need less attention than other personality types, they do enjoy playing with or being worshiped by their servants.

The Boss – Born rulers, like any boss, these Royals can be demanding of your time. They run a tight castle and micromanage their servants. Bosses want to rule every aspect of the kingdom and constantly be the center of attention—the way nature intended. They want what they want when they want it. Wake up. Feed me. Pet me. Play with me. Your spot? That's my spot! Bosses will use stick and carrots, whatever it takes to get their way. They will not hesitate to voice their displeasure but will also bless you richly with bonuses for your exemplary service, which makes it all worthwhile. Bosses may try to be dominant over other felions as well, especially if castle resources are scarce, like the prime viewing spot for Cat TV or a single litter box. That's high value territory and The Boss isn't big on sharing.

    Rayden is a Boss, which is fine, except for the fact that he is a total Jekyll & Hyde from moment to moment. This has made him wildly unpopular with our fur-brigade, who universally steer clear of him. As much as he and I love each other, we engage in a battle of wills from time to time when attempts to stop me from attending to the needs and requests of other rulers. He absolutely hates it when I sing or call him Ray-Dee Baby Boo; he will utter a low growl of disapproval, his broken tail swishing and flapping like he's waving a black flag at me. The word "no" is met with grumbles, hisses, and angry meows. Other times he can be a Boss in the most adorable ways. Quite often as I sat at my desk working on this book, Rayden would decide when I had written enough and needed to focus on him. He will gently demand my worship with love bites, or dance on my keyboard and lovingly threaten to delete the last chapter until I relent. All I can say is "as you wish" and enjoy Rayden's affection for as long as it lasts.

The Playful Explorer – Your Majesty is very curious and has a thirst for adventure. Playful Explorers are a lot of fun, with tons of energy, they're always up to compete in the Kitty Olympics. Daily activity is decreed to be a kingdom requirement. With a higher energy level than other personalities, these felions become bored easily when sitting upon a throne too long. There are adventures to be had and games to win, even if that means inventing their own solitary amusements at the expense of your stuff. They enjoy climbing and investigating, but much like kittens, without supervision, they can find themselves getting into trouble.

Our adorable Little Tiger was the poster cat for this personality type. For the crooked-headed tabby, every day was a new quest to explore the unknown. His wanderlust took him atop the highest cabinets, into the recesses of the deepest closets, and down to the dusty underworld that lurked beneath every piece of furniture. Little Tiger made up endless games to amuse himself, most of which involved knocking things down from high places. Anything on top of the refrigerator: goodbye. Stacks of DVDs were reduced to a pile of rubble on the floor. My coffee cups were routinely spilled and shattered. Nothing was safe from his paws. If there was a crash, thud, or clang anywhere in the house, there was a 95% chance it was caused by our little Magellan.

The Cat's Cat – These cats aren't always the biggest proponents of fraternizing with help, but a cat's cat is very content and social around royalty. While felions are not pack animals like dogs, these cats can easily form a friendship with a single co-ruler or even within a conclave. Agreeable, they display a willingness to share, groom, snuggle, and play with other Overlords. Most times, these cats love being around their own kind even more than their loyal servants, for whatever reason. They are perfect co-rulers to consider if you already serve an Overlord that would benefit from a furry companion. For your part, you must work hard to earn their affection, but eventually, they will reward your patience and loyalty.

Scaredy Cat – Often described as shy, nervous, or skittish, these reluctant Rulers may not have had a lot of human exposure/socialization as kittens. Others may simply have been born with a naturally fearful disposition. For whatever reason, scaredy cats lack trust, confidence, or both. Most people overlook the more anxious cats and kittens, but a little TLC can go a long way. With some time, patience, and effort, these shrinking violets can blossom into confident, independent, or social felions. With your help, they will claim their cat-given right of lordship over their castle. Speaking from personal experience, it is so rewarding when you help bring out their inner lion.

If you already have a cat in the castle, a timid felion may evolve into a cat's cat, finding it easier to form a Royal bond. Ever observant, these felions learn the benefits of trust and human companionship by observing the interactions of their co-ruler. For example, Petey and Puff Daddy became guests of Hotel Mancuso at six months old, and with little prior human contact, they were wary of the hotel staff. These two feared everything, including our resident rulers. In the beginning of their stay, they only made brief appearances during mealtimes, otherwise they only skulked through the kingdom like shadows in the night. However, they soon adjusted to amicable time sharing of territory with the fur-brigade. Over time, they joined the clique and eventually worked their way up through the ranks. For nearly two years, Puff Daddy and Petey resisted our solicitations of friendship. Both kept human interactions to a minimum. Not so much as a thank you for our service. It took years for them to fully embrace their roles as Overlords, but through spectating daily worship services, they began to feel left out of the fun. They gained enough confidence for active participation in social activities. Since that time, Puff Daddy is much bolder and will share a throne with me, while Petey uses his irresistible squeaks to demand proper worship—after all, he has years of missed petting to catch up on.

As much as cats love boxes, I am reluctant to organize their personas into proverbial boxes—they are much more complicated than that. Since each felion is an individual, they can and do have multiple traits incorporated into their temperament. While Overlords are notoriously stubborn, your lifestyle and even your own personality will influence that of your felion ruler.

. . . .

FUR FACT A cat's nose print is as unique as a human fingerprint; no two sets of bumps and ridges are identical.

. . . .

LIFESTYLE

When looking to add a felion ruler to the head of your family, it's essential to find one that will match your lifestyle. Consider your own routines and the time you have to dedicate to serve an Overlord, because your entire world—and theirs—will be greatly affected. To the extent you can, choose wisely whom you will serve.

Velcro cats are love bugs, but to be truly happy, they need as much attention as they give. If you work a lot or are out of the house most of the day, consider getting a more independent cat that is less likely to get depressed or suffer from separation anxiety if left alone for longer periods. If you have a busy, chaotic, or loud household, a timid cat will likely have a much harder time learning to thrive in that type of environment; they prefer a castle with little fanfare. Active cats are a lot of fun, but they need to be kept entertained and burn off plenty of energy, otherwise they may keep you awake at night or amuse themselves by knocking everything you own to the floor.

Be honest with yourself about what you want out of felion servitude, and always consider how the Overlord will acclimate to all the facets of your life. Make sure everyone else in the home is on board with crowning a king or a queen as their rightful ruler. It's always best if everyone in the royal court is involved in the Overlord's care; their hearts are big enough to gratefully accept worship from all their subjects. The kingdom will be a much more joyous place.

5

WHAT TO EXPECT WHEN EXPECTING A CAT

"I HAD BEEN TOLD THAT THE TRAINING PROCEDURE WITH CATS
WAS DIFFICULT. IT'S NOT. MINE HAD ME TRAINED IN TWO DAYS."

—BILL DANA

CAT PROOFING

Chances are you've heard the expression "curiosity killed the cat." This saying isn't without merit; by nature, felions are inquisitive animals. They like to explore their kingdoms and perform routine safety inspections. If you're not careful, Your Majesty can and will get into things. And I mean everything. Seriously. Everything. Although not deliberately or with malicious intent, felions can break your valuables and potentially injure themselves in the process. So, before you bring a cat or kitten into your home, take some time to "cat proof" it first.

By adhering to the following tips, you will be protecting not only your Troublemaker in Chief, but also your own possessions. In my early days of being owned by cats, I was known to leave coffee mugs and drinking glasses unattended on not so rare occasions. That meant spills and thrills for my tribe, who were either trying to train me or get me into trouble with the wife. Whatever their motivation, it worked. My coffee mug has since become an extension of my hand, and Catherine has threatened to allow me to drink only from sippy cups. Well played, kitties, well played.

Don't Leave Coffee Mugs and Drinking Glasses Unattended! – Cathy has obliged me to place this one at the top of the list. Heed this warning, or you too may be forced to go the way of the sippy cup. Good luck.

Lock Away Household Cleaners – Pine cleaners, bleach, and other household chemicals can poison your cat. Keep them secure and out of sight in a cabinet. If your cat has access to your garage, store all chemicals like fertilizers, insecticides, paint, and rodent bait with your cat's safety in mind, especially antifreeze, which smells sweet to animals but is deadly. Even if a cat gets some antifreeze on his paw and licks it off, it could be a fatal accident.

Secure All Medications – Pill bottles are prime targets for a fun game of kitty-cat karate. Secure all lids, even the pain-in-the-ass, childproof kind that take me five minutes to line up the stupid top. Don't leave medicine bottles on countertops, dressers, or vanities—it's called a medicine cabinet for a reason; use it. This includes prescriptions as well as over the counter drugs. Ibuprofen and acetaminophen can kill a cat. And I shouldn't have to say it, but I will: This also refers to any "recreational" narcotics you're "just holding onto for a friend." I'm not going to narc, and I'm not going to judge . . . unless you recklessly leave out your stash and endanger your felion's life. Secure all medications. I can't stress this enough.

Keep Breakables Out of Reach – Anything fragile or valuable should be kept safe in either a cabinet or display case as opposed to sitting out on open shelves, unless it's one of those ceramic clown figurines—in that case, just toss the horrid monstrosity in the trash. Or better yet, pulverize it to dust and send it back to the depths of hell from whence it came.

Close Windows and Exterior Doors – Unless you install pet resistant screens, you should be careful opening a window too far or leaving sliding screen doors exposed. Cats have been known to break through normal screens and fall out or escape. Much the same way we enjoy a good television show, cats delight in staring out the window at the Great

Backyard. This is what we refer to as Cat TV. Place a perch or kitty condo near the window so your cats can safely enjoy their daily episode of As the Bird Chirps without having to sit on the windowsill to do so.

Speaking from experience, always close the windows when you're not home. One of my fur-brigade pulled a Freddy Kruger on the window screen in my office. I'm not sure which one did it, but everybody's a suspect. Although we discovered the holes before they allowed for a break-out, our windows are now only ever open a few inches. Even though I'm not the one with claws, whom do you think my wife blames? Case closed.

As ambush hunters, cats are not only quick, but also stealthy. Give extra care when coming or going so that your cat or kitten doesn't sneak by you and slip out. I've lost count of how many times I've read of felion escape artists in online lost pet groups. This is probably the biggest cause of lost cats, and for the most part it's preventable. Avoid worry and heartbreak; be persistent and consistent when it comes to keeping the Overlord safely indoors.

Keep Closet Doors Closed – There's a reason for the oft-used horror movie jump scare when a random cat leaps out from the closet at the height of tension. Dark and quiet, closets are an attractive location for cats to chill when they want to be left alone. Trust me, if you're not hyper-aware, Your Majesty could easily sneak into a closet right under your feet. You may not even notice they're gone for a while, possibly hours. Maybe not until your wife later hears Shinobi meowing from within, indignantly demanding to be let out. And then you find yourself in hot water because that furry brat peed on her shirts.

Closing doors is only part of cat safety. Equally important is to always be cautious when doing so, especially with kittens. Whether you're going outside or just into the bathroom, whenever you shut a door, keep a watchful eye. Some kittens will follow you around the castle. They're so tiny that it's easy to overlook them, and if you're not careful tragedy can strike . . . like with our Gacelyn, who arrived at Hotel Mancuso after a closing door caused irreparable spinal injuries that landed her on a list to be euthanized (her full story appears in chapter nine, Special Kneads Cats).

Shut/Latch Appliances and Cabinets – If you're fortunate enough to have an in-home washing machine and dryer, close the lids or doors immediately after use. Open washers and dryers can be invitations for a catnap. Remember to always double check before shutting the door and turning on these appliances. Take the same care with cabinets, as they are tempting chambers of secrets for adventurous felions to explore or escape from the stresses of kingdom rule. If necessary, install latches or other preventive measures. Since our clever mischief makers at Hotel Mancuso learned how to open the cabinets, we installed door magnets to prevent them from being opened. Ha-ha! Can't get in anymore, can you now, Mr. Bitey? A worthy purchase to keep our cats safe and out of trouble, but who's keeping score? Chris: 1 – Cats: 57.

Cover Electrical Cords, Wires, and Cables – Hanging pull cords for blinds and curtains are a tempting toy, especially for kittens. Tie them out of reach or you may end up with a furry Tarzan. Don't forget to put away your phone chargers, too. Cats love to chew on stringy objects. I'm not totally sure why; it's a cat thing, right Rayden? But it's a compulsion that can get them shocked, potentially fatally, or accidentally strangled. If a cat ingests any strings or wire, it can cause a blockage by wrapping around their intestines, needing to be removed surgically. To help prevent such a catastrophe, you can tape your cords to the floor, or purchase tubing to keep your wires and kitty safe.

Hide String, Yarn, Thread, Dental Floss, Hair Ties, and Rubber Bands – Same rules as above, but it's important enough to reiterate. This can also apply to shoelaces. At the very least, tuck your laces into your footwear. Two of my royals, Legolas and Rayden, must own stock in a shoelace company. If I leave my shoes out, there's a good probability I'll find at least two inches missing from at least one lace, only for Cathy to find it in a litter box a day later. Honestly, we've been extremely lucky they only chewed off small pieces, but we no longer take chances. I've been trained to immediately put my shoes back in their boxes as soon as they come off my feet. As for the sneakers I wear around the house, I removed the laces years ago.

Anchor Top-Heavy Objects and Furniture – It's a known fact that felions love to climb to the highest perch to survey their kingdoms, burn energy, or just satisfy their curiosity. With 500 muscles in their bodies, these champions of the cat Olympics can vertically jump up to six times their height in a single leap. Springing horizontally can propel them nearly as far. For flat-screen televisions and any unstable furniture like shelving units, your best bet is to mount it to a wall so it doesn't come tumbling down in a dangerous heap when your brave explorer tries to scale it.

Close Toilet Lids and Garbage Containers – As you may or may not realize, your bathroom is a potential danger zone. From the contents of your medicine cabinet to your razor to uncapped toothpaste, bathrooms contain a load of hazards just waiting to injure a curious cat.

Ladies, as Cathy would surely tell you, having a new fur kid in your home is one more reason to make sure the man in your life always puts the seat down (and the lid) as if you needed another reason. Fellas, trust me, the wrath you will incur if you leave the seat up and the cat makes a splash will be epic, from the woman in your life or your sulking sultan when you try to bathe them afterwards. Not that I would know personally or anything. On a more serious note, cats in the toilet lead to nothing good, and a small kitten can actually drown from falling in the toilet.

Whether you're an exceptional cook or more of a Chef-Boyardee aficionado, be sure to secure lids on your trash receptacle. If it has a locking mechanism, use it. If it has a foot pedal, all the better. Even if your Overlord isn't hungry, the aroma can draw them like a magnet. Or maybe they just want to make sure you're properly recycling! Either way, with open trash receptacles, you could end up not only with a mess to clean, but also a sick cat who ate something she shouldn't have . . . which is pretty much everything you toss in the trash.

Protect Your Furniture – In case you don't already know, Overlords tend to scratch furniture. Why not? That's what it's there for, isn't it? They do so to stretch muscles, remove old claw sheaths, and claim ownership of the object with their scent. It's unfortunate, but it happens. You can put a cover on your couch or chairs for added armor against unwanted scratching, or use some double-sided tape as a deterrent. Your Majesty will be put off when they find their paws sticking to the tape and opt for a paw-friendly surface to scratch. Additionally, there are sprays on the market that help make furniture unappealing to cats.

I'll discuss additional ideas for furniture protection in the *Breaking Bad* section. But before we move on, hear this: DO NOT DECLAW YOUR CAT! Yes, it's in all caps, because I'm shouting. Do not declaw your cat, please. More on this later, too.

IT'S A JUNGLE IN THERE

Whether you're an amateur botanist, have an indoor garden, or just like pretty flora to liven up your living space, it's important to know which plants are toxic to felions before bringing one into the castle. Not only have the Overlords been known to chew on plants, but pollen can also stick to their fur and be ingested during grooming. Effects from the plants can be serious, and in some cases deadly. The following list of houseplants that are dangerous to cats is not exhaustive, but it's a great place to start.

- Aloe Vera
- Amaryllis
- Arrow-Head Vine
- Asparagus Fern
- Azaleas
- Bay Laurel
- Begonia
- Bird of Paradise
- Caladium (Elephant Ear)
- Chrysanthemum
- Clivia
- Daffoldils
- Dieffenbachia
- Dracaena
- English Ivy
- Eucalyptus
- Ficus
- Geranium
- Hyacinths
- Indian Rubber Plant
- Jade
- Kalanchoe
- Lilies
- Marijuana
- Milkweed
- Mistletoe
- Onion
- Oleander
- Poinsettia
- Pothos
- Sago Palm
- Snake Plant (Dracaena trifasciata)
- Tulip
- Yew [13]

Having a felion doesn't mean you can't keep any plants in the castle. You just need to find ones the whole family can enjoy—including your Overlord. Let's face reality, even the best-behaved cat can chew on your plants. Once upon a time in my castle we had two plants. Had. VanDuzer would use them as alternate litter boxes. Eventually, our only solution was to get rid of both plants. Better for me anyway, the Mr. Brown Thumb I am. However, I know more than a few loyal subjects who keep safe plants in their kingdom. And you can, too. House plants safe for cats include:

- African Violet
- Baby Tears
- Bird's Nest Fern
- Boston Fern
- Bromeliad
- Calahea Orifolia
- Cat Grass
- Catnip
- Date Palm
- Friendship Pant

- Gloxinia
- Orchid
- Parlor Palm
- Polka Dot Plant
- Ponytail Palm
- Rattlesnake Plant
- Spider Plant
- Staghorn Fern
- Venus Fly Trap[14]

A Word About Catnip and Cat Grass – Mother Nature's gift to the felion species, catnip mimics feline sex hormones, so needless to say, Overlords really enjoy this substance. And catnip can help relieve stress and reduce anxiety. There's nothing cuter than watching our cats bug out on catnip, rubbing, rolling, tap-dancing on the fronts of their paws. After whiffing some catnip, your Catsanovas may show overt signs of affection, relaxation, and happiness. Lucky devils. Of course, not every cat will react the same. Certain royals will display active behaviors, such as playfulness or sometimes even aggression. For others, catnip seems to have no effect at all—I guess they're like the designated drivers of their species. Cat toys are commonly stuffed with catnip for enhanced fun, even the laziest of felions find it hard to resist. It can also be used as an attractant; rubbed on a surface, catnip can encourage Your Highness to use the litterbox and scratching posts.

As if catnip wasn't enough, living room lions even have a type of grass specifically engineered for them. Cat grass is grown indoors and is a safe option for Your Majesty to enjoy. It's not its own strain of plant but rather a grass mixture of wheat, oats, rye, and others seeds. Cat grass aids digestion and acts as a laxative, helping your felion eliminate hairballs into the litter box instead of puking them up on the floor for you to later step on during a barefoot, half-asleep trip to the bathroom. Or something like that. My cats know exactly what I'm talking about!

Like humans, cats can also have allergies to certain plants, so even the ones listed as pet safe may still cause an adverse reaction if the Overlord is allergic. Common allergy symptoms in cats include:

- Coughing
- Sneezing
- Wheezing/snoring
- Ear infection
- Excessive scratching/ patches of missing fur

- Runny eyes/itchy eyes
- Sensitive/swollen paws
- Diarrhea
- Vomiting

As I've learned from my veterinarian, ear infections are a common indication of an allergy in cats. If you notice Your Majesty shaking their head, scratching their ears excessively, and losing balance, then an ear infection may be to blame, and an allergy may be the root cause. Other noticeable symptoms include bright red ears, crust/scabs from scratching, and a strong pus odor emitting from the ear canal. The same applies to foods. Cats sometimes have allergies to grains, chicken, or fish or perhaps some other ingredient. Dr. Singh was able to tell that my sweet little Miyagi was allergic to her food due her excessive scratching. Even though I keep her nails trimmed, she managed to rip her neck so badly that fur will never grow back in certain areas. Dr. Singh has since put Miyagi on a prescription diet, which has minimized her allergies. If you suspect Your Highness has allergies, too, please schedule an appointment with your veterinarian.

FIND A VETERINARIAN

Even before you take your new cat home, you should find a veterinarian, preferably one in relatively close proximity to where you live. If you're adopting your cat from a rescue, ask whom they use and see if that veterinarian is a viable option. Get recommendations from other servants. Before the coronation is the time to do a little investigating and price hunting. Not all veterinarians are created equal. Some veterinarians take a more holistic approach, while others follow more traditional treatments. It is important to find one that you like, and trust to care for the Overlord's health, so don't just blindly settle for any vet. Pay a visit to the office; see if the staff is friendly and helpful. Inquire as to what services they provide in office, take note of their business hours.

It's also a good idea to have an emergency backup. Vet offices open 24 hours a day are typically more expensive, but when it's after normal business hours and you have a royal emergency, you'll be thankful you have somewhere to turn for treatment. Don't wait until there is an urgent situation; the more prepared you are, the quicker you can act to get immediate help if needed.

VACCINES & CHECK UPS

Your Highness should have an annual checkup with your veterinarian. This will help you keep on top of any health concerns before they become serious. For their own protection, you will also need to keep your cat updated on their vaccines. FVRCP and Rabies vaccines are typically boosted on a three-year basis. The vaccines are especially important if you choose to take your cat on outdoor excursions. Additionally, make sure you only use flea/tick prevention recommended by your vet and carefully follow directions for use.

STOCKING THE OVERLORD'S DOMAIN

Of course, when converting your home into kitty castle, safety proofing is only part of proper preparation. As you plan for Your Majesty's coronation, you must ensure the domain is well suited for felion rule. On day one you should have all the essential supplies in place for when kitty assumes the throne.

- Food
- Litter
- Litter boxes
- Food & Water Bowls

- Pet bed
- Toys
- Scratching post
- Nail clippers

- Brush
- Travel carrier
- Cat tree/condo

Optional Amenities – These items will help with maintaining health and adding enrichment to enhance quality of life. While I am listing these as optional, I strongly recommend many of the items on this list. If not stocked for the coronation, not to worry, they can always be incorporated later.

- Pet vitamin supplements
- Water fountain
- Litter/ food mats
- Cat grass/catnip
- Pheromone diffuser
- Collar and tags

- Harness & leash
- Double-sided tape
- Puzzle feeder
- Toothbrush & Pet Toothpaste

Where Does He Get Those Wonderful Toys? – Sometimes all the bureaucracy of running an entire kingdom can be a drag on the Overlord. There are couches, beds, and chairs that need to be slept on. The furniture sure isn't going to climb itself. Who's going to kick litter all over the floor if not them? Not to mention the daily inspections and supervision of their servant, because good help is hard to find these days.

Play is an important aspect of the daily routine. Provide a variety of toys to engage your felion's natural instinct to hunt and pounce. Crinkle balls, toys that jingle, and rattle mice are all good options to have available. Introduce a plushy, catnip-filled foe for your furry hero to wrestle and conquer. Trackball toys, hanging-danglers, and springy, punching kooshes can all be a wonderful source of entertainment for cats to enjoy on their own.

When you are able to have playtime together, engage your kitty using stick toys, laser pointers, or clicker training. To avoid felion frustration and displeasure, make sure Your Majesty always finishes as the victor of any game. Allow your purry predator to satisfy their primal urge of catch and kill. A happy Overlord leads to a peaceful kingdom.

Even if you don't have the budget to spoil Your Highness with store bought gifts, you can still offer plenty of enrichment on the cheap. Cats love paper bags and empty cardboard boxes. Ah, the simple pleasures. Put your online shopping addiction to good use—form some empty Amazon boxes into a cat maze for your brave adventurer to explore. They'll have a glorious time knocking around pieces of wadded up paper. Get creative. If you're crafty, you can discover plenty of ideas online for homemade toys and puzzle feeders.

Itching To Scratch – Scratching posts should be an essential fixture in any kingdom. They offer an approved space for your Overlord to scratch, which will help to protect your furniture. Posts are available in a variety of materials including sisal, cardboard, and carpet. Scratchers can be vertical, horizontal, or inclined, and each type works different muscles. If you are able, provide a variety of scratchers throughout the castle to satisfy all their needs. Every room should have a scratching option other than furniture or carpeting.

For a vertical post, my personal recommendation is one tall enough (at least 30 inches) for your felion to really get a good stretch. I was introduced to this type of scratcher when I first got involved with fostering. Several other loyal servants highly recommended it, so I ordered one the next day. It towered over our other posts and had a wide, sturdy base. It quickly became a felion favorite in Hotel Mancuso, and now we have at least two in each room.

Kitty Conveyance – The Royal Mews at Buckingham Palace is responsible for all road travel arrangements for the King of England and members of the Royal Family. Likewise, as the royal chauffer of kitty castle, it's up to you to choose a pet carrier suitable for any necessary transport of the Overlord. From hard shell to soft bags to backpacks, with so many brands and styles, there are nearly as many options for kitty conveyance as there are models of cars. One thing is certain. No matter which type of cat carrier you purchase, there's a good chance the Overlord will disapprove of it on principle, so choose a carrier you can easily get your felion into. My preference is a hard-case top-loader. These carriers have a top hatch as well as a front door. The chore of getting an unwilling felion into a carrier is so much easier when you can just lower them inside from above. A rooftop entrance is also less stressful for your meowing monarch.

Rubik's Food – Food puzzles require Your Highness to work for meals or treats by using their brains and dexterity to release kibble from a variety of challenges. These are a great source of enrichment as they cater to a felion's natural instinct to hunt for their food. You can use these puzzles for their favorite treats or even for royal feasts. Cats are problem solvers and enjoy a good brainteaser. In the battle against felion boredom, puzzle feeders promote mental and physical stimulation. They are a great way to keep the Overlord busy while you're out of the castle for hours at a time.

There are several types of puzzle feeders available. Some are balls that dispense treats. Others are stationary and include food mazes, sliders, or fishing kibble from cups. Much like with toys, you can easily make some affordable food puzzles on your own with empty plastic water bottles, egg cartons, or even the left-over cardboard tube from a roll of toilet paper. Just search online for creative, budget-friendly ideas.

To The Trees – Investing in a Cat Tree or Tower Condo with many different levels, perches, scratching posts, and dangling toys will be extremely beneficial to your felion's health. Be sure to place the tall structure in an area where they can overlook their domain. Placing it close to a window is also a great idea. A tall tower or condo with a hidey-hole will give Your Majesty a sense of control while also providing an escape route other than dashing under furniture and becoming a dust bunny.

If you notice your Overlord isn't using the tree, try rearranging its placement. Find a spot where your felion can feel safe and have a perfect view of the room. And don't be afraid to mix things up; over time the cat tree may become less exciting for your cat. Consider repositioning it so that a different side is accessible or moving the tree to another room. You might even want to purchase a couple of trees to have in different chambers of the castle and occasionally swap them. Variety is the spice of life. If the castle is short on square footage, try staggering wall-mounted perches, which will still satisfy the Overlord's desire to rule from on high.

DECOMPRESSION

Postpone the fanfare. The Overlord will likely require some decompression time when transitioning into a new palace. Past experiences and comfort levels will determine how long it will take to decompress and accept their role as ruler. Some cats handle the transition with ease, while less social cats or ones that have had traumatic experiences may take much longer to adjust. Felions are creatures of habit, so it's understandable that such a huge change in their lives can cause lots of stress. But fear not, with love and patience, Your Majesty will soon fill your schedule with plenty of worship time and social obligations to the crown.

The Throne Room – On day one of the coronation, when your new monarch arrives at the castle, immediately usher them to the Throne Room. It does not matter which room you choose, but do pick only one to serve as Your Majesty's temporary living quarters for the next few days or even weeks as they unwind and settle in. The room should be cat-proofed with accommodations becoming of royalty, including food, water, toys, and a litter box. To avoid becoming overwhelmed by an influx of adoring felion enthusiasts all at once, only one-on-one audiences should be permitted. As the Overlord becomes comfortable with greeting their loyal subjects, access to the rest of the castle can be expanded.

Hidey-Holes – Even when one of our royal guests has a single occupancy suite, I always set up a hidey-hole—an enclosed space in a non-centralized location of the Throne Room where the Overlord can retreat if things get too overwhelming. Having a sanctioned hiding spot is preferable to one that is not easily accessible to human servants, like under furniture or behind large appliances. I like to use a decent-sized cardboard box (usually from one of my Amazon or Chewy deliveries) and cut an entrance hole in one side. To make it more appealing and comfortable, I line the inside with a soft blanket or cat-bed. If the Overlord retreats to their secret cat cave, it's a good indication they are feeling stressed, threatened, or just want to channel their inner hermit. At these times, you can lobby for the cat to exit of their own free will, but you should never try to force them from the sanctuary of their hidey-hole.

As Days Go By – Decompression will allow the Overlord to become more comfortable with castle life on their terms. You and your family are no longer perceived as potential threats. Relationships form, and loyal servants are slowly accepted into the fold. And as they grow more confident in their leadership role, a felion's true personality will rise to the surface. As days go by they will be more playful and affectionate.

CAT TALES: *Mr. Bitey*

Fostering so many kitties over the years, I have seen my share of cats that desperately need time to decompress and learn to trust people again. A perfect example of this is my gray devil, formerly named Luna. A friend of a friend was concerned about her coworker looking to surrender her cat to the shelter. I received the following plea for assistance in my inbox. Certain information has been redacted for privacy concerns.

Chris . . . This is all the info I have. A student found Luna in the Bronx, and he lived with the student and his family with another cat until March. As far as I know, he didn't show any of the behavior he's showing now. They said he was very affectionate, liked to sleep on plants or the kids' shoulders, and got along with the other cat.

In March he went to live with [my coworker]. He was scared and stayed under the bed for a day or two. After that, he wanted to be near her and sleep against her shoulder, but she didn't like that and would push him off the bed. He wanted to sit in her lap, but she didn't want that either and would "toss" him off. She said he would "walk too close to her feet and get in her way" and rub against her leg so she would kick him away or put him in the bathroom. She has a studio, so I suspect she likely put him in the closet. She said he scratched her leg and acted like he is now after about two months. Based on how I've seen her interact with students (she screams and threatens violence), I'm thinking she probably yelled at Luna and did other traumatic things.

Needless to say, I was shocked and angered to read this. Sadly, poor Luna was being traumatized in his own castle. His only transgression was unsolicited affection and constant attention seeking behavior. Luna's defensive and aggressive reaction to his mistreatment was only a natural response. His human was unfit to serve! The sooner he was out of that situation, the better. Even though I was on a self-imposed hiatus from fostering, Cathy and I agreed to take him in, and the woman who contacted me agreed to transport him to us.

I set him up in a crate in my office as per Hotel Mancuso protocol for isolation and decompression. The crate was four feet long and three feet wide, big enough to comfortably house a large dog; it was our luxury suite. As we prepared for his arrival, Cathy included all the amenities we had to offer. When he finally arrived, Luna was not a happy camper. He greeted me with a wide-eyed hiss, his ears flat.

"Hey buddy, you're safe now." I smiled at him and offered a slow blink.

Luna did not want to be buddies. He definitely did not feel safe. He hissed again and backed away.

"I know. I get it. You're just mad that some dumbass named you Luna, aren't you?"

He responded with a growl. Clearly this cat had no sense of humor, because everyone knows I'm hilarious.

Mr. Bitey, the gray devil. But yeah, I love him.

I sat in my office at the computer and went about my work editing school yearbook videos. Luna tested the bars with his teeth, beat on them like a desperate prison inmate. He climbed the sides, looking for an escape. He anxiously paced back and forth, lunging and spitting if I dared to walk past. I made it a point to ignore him. Let him chill and get comfortable being in the same room with me.

By the second day of his stay at Hotel Mancuso, I figured our newest guest would be a bit more relaxed. Boy was I wrong. He had already scared off Cathy when she tried to feed him breakfast. Swatting and lunging, he almost sank his teeth into her arm. I was left in sole charge of his care. Scooping his litter box, feeding him, and changing his water bowl were challenging tasks as he would swipe at me whenever I reached into the crate. Like Whack-A-Mole with claws. I used a piece of cardboard and the crate door as a shield.

He was not adapting to being kept in a crate, likely due to his trauma of having been locked in a closet. At this point I made a gesture of trust and opened the crate door to allow him to freely roam my office. Luna took a cautious step out of the crate, and as I turned to go back to my desk, he thanked me with a bite on my bare foot. I found his lack of gratitude to be a bit discourteous, but I was willing to chalk the incident up as a mishap. I left the room to disinfect the bite and give him an opportunity to explore his surroundings on his own terms without worrying about my presence.

When I came back to check on things, Luna was hiding somewhere. I didn't bother to look for him. No need to risk upsetting him further. I sat down with a cup of coffee and went back to work. Throughout the day I spoke aloud in a conversational tone about changing his name to something more suitable to his personality. I even threw out a bunch of suggestions: Graywind, Maximus, Rocky, Titan. Luna didn't seem enthused. He was still in hiding by the time I went to bed.

On day three, half asleep and sliding across the floor in my socks, I went to check on Luna. He was still in hiding. Looking in the open crate, I noticed he had eaten some food and used the litter box overnight. This was a good sign. He must be feeling more comf—*Motherfluffer!* I'd been ambushed with a quick bite on my Achilles tendon, like a nasty wasp sting. Then Luna was gone as quick as he came, but his attack betrayed his hiding spot, crouched under the printer stand. Now I knew where he was, and he knew I knew it. He uttered a strange sound, a mix of a meow and a growl, a greowl: *A bite a day will keep the fat man away.* We stayed away from each other the whole day. The next day would be better. Time and patience, I told myself; he'll come around.

The next morning's feeding I was on alert, wearing sneakers and prepared for Luna to come out from under the printer stand and bite me again. To my surprise I found him out in the open, sitting on a storage shelf. Not an optimal throne, but I was happy to see his body posture was much more relaxed.

"Are we going to be friends today?" I remained cautious but optimistic.

Luna jumped down from his perch, his tail up. He meowed as he circled around, rubbing his body against my legs. I dared a smile. Had I finally reached him? I leaned over slightly, and he booped my hand with his head. Progress. Maybe he felt bad that he had misjudged me and was trying to make amends—*OWWW! Son of a hiss!* It was a preemptive strike, an ankle bite just above my sneaker, adding a double whap to the back of my foot for good measure. He clearly hated feet, not that I could blame him, but mine were completely innocent. As a barrage of colorful expletives exploded from my mouth, Luna retreated, assumed a defensive posture, expecting retaliation. He crouched and hissed fearfully. Seeing him like that melted away any anger or frustration I had in the moment, and I could only feel sorry for him.

Time and patience, I thought to myself.

At that point, I chose to ignore him, sit at my desk, and start working. I certainly wasn't going to allow myself be chased from my own office by a seven-pound cat. I had to pay the bills, and he certainly wasn't chipping in for rent!

Soon Luna was back on the shelf, just watching me from across the room. Occasionally, I would turn to him and offer slow blinks. In cat speak this is a sign of love and trust. He didn't return the blink. However, later that afternoon, he came to me for affection, rubbing his body against my legs. He received some cautious petting for his effort to make friends. There was hope. Tomorrow will be better.

The next day, Jaws was at it again, then again and again on the days that followed. Each time I thought we had made a real connection, there was always a step back. Since my feet were protected, he moved up to my legs for a total of six unprovoked bites in seven days. The last one was the deepest: two sets of bloody fang holes in my left calf as if I had been bitten by tiny Draculas. I felt like a damn pincushion and left with a sense of hopeless exasperation. Being totally honest with you, I was close to giving up on him . . . for about fifteen minutes.

"Wifey, get me the carrier. That biting hisshead is out the fluffing door!" I was ranting and raving, hissing in pain as I disinfected the bites. "Say goodbye, Mr. Bitey."

A moment later, Cathy appeared with the carrier and offered it to me with a blank face. I was surprised. I had expected some kind of protest or plea from her on his behalf. "Here," she said, daring me to take it.

I did. More forcefully than I had intended.

"Go ahead," she said. "That's what everyone else did. Then what?"

Then I will have failed him, too.

As usual, she was right. Her eyes softened as she watched it sink in. Without a word, she took the empty carrier out of my hand. Well played, Wifey.

I realized that if I deserted Luna, I couldn't expect more from anyone else. Once placed in a shelter, he would surely scratch or bite someone else and would inevitably end up on the list for euthanasia due to his temperament. I had no doubt. He clearly wanted love, but until now humans had failed him, forcing him to react with fear and mistrust. I couldn't let it happen again, not with his fate resting in my hands. I was all he had. The bite on my leg would eventually heal with some antibiotics, but if I gave up on Luna, I would have an open wound on my soul for the rest of my days. I had the time; all I needed was the patience.

Well, at least I had finally come up with his new name: Mr. Bitey.

It took weeks for Mr. Bitey to fully decompress and feel safe in his suite at Hotel Mancuso. Once we got him neutered, his more aggressive tendencies faded. Slowly he and I began to trust one another. Being that I was on a tight work deadline, we spent ten hours a day together in my office. I taught him how to edit video, and he let me know when it was time to take a break by jumping on my lap or walking across the computer keyboard. Throughout the process we had plenty of setbacks in our relationship, but our foundation was solid. Bites were replaced by love nips and lap naps. Eventually Mr. Bitey became very attached to Cathy and me. He finally had come to know real love and contentment.

We ultimately decided to make him an official part of the family. Even then, however, I knew it wouldn't lead to a fairytale ending. After all, Mr. Bitey was still a work in progress. We would still need to introduce him to the fur-brigade, and judging from his hisses at the curious paws reaching under my office door, I was well aware more challenges lay ahead.

Hey, no one ever said rescue was easy. ☙

THE KITTY COLD

As I've stated previously, cats are very sensitive to change. The bigger the change, the more stressed they become, and the first week in a new castle is no exception. The anxiety can put a strain on their immune system and induce an upper respiratory infection that rescuers often refer to as a "kitty cold." It's similar to the common cold for people and equally as contagious, which is why it is so important to isolate Your Majesty from any resident pets for the first week.

Of course, cats adopted from a shelter are very prone to upper respiratory infection, not only due to the increased stress, but also their exposure to more viruses in other stressed, sick animals. But any new cat in your home, even one purchased from a breeder, is susceptible to developing a kitty cold. I've had perfectly healthy cats and kittens come from people's homes and get sick just from the stress of the transition, likewise some of my foster kitties also developed a cold in their new castle following an adoption. It can take several days for kitty cold symptoms to appear, and they may include:

- Nasal Congestion
- Sneezing/Coughing/Wheezing
- Runny Eyes/ Runny Nose with discharge
- Squinting
- Conjunctivitis (pink eye)

Cats with an upper respiratory infection will also lack an appetite and seem lethargic, but even healthy cats in a new environment may be reluctant to eat or explore in the beginning, so the best indicators will be the symptoms listed above.

(L) Rescue kitten with a severe upper respiratory infection. (R)The little fighter, one week into his medical treatment.

If your felion is showing symptoms of an upper respiratory infection, make sure to schedule an appointment with your veterinarian. While common and easily remedied with a ten-day course of antibiotics, an upper respiratory infection can get worse if left untreated.

During recovery remember to wash bedding and bowls frequently to protect against re-infection from contaminated objects. Don't worry, the kitty cold cannot be transmitted from pet to humans. However, if you have another pet in the home, be sure to wash your hands often to prevent spread.

TRACKING THE ANNALS OF OWNERSHIP

If you read that and think I'm referring to anything other than registering your felion's microchip in an online database, get your mind out of the litter box. Chances are good that if your Overlord comes from a rescue or shelter, they will have been tagged already. In the unfortunate instance that Houdini pulls a fast one and disappears out of your castle, if they are found and brought to a shelter or veterinarian, a quick scan will be able to help track down the head servant.

A microchip is an identification chip implanted under the skin, not to be confused with a GPS tracker, which is a more recent technological advancement in loss prevention. A pet GPS tracker is a special collar that uses satellites to pinpoint and send their location to an app on your phone. Some trackers will show where your cat has been or even light up at night, making it much easier for a worried servant to retrieve their missing monarch. Of course, this technology requires a monthly subscription fee for service, but all in all it's a small price to pay to be able to find a lost cat quickly.

Remember to have the microchip registered in your name. Should your kitty not come with a microchip, one can be implanted by your vet during their first exam. Always keep your contact information up to date.

Some sites offer pet registration in a national database for a small annual fee. Michelson's Found Animals is a free national pet registry where my cats are registered. Be as detailed as possible when describing your cat's physical attributes, and include photos. To register your pet visit: www.foundanimals.com.

HAPPY MEALS

Proper dietary nutrition is vital for the Overlord to be happy and healthy. They are obligate carnivores, which means they require higher protein intake, relying entirely on meat as their source of sustenance. If you're a vegan or vegetarian and you're considering submitting to felion rule, please understand that in spite of your objections to the consumption of animal flesh, cats simply cannot survive as vegetarians. You'll being doing a disservice to your ruler and put their health at great risk. Occasionally, they may enjoy a fruit or vegetable as a treat. It should always, however, be in moderation and in addition to a meat-based diet.

For adult Overlords, royal feasts should be served twice a day, ideally twelve hours apart. Some servants allow their cats to "graze-feed," leaving out a bowl of kibble all day and refilling it as needed. If you decide to use this method, be sure to only do so with kibble. Wet food should never be left out for more than a few hours or it will start to collect bacteria and cause digestive issues. Although graze feeding allows your cat to eat small meals throughout the day, it can lead to obesity if you're putting out too much dry food. If you choose to let your felion free feed, it's important to limit how much food is portioned out per day. Also, after sitting out for a day kibble becomes stale, so it's always best to replace it daily with food fresh.

Graze feeding is a viable choice for servants who need to be out the house for long periods of time, but whenever possible, scheduled feedings are a better alternative because they allow you to feed the Overlord and at the same time every day. It's imperative to their emotional and digestive health that feedings stay consistent. As you'll read over and over in this book, cats thrive on routine. If you're running late serving breakfast or dinner, Your Majesty will be sure to inform you of their displeasure . . . loudly.

There are pros and cons to serving royal feasts from a bag or can. Bagged kibble is easier, cheaper, can be left out longer, and can benefit oral health by reducing tarter build up. Dry food, however, contains significantly less moisture, and if not properly regulated, it can lead to obesity. Canned or wet food is more expensive and less convenient, but it's still a good idea to incorporate it as part of their regular diet. Canned food helps prevent constipation, promote urinary health, and assist with weight management. My recommendation would be a combination of both wet and dry food.

Whatever type of food you decide to serve, there are plenty of choices on the market. Not only can you find a variety of flavors, but also grain free, hairball control, age specific, and food for cats with more sensitive digestion. Commercial cat foods are specifically formulated to include all of your cat's nutritional requirements. My one suggestion would be to mix things up, incorporate a variety of brands and flavors into the menu. This will help keep Your Highness from becoming a famously finicky eater. If you decide to switch flavors, brands, or alter your cat's diet, one thing to keep in mind is that cats need to be transitioned gradually. To minimize any digestive issues, please follow the transition schedule below.

DAY 1: 25% new brand 75% old brand
DAY 4: 50% new brand 50% old brand
DAY 6: 75% new brand 25% old brand
DAY 9: 100% new brand

Another dietary consideration is home cooked meals. This is a great option if you have the time and dedication to become the royal chef. This method comes with some drawbacks, however. Aside from being a more expensive alternative to commercial foods, you'll need to ensure that your cat is receiving enough of the specific nutrients they require. You'll need to research the tomes of recipes, making sure to add supplements such as Taurine, which are vital to a healthy felion diet. Cats that are not getting enough of these nutrients may seem fine for a while, but a deficiency can be a serious health concern. If you're considering a home prepped felion diet, I'd recommend prior consultation with your veterinarian.

Some servants may prefer to feed their Overlord a raw meat diet, but that brings a whole host of potential risk. While a raw meat diet more closely mimics the way felions would eat in the wild, in my opinion, the dangers of bacteria like E. coli and Salmonella, as well as possible parasites, render it too dangerous for Your Highness. Bacterial infections can not only impact the health of your felion, but if handled incorrectly, can also put everyone in the kingdom at risk. If you insist on considering a raw meat diet, I implore you to please consult your veterinarian first for a professional opinion and guidance.

· ·

FUR FACT   Cats are the only species of mammal that cannot taste sweetness. However, cats do have a special receptor on the roof of the mouth, the Jacobson's organ, which allows them to "taste-smell" aromas around them.

· ·

THE TRICK TO TREATS

Limit treats to no more than 10% of your cat's daily caloric intake. Unlike commercial cat food, treats are not a balanced source of nutrition and need to be used sparingly. It's like us trying to survive off candy; a Snickers bar tastes better than kale, but the ramifications of subsisting on chocolate, caramel, and peanuts will have a severely negative impact on our health. Feeding Your Majesty too many treats can lead to obesity or even refusing to eat their regular meals. Nevertheless, treats have their place. If your Catsandra Furpaws is food motivated, using treats as a reward will help you to train her—that is if she doesn't train you first!

Although the fur-brigade goes crazy for Temptations, I try to limit commercial treats and opt for healthier choices whenever possible. Certain fruits and vegetables are safe for felion consumption, and I sometimes offer small portions of tuna fish in water. Most of my cats enjoy boiled chicken, including the gizzards and the liver.

Human foods considered safe for cats include:

- Beef (lean cuts)
- Chicken (skinless)
- Eggs (boiled or scrambled without butter or seasoning)
- Fish
- Lamb

As I mentioned, it's best practice to avoid feeding Your Majesty raw meat; be sure to either bake or boil these tasty treats and cut up into bite-sized bits. Avoid frying as it is particularly unhealthy. Seasonings are unnecessary for a refined felion palate, not to mention some can be toxic.

Although felions are strict carnivores, they can occasionally indulge in some plant-based Hors d'oeuvres. These fruits and veggies are deemed cat-safe, but I'd recommend feeding them to Your Highness in strict moderation:

- Asparagus*
- Bananas
- Blueberries
- Bread
- Broccoli*
- Cantaloupe
- Carrots*
- Corn*
- Green Beans*
- Honeydew
- Lettuce
- Oatmeal*
- Peeled Apples
- Pumpkin
- Rice*
- Spinach**
- Watermelon

* *Cook: boil or steamed.*
** *Don't feed spinach to your cat if it has or previously had any urinary or kidney problems. Spinach can cause crystals to form in the urinary tract, which can lead to potentially fatal urethral blockage.*

Keep in mind that as the royal chef it is your responsibility to properly prepare these delicacies and limit portion size. As a loyal servant you must also familiarize yourself with which foods to avoid. Some foods are unhealthy, and others are downright toxic. Fruits should have their seeds removed during preparation. Bones, especially cooked, could cause choking or severe digestive damage. Human foods toxic to cats include:

- Alcohol
- Avocado
- Bones (cooked)
- Candy
- Chives
- Citrus Fruits
- Chocolate
- Coconut
- Coffee/Caffeine
- Milk/Dairy Products
- Fat Trimmings
- Garlic
- Grapes/Raisins
- Leeks
- Mushrooms
- Nuts
- Onions
- Salt
- Seeds
- Scallions
- Shallots
- Uncooked Potatoes
- Uncooked Tomatoes
- Xylitol/artificial sweetener
- Yeast/Raw dough[15]

WARNING: The symptoms of eating these foods can range from mild to extreme. If you know or suspect that your cat has eaten something on the toxic foods list, immediately call your veterinarian or the ASPCA Poison Control Center at 1-888-426-4435.

PEARLY WHITES

Tooth decay and gum disease are common issues in cats especially as they get older, so be sure to keep up with your felion's oral hygiene. Tooth and gum infections are not only painful but can often lead to other health concerns. Keeping your Overlord's teeth white will also help you keep extra green in your wallet over the long term. Optimally, a cat should have their pearly whites brushed daily. This can be done with a special cat toothbrush. It's important to only use toothpaste specifically designed for cats, as human products can be toxic.

As you can imagine, brushing your felion's teeth is easier said than done, especially if they've never had it done prior. Start this chore as early in their life as possible. However, if you're like me and find that you're unable to brush your cat's teeth, schedule a dental cleaning with your vet at least twice a year, or at the bare minimum as part of Your Majesty's annual vet visit. Regular cleanings can help prevent tooth decay and gum infections. Proper dental care can also reduce the risk of certain types of oral cancer and even heart disease. Not only will you keep Your Highness healthy, but in the long run you'll also be much less likely to empty the coffers for preventable veterinary expenses.

. . . .

FUR FACT   Unlike humans, a cat's kidneys can filter the salt out of seawater, allowing them to drink it in order to survive. That being said, you should NOT be giving your cat saltwater to drink unless you're adrift at sea in a lifeboat.

. . . .

DRINK UP

Making sure Your Majesty is drinking enough water is critical to maintain good health and help prevent dehydration. Cats that consume a dry food diet will need to drink more water than cats that have wet food incorporated into royal feasts. Proper hydration prevents the development of urinary and kidney-related health problems. The recommended intake of fresh water for cats is 4oz for every five pounds of body weight. So a ten-pound felion should drink at least 8oz of water per day.

Water bowls should be cleaned and refilled daily. If you use a gravity water dispenser, you've bought yourself a little time and can wash these every few days. Consider using steel or ceramic bowls instead of plastic, which can harbor more bacteria and lead to cat acne on their chins. As with food bowls, wider bowls reduce whisker stress and are usually preferable for cats.

Fountains are a great way to encourage the Overlord to drink more since they are instinctually attracted to running water. In the wild, a flowing water source is far more appealing to cats than a standing puddle, which can be stagnant and full of bacteria. The same holds true for Your Majesty who views running water in the castle as fresher and cleaner. This is one reason why some felions enjoy drinking from sink faucets. The fur-brigade absolutely loves our water fountains, and I highly recommend getting one for your kingdom. Fountains can be a little more difficult to clean, and you'll need to schedule regular filter changes, but overall, it's definitely worth the extra time and investment.

If you're concerned your felion isn't drinking enough on a normal basis, you can add some extra water to their food. Other tricks we have used include adding a few drops of tuna juice, clam juice, or sardine juice (from the can) to their water for a little flavoring.

THE GAME OF THRONES

Any felion will tell you, being awesome is exhausting. This is why the Great Ones sleep anywhere between twelve and eighteen hours a day. Fortunately, that makes them perfect companions if you're like me and enjoy spending your off time relaxing. Kittens and seniors can sleep even longer, up to twenty hours a day. Since felions are hardwired as predators and hunting prey takes an enormous amount of effort, they naturally try to conserve energy, not to mention they have to supervise your fulfillment of duties to ensure compliance. Like lions and other wild members of the felid family, Your Majesty tends to be most active during the magic hours of dusk and dawn.

When settling into their new castle, the Overlord will likely spend late night hours exploring their territory, claiming one throne at a time. A chair. A pillow. A lap. As they continue to expand their rule, Your Majesty will nap wherever and whenever they please. You'll find them in some awkward and hilarious positions. *I claim this fruit bowl for the House of the Cat.* Day or night, high and low, you can find felions napping in their favorite places, some of which will also happen to be your favorite places. In the game of thrones, if you move your feet, you lose your seat.

Most monarchs, in their benign wisdom, will be more than happy to share space and warmth with you. They feel safe knowing that you will protect them while they sleep. For the lucky, our most honored prize is to personally serve as Your Majesty's throne.

THE SANDCASTLE

Unlike dogs, cats don't need to go outside multiple times a day to do their business; they use sandcastles, also known as litter boxes. There are a wide variety of boxes and litters available. Litter types include clay, silica, pine pellets, paper, clumping, non-clumping, scented, unscented, and even multi-cat formula. When choosing a type of kitty litter, it's not as simple as one size fits all. While my Overlords seem to prefer the sandy clumping litter, yours may not like the granular feel on their paws and prefer pellets or paper. It can sometimes be trial and error until you find a litter to their liking.

Cats instinctively bury their waste, but it's not a courtesy for our benefit. This behavior traces back to their roots. In the wild, cats aren't at the top of the food chain. Burying their waste is an effort to hide their presence from predators. If you notice that Your Majesty is not covering their poop, this could mean several things. Either they are alerting you to an underlying health issue, letting you know they are not pleased with your choice of litter, or if you have a multi-cat household, it could be a display of dominance.

Sandcastles come in all different shapes and sizes. Whether you choose a standard tray/pan type, one with high sides, or one with a covering, make sure it's large enough to accommodate your cat's entire body. Pour about three to four inches of litter into the box so they have enough to bury their treasure. Litter box placement is also important. Keep the sandcastle away from their food and water. If possible, choose a quiet location in the kingdom, but make sure the royal privy is always easily accessible.

Because some finicky felions prefer to use one box for pooping and the other strictly for urination, some cat behaviorists recommend one litter box per cat, plus one: 1 cat = 2 litter boxes; 2 cats = 3 litter boxes, etc. In my experience, however, a lone ruler can do just fine with one litter box as long as it is kept clean. Before we added a second cat to our family, Sunny Girl had only one box and there was never an issue, and I know more than a few people with one cat and one sandcastle. However, if you have more than one cat, you really should also have more than one box. That's only fair. With so many kitties of our own, not only do we scoop out boxes two to three times a day, Cathy gives each box a thorough washing every week. You really don't want to know how much money we spend on cat litter every month unless you could use a good laugh!

FUR FACT   Kitty litter was an accidental discovery made by Edward Lowe in 1947, and he later developed the Tidy Cat brand of litter. Prior to that, humans provided boxes of paper, ashes, dirt, or sand, none of which did a proper job of absorbing the smell, which is one of the reasons most felions were kept as indoor/outdoor pets.

Have you ever stepped into a public restroom to find it was an assault to your senses? The rank smell causes you to hold your breath, you're afraid to touch anything, and you're considering burning your shoes after having stepped in a wet spot! If so, you should be able to relate to the Overlord not wanting to use a soiled litter box. Even though they bury their waste, a cat's sense of smell is fourteen times better than a human's. This is a huge reason for "accidents" right outside the box. Cats know they are supposed to relieve themselves in the box, but it smells horrible, and they likely can't find a clean space. Do yourself and your kitty a favor and always keep the sandcastle clean. Scooping twice a day is recommended, but you can probably get away with once a day if you serve a single monarch. Don't let your sandcastle become that disgusting public bathroom. It's a dirty job, but someone's got to do it.

FUR FACT   A royal coat is actually made from three different types of hair. Cats have a layer of hairs that make up the undercoat, awn hairs that insulate the body, and longer, thicker outer hairs that protect the skin and prominently display colors and patterns.

ROYAL GROOMING HABITS

Very clean animals by nature, cats don't require bathing, not to mention, it's totally undignified. Bathing Your Majesty is stressful and unnecessary . . . for both of you. You think you can do a better job than they can? Felions are fastidious self-groomers with the highest standards of hygiene, spending 30% or more of their waking hours cleaning and preening themselves. They'll lick their paws and comb their furry faces with them. Call it vanity, but the Overlords love their own scent, and there's nothing like a good tongue washing to deposit their favorite cologne.

Even though they always like to look and smell their best, the Overlords aren't total narcissists. Denticles on their tongue acts as a wet brush, not only removing dirt and excess fur, but also helping to keep kitty cool. Additionally, cats use grooming to self-sooth in stressful situations. This coping mechanism, however, can lead to over grooming, which in turn can lead to patches of missing fur and skin irritations.

An absence or lack of grooming could be a sign of a health issue. This could also be accompanied by a lack of appetite and low energy. Obese cats have difficulties grooming, unable to properly reach their backs and hindquarters.

Anyone owned by a cat will tell you that fur is the gift that keeps on giving. You know the Christmas tree tinsel you keep finding around the house even months after the holiday? Cat hair is like that, but everywhere, and all the time. In my house, with so many in our fur-brigade, it can look like we're being invaded by Tribbles. *Star Trek* reference aside, shedding is unavoidable, and indoor felions shed all year round. If you think you're going to keep Your Majesty from sitting on your couch, chilling on your bed, or sleeping on your clothes, don't bother. It's a losing battle. Once owned by a felion, you must submit to this behavior, so vacuum regularly and invest in some lint rollers.

Shorthaired cats will benefit from a gentle brushing of the royal coat once a week, which will help cut down on shedding and reduce hairballs. However, if you choose to be owned by a longhaired cat, you will want to brush them daily to avoid matting and clumping. If you do so regularly and correctly, many Overlords will enjoy the brushing as part of worship, and it can help you bond. Not so much if you if you end up only combing out the knots or need to cut the knots out of a felion like our shaggy Shinobi-Kenobi. He rolls around on the floor, tangling his fur while being cute all day long, then cries like a baby and swats my hand when I attempt to brush him properly! Caring for Shinobi's fur can be a lot of work, so we treat ourselves by getting him a short "lion cut" shave to sport once or twice a year.

. . . .

FUR FACT   Cats have up to thirty-two whiskers on their face, twelve on each cheek, up to eight over their eyes, and between six and eight on each of their front paws.

. . . .

Whiskers are also a type of hair, only much thicker. Although they're quite stylish and regal, they are not merely for good looks. Like magic, the Overlords gather information through their whiskers, which are embedded in their nervous system and provide sensory input, not unlike insect antennae. Lengths vary by cat; the bigger the felion, the longer the whiskers. They transmit information about the size, shape, and speed of nearby objects, which helps cats navigate. The Great Ones' whiskers will help determine if they can fit through a small space without getting stuck. Whiskers are so sensitive they can detect the movement of air, acting as a kind of cat radar, allowing them to locate food and keep from bumping into walls. Proprioceptors located at the ends of whiskers alert the brain regarding the position of the body and limbs and are partly responsible for how cats almost always land on their feet. Unlike fur, these valuable hairs should never be trimmed or cut, which would drastically decrease a Your Majesty's sense of spatial awareness and cause confusion.

PAWDICURES

Congratulations, you're officially hired as the royal pedicurist. As you will learn, this is a thankless but necessary duty to fulfill. While the Overlord may not appreciate this service, hopefully they will learn to accept it with dignity and grace, like my sweet Miyagi. She spreads out her toes to make my job easier. Despite her well-mannered example, reactions from my other cats range from begrudging tolerance to angry protests.

You should trim your cat's claws every few weeks. It's best to start this practice early; regularly clipping a kitten's nails will make the process easier when they reach adulthood. Since felion claws are curved inward, there is the possibility of puncturing your cat's paw-pad if they get too long. This can be extremely painful (ever had an ingrown toenail?) and cause an infection. Not only is nail trimming beneficial for your cat, but they'll be also less apt to scratch your furniture. As you may or may not know, some Overlords like to knead on their favorite servants, and while this is a truly adorable sign of their affection, if their claws aren't trimmed it can be a less pleasant experience than intended.

How to Trim Claws

- Reverently take Your Majesty's paw in your hand and, using your thumb and forefinger, gently press on the digit to expose the retracted claw.
- Using a pet nail clipper, snip off the tip. Be quick and efficient; the Overlord doesn't appreciate dillydallying and will grow impatient should you take too long. Be careful not to get too close to the quick (the pink part) as that has blood vessels and will cause pain and bleeding. Not to mention hours of guilt and profuse apologizing to Your Highness.
- If your cat becomes overtly stressed and starts throwing a royal hissyfit, stop and try again at another time. Of course, this could result in you only being able to trim one paw, or even claw at a time. Be vigilant. Hopefully, the repetition will slowly cause them to accept the process.
- When you're finished, commend them on a job well done, and reward their courage with ample worship. Celebrate your Overlord's triumph by offering a favorite treat so they can start to make a positive association with the practice.

For Overlords that are not accustomed to receiving regular pawdicures, the process can be unsettling or even frightening. If you're not able to restrain them on your own, you may require an assistant to help. When it comes to nail trimmings, my wife and I often have to work as a team on some or our more difficult cats.

. . . .

FUR FACT   Cat's claws grow inward. While this makes them adept at climbing up trees, it makes climbing down headfirst almost impossible. This is why cats are notorious for getting stuck in trees or on top of poles.

. . . .

Tips for Clips

- Try to make the process as stress free as possible. Prepare everything in advance; make sure supplies are laid out within arms-reach. Eliminate distractions, especially anything that could startle your cat like phones, kids and even other pets.
- Wear long sleeves to protect your arms. If you're dealing with a habitual scratcher, armor up in layers or consider purchasing specialized handling gloves.
- Be calm and cool. Your Majesty respects confidence. The more you stress out, the more your cat will as well.
- Personally, I like to give impromptu homilies in an effort to keep their attention focused on my voice rather than on what I'm doing.
- Get Your Highness tired from a royal feast or play session beforehand.

The Purrito Wrap – This technique involves swaddling your cat in a towel with only their head and paws exposed, leaving Your Highness looking like a kitty burrito. Being wrapped in this way is comforting for some cats. It also keeps them from thrashing too much and injuring themselves or their loyal servant. The aptly named "Purrito" is a safe and effective restraint which can also be employed for other unappreciated duties such as giving medications, cleaning ears, and brushing teeth.

Go Pro – If you're really struggling or anxious, you should get an appointment with your vet, or even a groomer. Nail trims are relatively quick and inexpensive, usually starting around $10-$15. On the plus side, your vet might also be able to detect any health issues during a curt, visual inspection, like checking their ears or paws for any signs of infection.

Grooming Helmet – Consider this alternative to safely trim the claws of uncooperative cats. The grooming helmet resembles a fishbowl, or an old astronaut helmet from those 1950s sci-fi films, it is placed around the Your Majesty's head and will keep you free of bites during pawdicures. One drawback with this bubblehead approach is that they can still see what you're doing and may put up a fuss in resistance.

The Cat Muzzle – The cat muzzle is an adjustable fabric hood that covers the face of your extra feisty felion so they can't see what's going on. A small hole for their nose allows them to breathe but prevents them from opening their mouths enough to bite. For some felions, covering their eyes can be soothing, but other cats may totally spaz out. If you choose to use a muzzle, you must watch your cat closely and be ready to remove it immediately if your cat starts to vomit or has difficulty breathing.

A muzzle shouldn't be your first option; it's much better for Your Highness if you take the time and have the patience to get them comfortable with nail trimmings. I only use a muzzle on my biters, and only after trying everything else.

CAT TALES: *What Goes Up*

"This cat has been on top of this pole since noon today. The police said it's not their job, and the Fire Department won't help. It's on Tessa and VanDuzer."

It was 10:30 pm on February 2, 2017, when I saw that message from a woman named Michelle on the Staten Island Hope Facebook page. There was a photo attached as well. Through the bare tree branches I could see the silhouette of the kitty sitting atop the narrow pole. Poor kitty must've been absolutely terrified.

The temperature had dipped below freezing since sunset. The cat had no shelter from the brutal cold and had gone without food or water for nearly twelve hours. Possibly more. There was no telling how long the cat had been up there, and I wondered what drove him up the pole in first place. Most likely hunting a squirrel, or perhaps he was chased up there

Help! Cat stranded on top of a pole for 12 hours.

by a predator. Nevertheless, a rescue was in order, and I pondered how best to get him down.

Before a plan formulated in my head, I responded to Michelle's plea for help, saying I would be there as soon as I could. She messaged me her phone number and asked me to call her when I arrived. Honestly, I was not prepared for this type of rescue, but I had to do something. I just wasn't sure what. I didn't even own a ladder. My father-in-law had one, but it only extended to twenty feet, and it wasn't like I could safely fasten two ladders together . . . or could I?

Don't even think about it, Mancuso. You're no MacGyver.

I was glad the rational side of my brain decided to speak up, because (God help me) the emotional side was already entertaining the idea of using duct tape.

Whatever action I was going to take, I knew I needed to recruit help, so I reached out to Michael Dietrich, a fellow rescuer and SI Hope volunteer. Mike had plenty of experience with trapping stray and feral cats; he'd know what to do. Maybe he would even have a tall-enough ladder.

He didn't.

Mike and I decided to make a few calls and then meet at the location. I knew of only two people I could ring at this late hour to ask for a

30-foot ladder. Both calls went to voicemail. I could only hope Mike was having better luck on his end. Within five minutes I was grabbing my coat from the hallway closet.

Catherine's sleepy voice called out from the darkness of our bedroom, "Chris? Where are you going?"

She turned on the bedside lamp, and I briefed her on the situation.

"You're going by yourself? Now?" There was concern in my wife's voice, not only for the safety of the cat, but mine as well. "How are you going to get him down?"

I crossed the room to give her a kiss. "Don't worry, I'm going to meet Mike." Of course, our calico, Caramel, demanded a tribute as well since I had also interrupted her sleep. Satisfied with a peck on the head, she curled back into a ball at Cathy's side. "Sorry I woke you, Wifey. Go back to sleep."

"Are you bringing him back here?"

"Who, Mike or the cat?"

She rolled her eyes. "The cat."

"I don't know. I'm not sure what's gonna happen. Maybe Mike will take him. We have to get the cat down first. That's the top priority."

"But how?"

I had no answer. I kissed her instead.

The worry again: "Honey, please be careful."

"I promise." I stole another kiss and was out the door.

On my way out I grabbed my camera bag and a pet carrier. In the event we were unable to get the cat down, I wanted to record footage and post an online plea for help.

It was a twenty-five-minute drive. The heat in my van was finally kicking in by the time I parked on VanDuzer street. Mike was already there, standing on the sidewalk, a shadow among shadows.

"Mike! Thanks for meeting me."

"Of course," he said. "No luck tracking down a ladder." It wasn't a question. "Yeah. Me neither."

"I brought a carrier." I said, proud of my forethought.

Mike had brought a carrier as well, but his was much larger. All things considered; it was obviously the better choice.

"Okay. We'll use yours," I said. "Show off."

Mike laughed. "Don't feel bad, it's genetics."

"Did you get eyes on the cat?"

Mike pointed. I craned my neck as my gaze followed his finger above the skeletal tree line. Above the two-story house. It took a second for my eyes to recognize the tiny shadow outlined against the night sky. The cat was hunched, silent and motionless with fear. Just looking up, I experienced a brief moment of vertigo, my own acrophobia tickling my insides with nervous electricity.

We stared up at the cat before looking at each other.

"Damn," I whispered, swallowing hard.

Michelle, a middle-aged woman, came outside to greet us. For her, the last twelve hours had been filled with fraught phone calls and pleas for help as she watched the stranded felion from her window. She looked tired and worried but managed to give us a grateful smile as we shook hands.

"What now?" she asked.

Indeed. We watched. We waited. The minutes ticked by.

Home Depot opened fairly early, and we talked about renting an extension ladder. Maybe SIACC would send a field worker, but they did not open until 8:00 am, and who knew how long it would take for field rescue to arrive? In the freezing cold, every minute counted.

A light bulb went off in Mike's eyes. "Let me see what I can do . . ." He reached into his pocket for his phone. "I'm gonna call my job and see if they'll send someone with a cherry picker."

Mike worked for Con Edison, the local power company. It was a Hail Mary, but we clung to the sliver of hope, not unlike the cat we were trying to save.

He hung up with a smile. "A truck is on its way. Should be about forty-five minutes to an hour."

"Oh, that's wonderful!" Michelle exclaimed.

"Dude! You are the fluffin' man!"

Mike waved off my compliment and turned his attention back to the cat. "Don't worry cat, somebody's coming to get you down."

Michelle went back into her house to wait, but I promised to call her as soon as Con Edison arrived. Mike and I froze our butts off on the sidewalk waiting to flag down the truck. We occupied the time with good-natured banter and caught up on cat-guy talk.

The lineman, Michael Amatrudo, got out of the vehicle and introduced himself. The Mikes did most of the talking. Michael A had no experience with cats but was an animal lover and assured us he would do his best. Mike D handed him the carrier into which we had put a can of food, hoping hunger would help lure the cat inside.

The truck's engine continued to rumble; hydraulics whined. Michelle joined us outside and the three of us stood together, our necks craned, watching the bucket ascend and slowly maneuver towards the pole.

Although the top couldn't have been more than twelve inches wide, the cat was moving precariously from one side of the pole to the other as the worker tried to coax him into the carrier.

"Come on." We rooted. "Go on, get in there."

As the lineman repositioned the bucket, I zoomed in with my camera lens, trying to hold a steady shot. It was difficult to see what was happening, but then I caught the glow of the cat's eyes in my camera light. He was staring with wide-eyed fear, desperately trying to avoid the worker. My heart was in my throat as the kitty maneuvered as if to climb down on his own but thought better of it.

The bucket moved again, completely obscuring our view from below. We waited long minutes with bated breath and crossed fingers, unable to drag our eyes away despite not being able to see what was happening.

"I got him!" The worker finally called from above.

Joyful cheers. The three of us gave him a round of applause.

Two minutes later we got our first up-close look at the pole-cat (who turned out to be a female). She was a beautiful, solid gray with big yellow eyes. Staring out from the carrier, she didn't seem fearful, which I took as a good sign she was at least relatively friendly.

With the cat safe, it was decided that I would take her to Hotel Mancuso. After securing the carrier in the front seat, I said goodbye to Mike with a manly man hug. During the drive, I did most of the talking. When I got home, I saw that Cathy had set up the isolation crate in my office before going back to sleep. She really is the best!

As it turned out, Tessa had a very sweet disposition. She recognized that I was one of the good guys. After spending hours in the freezing cold, she was more than happy to have a meal, curl up in some warm blankets, and take a nap. The next day she received a clean bill of health from our awesome rescue vet, Dr. Singh. She also was tested, vaccinated, and scheduled for spay.

Tessa, down safe and sound. Time to take a trip to Hotel Mancuso.

I shared the video of her harrowing midnight rescue on social media. The story was even picked up by the Staten Island Advance, with Michael Armatrudo and Con Edison receiving well-deserved praise. Despite all the shares and views of my video, no one had stepped up to reclaim Tessa. Several families reached out with adoption inquiries, though, and two weeks later, Tessa selected her new servants, who came all the way from Pennsylvania to meet her. ☙

THE COMPLAINT DEPARTMENT

Effectively ruling an empire can be very demanding for any Overlord. Boundaries must be marked and protected. Daily safety inspections are required to be completed on schedule. Everything in the domain has its place and reason. Order must be kept at all times. Not only do cats have their own schedule to keep, Your Highness also must supervise their humans to ensure quality of service.

Apparently, overseeing the realm also involves a lot of administration. No detail goes unnoticed. Meticulous note takers, cats are fans of bureaucracy. Rules are meant to be followed. However, felion rules are quite different than ours, and the Overlords give little thought to our customs and behaviors. In order to maintain peace within the kingdom, as devotees it is we who are expected to fall in line. Depending on their personality, Overlords have varying standards and expectations with which to comply. Each day the meowing monarchs will review the state of their dominion and determine what, if any, action is necessary to refine the kingdom to their will. Obviously, filling out paperwork is beneath the Overlord. They have wonderful memories and do all their management internally. Your Majesty will be sure to issue an official doctrine of complaint should they find any aspect of castle life unsatisfactory.

It is your sworn duty to ensure harmony in the realm, as such you must address all the royal complaints in a timely manner. It's of great importance to learn the secret language of Meow and pass this felion wisdom on to all citizens and ambassadors who serve at the pleasure of the Overlord.

THE SECRET LANGUAGE OF MEOW

"CATS SPEAK ONLY TO THOSE WHO KNOW HOW TO LISTEN."

—SIGMOND FREUD

CATS CAN OFTEN SEEM aloof. You call your dog's name and he happily comes plodding over, tail wagging, looking for your approval. If you call for Your Majesty, don't expect too much. The chances of them "here, kitty kitty-ing" are fifty-fifty at best. Most likely you'll get an ear twitch, or maybe a head-turn as an acknowledgement. But just because your felion doesn't always come at your beck and call doesn't mean they don't give a fluff. It's just the way they are hardwired.

Unlike dogs, cats have an independent streak and are most comfortable when things are on their terms. They are not as eager to please humans as their canine counterparts. As our Overlords, cats like to be in control at all times, and they want us to know it. They will often ignore our solicitations on principle, only coming to us when they desire to be worshiped. And when they do, we feel honored to have been chosen!

The truth is, despite seeming indifferent to their servants, the Overlords are more than happy to have us around. I've learned to recognize that they show us their love in subtle ways, like sitting next to us or simply being in the same room. The latter is perhaps one reason cats seem to hate closed doors so much, especially when their favorite people are behind those doors. They may meow or scratch at the door to be let inside . . . even if we're in the bathroom. *Whoa, slow your roll, buddy. You wouldn't like it if I stuck my head in your litter box while you were answering nature's call!*

Scientists believe cats can recognize anywhere from twenty-five to forty words. While they don't understand the meaning of words, felions understand them by association and repetition. They can definitely distinguish their name—whether they choose to acknowledge you is a different story. The same holds true for certain sounds. Opening a can of cat food will cause an excited stampede as dozens of paws rush into the kitchen expecting a royal feast. However, the fur-brigade doesn't realize the difference between opening cat food or a can of tomato sauce; they still scamper into the kitchen eagerly meowing. That being said, the fur-brigade knows the difference when I am opening a bag of treats versus opening a bag of potato chips. But these sounds are subtly different, and I always shake the bag of treats first.

Although they can recognize and respond to our words and various sounds, cats can't speak to us in return. Or can they? They communicate in their own language, but it's up to us to learn how to speak cat. Learning their language will greatly please the Overlord and improve your relationship.

LANGUAGE OF A HAPPY CAT

Cats may lack the ability to smile, but the Overlord can convey their good mood in many other ways. By learning how to decipher felion body language, you can earn trust, deepen the bonds of affection, as well as prevent misunderstandings and potential aggression.

We can learn a lot about what cats are trying to say by watching the position of their ears, tail, fur, and eyes. Body language speaks volumes in cats. Every behavior is saying something about their feelings or health. Granted, cat speak can be a little confusing at times, like how a word can have multiple meanings in English. For example, they're, there, and their all sound the same despite being spelled differently, each with its own meaning. The same is true for cat speak, therefore, it is important to take all cues and behaviors into account so you can have a complete context of what the Overlord is trying to tell you.

Good Vibrations – An obvious indicator of mood, a cat's tail is tail like an emotional barometer. If Your Majesty's tail is straight up and vibrating like a tuning fork, this signals love and excitement. Frequencies of joy are being broadcast through their rear transmitter. You are the Chosen One. Consider yourself lucky; the Overlord is extremely happy to see you. Reward their favor with extra snuggles and one-on-one time.

Tall Tails – When Your Highness parades around the castle with their tail held high it signifies a happy mood and a willingness to be social. An efficient and confident salutation, a raised tail is the equivalent of a friendly greeting. A furry banner of good will, a tall tale displays approval. Well done. If the tip of the tail is hooked like a question mark, the Royal Highness is feeling altruistic and inquisitive. Consider yourself very fortunate for being granted an audience. The Overlord is willing to accept your worship or engage in fun, felion games. Make the most of this opportunity.

The Cat Hug – When showing love and affection Your Majesty will often curl their furry butt-arm around you. This highly flexible appendage, sometimes referred to as a tail, is a felion's special way of hugging their favorite people or other animals.

Now Hear This – With thirty-two muscles in their ears, cats can rotate each independently of one another, up to 180 degrees. The position of a cat's ears in relation to posture can be telling. Neutral refers to the ears' natural direction. In this case, the Overlord is feeling relaxed and agreeable. They are more than happy to listen to whatever you have to say. When a cat's ears perk straight up, Your Majesty is on alert, and something has their attention. Trying to collect as much auditory data as possible, a felion will face their ears forward and focus their superior hearing. Perhaps kitty is feeling curious or playful, like when they're checking out a new toy. Maybe ninja cat is ready to go on the prowl.

Snake Eyes – When it comes to nonverbal felion communication, there's more than meets the eyes. Felion pupils are vertical and shaped like slits. They fluctuate in size and shape based on light and emotion.

When a cat's pupils are visible as slits, this is like a vertical smile. The Overlord is content and relaxed. Droopy lids may signal they are about to take a catnap and they trust you enough not to have to find a private space to catch up on some beauty rest.

Slow Blinks – Even when on the other side of the room and not necessarily seeking affection, your willingness to serve pleases Your Majesty. Think of slow blinks as long-distance cat kisses. Although slow blinking is a subtle communication, it is a significant expression of love. Do not take it for granted.

Happy Dance – *I'm so excited, and I just can't hide it.* When the Overlord is overjoyed to see their favorite person, they will perform a ceremonial dance for your benefit. Furry little paws will joyfully bop in time with a musical recital of their favorite felion love song. Whether the happy dance is an intricate ballet or a simple two-step, the rhythm is gonna get you.

The Body Rub – When a felion rubs their body against you, it is a clear sign they want something. They could want some worship time. They may be hungry. They could even be telling you it's time to scoop the sandcastle. Your best bet is to just go ahead and perform all three tasks.

Blessed Boops – In Cat World, head, nose, and cheek bumps are felion blessings. With the power to sanctify, the Great Ones will boop the faithful with approval. Sure, you were late serving dinner and you missed worship service, but with a loving boop, all is forgiven. With scent glands in their cheeks and foreheads, the Overlords are reinforcing their ownership and depositing their kitty cologne on you because it's always important for you to smell their best.

Paws of Pause – When you are occupied by non-felion related activities, the Overlord reminds you of what is truly important: petting, playing, and snuggles. Using a paw to gently tap your arm, your leg, or even your head is a royal decree, *"Excuse me, but I require your undivided attention."* You are relieved of your current obligation, at least long enough to satisfy Your Majesty's need for worship.

Felion Baptism – Many Overlords are affectionate and will shower their staff with sandpaper kisses. A benevolent sign of felion adoration, baptisms are a sacred gift awarded to the pious. With the healing power of their tongue, the Great One is washing negativity away and purifying you in the name of the Celestial Meow. Taking part in this holy ritual strengthens the bond between felion and human. Although cat tongues are rough, felion wisdom dictates that all love comes with a little pain.

This End Up – A cat that feels comfortable enough to lie on their back and expose the most vulnerable part of their body around you is a tremendous sign of love and trust. This belly-up position is saying that Your Majesty trusts you with their life. Unlike a dog, a cat showing you belly is not a posture of submission. As tempting as it may be, you should not take this compliment as an invitation for a belly rub or risk springing the claw trap. Maybe Indiana Jones could escape the kitty Rickroll unscathed, but the rest of us are going to need some Band-Aids.

The Fluffening – Commonly referred to as fluffing or making biscuits, many cat experts speculate that kneading is a remnant behavior from kittenhood. Cats will fluff pillows, bedding, or anything soft in a display of happiness and comfort. True as that may be, kneading also serves a higher purpose; it is a form of therapeutic massage. Your Majesty possesses an ability to heal body and spirit, which she reserves for her most loyal servants. With a ritualistic Laying on of Paws, the fluffening focuses on precise pressure points that reduce stress, anxiety, and depression.

Some felions specialize in catupuncture, the ancient medical practice of inserting finely pointed claws into the skin to release toxins and cleanse your aura. Although intended as a gentle reward, felion acupuncture is often painful. Then again, your cat may simply be reminding you that it's time for a quadruple pawdicure!

The Blep – They are undignified and silly, but without a doubt cat bleps make the cutest photos. A blep is when a cat has the tip of their tongue protruding from a closed mouth without realizing it. This derpy look typically means that Your Highness is super chill. Or maybe they're contemptuously sticking their tongue out at you in the cutest possible way. Although a blep is adorable, as with the belly trap, you should resist the urge to touch it.

Certain breeds like Persians are more pre-disposed to having their tongue hang out due to their flattened faces. In some instances, like a constant blep paired with drooling, your felion may be dealing with a dental issue or mouth infection, and you should seek veterinary attention.

Elevator Butt – Going up? Does your kitty's butt go sky-high when you pet or scratch them? That's called the "elevator butt." Some cats will display the elevator butt no matter where they are petted, others may only respond in this fashion when you reach the base of their tail. Every cat has a different tolerance for physical affection, but an elevator butt lets you know you've hit the spot and to continue petting. Enjoy the ride.

Wiggle Butt – When she shakes that booty, Miss Wigglebottom isn't twerking. She's not about to pole dance on a scratcher hoping you'll toss her catnip. She is a mighty huntress, and that adorable wiggle is actually a precursor to pouncing that's connected to her wild instinct for stalking prey. Of course, butt-wiggling isn't limited to females, males shake their backsides, too. You'll often notice this hilarious behavior during playtime.

Butt-Faced – Relax, kitty didn't just punk you. When Your Highness puts their butt right in your face, think of it as an invitation for a gracious sniff. In Cat World, getting butt-faced is a special blessing. After all, you've earned this reward. Yeah, I know, the Great Ones have some strange customs, but who are we to question their wisdom? The good news is you don't have to kiss Your Majesty's asterisk to reciprocate. Instead, worship your cat with the standard pets and scritches.

Gift Giving – A dead mouse for me, really? It's not even my birthday. The Overlord is proud of their kill skills and is kindly offering to share their prize with you. If your ninja cat presents a fresh kill at your feet, try not to freak out, as hard as it may be. Instead, feign gratitude and commend them on their masterful hunting prowess. Remember, it's not the gift but the thought that counts. The fact that your felion is willing to share their prize with you is a high compliment. You are family— an adopted, clumsy bipedal, but family nonetheless.

Thankfully, not all gift offerings consist of the corpses of slain foes; many cats will bring their favorite toy to initiate a play session. Or perhaps they just want you to sing praises of their prowess and engage in an impromptu worship ceremony.

Suckling – If your kitty is suckling on your shirt, this is a sign of contentment and affection. It is also commonly paired with the fluffening. Suckling can also be a form of self-soothing, and Your Highness may suckle on blankets, towels, or other soft objects. As a young prince or princess, Your Highness may have been taken away too early from their Queen and still seeking the same feeling they had as a kitten.

Happy Drools – Equal parts adorable and gross, some cats will drool while they are being petted. Felions drool because they are extremely happy and their jaw muscles relax. You may also notice this commonly happens during the fluffening and when they suckle. It's totally normal. However, if your cat is drooling and it's not directly linked to petting, suckling, or fluffing, this could be a sign of illness, severe stress, or dental disease.

Love Nips – These little bites are not an act of aggression but a sign the Overlord holds you in high esteem. And what better way to show affection than to nibble their human? You're welcome. These little nibbles don't break the skin and are usually painless, or at least Your Highness will never intentionally hurt you. Love nips can also be an arrogant demand for attention in the cutest way possible. Every felion knows they can easily tear humans limb from limb with their powerful jaws, and these painless bites serve as a gentle reminder to us of that very fact. Either way, when the Overlord blesses you with a love nip, offer your humble gratitude and shower them with plenty of worship.

Kitty Kung Fu – Not only will cats Bruce Lee inanimate objects to amuse themselves, but they also like to find sparring partners to practice their Kitty Kung Fu skills and keep their reflexes sharp. Often when initiating a playful sparring session, Your Highness will slap another Royal seemingly for no reason, or perhaps ninja-slap a canine subject, or even one of the human servants. This ancient form of felion martial arts is used by the Overlords when hunting prey. Yes, cats like to play with their food. Don't worry, this furry flurry of strikes is done with retracted claws so as not to inflict injury on their opponent. That being said, you should still not engage in any of type of physical play with your hands; use an appropriate toy that kitty can chop, swipe and bap until their royal heart is content.

Zoomies – One minute they are calm and quiet, then, without warning, little Flash is zipping around the house *Fast & Furious*, bouncing off the walls and furniture like a pinball. Watching your monarch suddenly zipping throughout the castle can be curious, if not startling. The Zoomies are a normal release of pent-up energy and a good indication that Flash would benefit from some extra playtime added to the daily routine.

THE STOP SIGNS

As much as we'd like it to be, servitude isn't all purrs and cuddles. Part of your duty will be heading up the complaint department. Since the Overlords lack the ability to use facial expressions to convey emotions, they will communicate by using their ears, tails, eyes, and body postures. Paying close attention to these kitty cues will help you better understand your cat's emotional state and respond accordingly. Again, when trying to determine the disposition of your felion, remember to take all body parts as a whole, as each part is a piece of the puzzle.

Back Off – When approached, an anxious cat may slowly back away; they may even bolt towards their hidey-hole at warp speed. There's no mistaking this type of behavior for anything other than what it is. You can practically hear them whispering, "stranger danger." For whatever reason, the Overlord is not prepared to grant you an audience. For some rulers it may take time to earn their trust and friendship. Maybe they've been through some things. Until they become more comfortable with you, these felions will use avoidance. When they do, don't pursue. Chasing will only escalate their fear.

Lip Licking – Unless the Overlord has just finished a royal feast, if your cat is lip licking, this is a subtle indicator they feel uncomfortable. Although they may tolerate your or touch, it's likely they are mildly stressed, anxious, or even fearful. The Overlord is just not ready for this kind of closeness with you right now. Lip licking is a way cats soothe themselves and relieve stress. At this point, it's best to end the interaction before it can turn sour. Allow Your Majesty some time and space before requesting another audience.

Remember, cat speak can be a bit complicated as some gestures or behaviors have multiple meanings. Other potential reasons for lip licking include nasal congestion, dental pain, or nausea, all of which will require a vet check-up.

Airplane Ears – As mentioned, ears aren't just for listening. Airplane ears, when both ears are extended to the side of Your Majesty's head like wings, indicate that your felion is either angry or frightened. The flatter the ears are to the head, the more fearful the cat. Flattened ears are often accompanied by hisses or growling, especially if the Overlord is feeling particularly threatened. Airplane ears is a deliberate warning, the drawing back of the ears is a defensive mechanism to protect the cat's ears from an opponent's teeth or claws in a royal rumble.

Magical Mystical Mystacial Whiskers – Not only do the Overlord's whiskers magically pick up loads of sensory input from their surroundings, the mystacial whiskers, which are the whiskers on their muzzle, move independently from the whiskers or their chin or eyebrows, adding another layer of emoting to their repertoire. If a cat's cheek whiskers are rigid and pulled around their face, it means they feel threatened and possibly aggressive. As with their ears, cats flatten their whiskers to protect them during a fight.

The Black Holes – Fear and anxiety cause a cat's pupils to dilate, and you find yourself staring into black holes of a felion abyss. An Overlord's pupils dilate to take in as much visual information as possible about a potential threat. Keep in mind that wide, rounded pupils can also indicate playfulness or the hunting of prey. When in response to stressors or fear, Black Holes are typically paired up with crouching, as well as flattened ears and whiskers. Like with all of these stop signs, it's best not to force interactions.

Crouching Tiger – A crouching felion generally means fear, aggression, or possibly pain. To determine the which, a servant must also take external factors into account. There is nothing positive to say about a crouching kitty. As a means of conflict avoidance, a fearful or anxious cat may crouch, trying to appear smaller and less threatening, as if to say, "I'm not trying to mess with nobody. Look how small and unthreatening I am." As a form of defense, an aggressive felion may crouch, flatten their whiskers and ears, and narrow their eyes. In this way, they are strategically making themselves a smaller target but are also poised to spring into an attack and let their inner tiger loose. The absence of social stressors or environmental triggers could be indictive of Your Majesty suffering pain or illness.

Come At Me, Bro – A cat will usually prefer to avoid conflict whenever possible. However, as a matter of honor, some Overlords may feel the need to defend the crown when threatened. An unblinking stare will assert control and domination, but in the event subtle doesn't work, felions may choose a more aggressive tactic. They will raise their heads to show they will not back down from a royal rumble. Their ears go flat, and their whiskers pull back. This type of confrontation may be accompanied by a growl or hiss. Challenge accepted. Be advised, this escalating behavior is not a bluff.

The Down Low – Kitty is creeping on the down low. While this behavior is also utilized on the hunt, some scared cats will employ this method to attract as little attention as possible. A lowered tail signifies uncertainty or even aggression. By lowering their head, the cat is trying to convey a lack of interest and avoid potential conflict. Nervous and scared felions will creep low to the ground when they walk. They will move fast in hopes of going undetected, but they are also in a good position to spring into action if they fail to slip under the radar.

Tell Tail Stop Signs – Unlike their canine counterparts, cats generally wag their tails out of annoyance as opposed to a friendly wave hello. The speed of the tail swishing is a good gauge to determine the level of Your Majesty's irritation. A mere annoyance may cause a mild tail flick at the tip, whereas when angered the Overlord's tail will whip quickly back and forth, or even thump. Tail thrashing resembling an out of control metronome is usually a precursor to aggression, however you may also notice this behavior when your felion is on the hunt or involved in play. Oddly, my VanDuzer would wag his tail when he was happy (even though he had never been exposed to dogs), but he was an anomaly in that sense.

Tuck It Back – If your cat has their tail between their legs, it's a sign of extreme anxiety, stress, or insecurity. In an effort to appear nonthreatening, Your Highness may tuck tail in submission, especially if there is a more dominant felion around. A tucked tail can also be indictive of an illness. Whatever the reason, it's definitely a sign that the Overlord is disinterested in any kind of interaction.

The Glacier – The unknown world around a felion can be terrifying, even if it's just your living room. The terrain has yet to be conquered, and the Overlord is wary of unidentified dangers lurking everywhere. With the speed of a glacier, they will proceed on a covert mission to gather as much information as possible and make a threat assessment. They may not be frightened, but Your Highness is anxious. Slow and steady, low and ready. Step by step, they explore on high alert and proceed with caution.

The Statue – A fearful/anxious felion will not approach you no matter how much you try to coax them. Unsure whether to run or fight, a scared cat may completely freeze up, especially if they don't have an escape route. Their posture will be tense, usually they will appear hunched up with their tail protectively wrapped around their body or tucked between their legs. If Your Majesty freezes in place, they are terrified, and their next reaction is unpredictable. It's best to back off and allow them to escape to a more comfortable location.

Panting – This may appear cute (when it comes to cats, what doesn't?) but panting is a sign of distress or extreme anxiety. You will notice their mouth open, tongue partially out, and rapid, shallow breathing. Panting is rare for cats, unlike dogs, felions don't use this as a method to cool themselves—they employ grooming to help achieve that, so if the Overlord is panting, you can be certain something is not right. If this behavior is a result of interacting with a person or other animal, give your cat time and space to calm down. Once they feel safe, breathing should return to normal. Some felions have a particular aversion to car rides or pet carriers and will pant any time they are forced to go on a trip. Being exposed to extended stress for too long can have a negative impact on your cat's health. If you are unable to manage Your Majesty's anxiety, you should consider speaking to your vet about medications.

Like some of the other cues above and depending on the situation, panting can have multiple causes. A cat may pant after a rigorous play session or as a warning sign when they become over-heated. After rest and a cooling-off period, they should resume normal breathing. Sometimes panting can be the result of a serious health issue. If you suspect that your cat is panting due to pain or illness, see your veterinarian as soon as possible.

Halloween Cat – It's pretty easy to tell when a felion is utterly terrified; they resemble the typical black cat Halloween decoration. You can spot their flattened ears, pulled-back whiskers, and wide, black hole eyes. A terrified cat's fur puffs out and stands on end, and their back arches in an effort to make themselves appear larger. Some people may be inclined to view a puffy, wide-eyed kitty as adorable, but a Halloween cat is no cause for celebration. Like a live wire, a frightened cat may shake or tremble in panic. They will issue verbal warnings with hissing, growling, and spitting. A Halloween cat is likely to react aggressively towards any perceived threat. Never try to touch or interact with a Halloween cat or you could find yourself as bandaged as a mummy.

Crab Walk – This sideways walk-hop is commonly seen in kittens while they're playing or when they startle themselves in the mirror. Truthfully, it looks utterly hilarious, however in adults it's no laughing matter. A fear response, the crab walk is accompanied by the Halloween cat posture. Cats walk this way so they can safely retreat while still looking large and keeping their eyes on a potential attacker. If Your Majesty employs this strategic withdrawal, don't follow. Allow them to escape the situation and find somewhere to chill out for a while.

Talk To the Hand – Cats slap, bap, and swat for different reasons. Whereas a Paws for Pause is a gentle plea for attention, and Kitty Kung Fu is a slap-happy form of play, swatting is employed as a royal directive to stop fluffing around. As always, make sure to take cues from your monarch's body language to fully understand their intentions. Your Highness may not be feeling well, or perhaps they're just not in the mood for your shenanigans. A quick swat is a form of corporal punishment. Stop that! Ignoring or misinterpreting this sign can lead to escalation. If they feel threatened, a felion may activate their claws to ensure you get the point. All five of them.

Warning Bite – A warning bite is exactly that—a warning. The Overlord is extremely displeased with your conduct, and this physical reaction is yet another order to cease and desist. Perhaps in your eagerness to worship, you touched a vulnerable spot or startled them. Either way, your felion has had enough. Only moderate bite-pressure is applied, but this is your last chance to back off before things gets too serious. While these warning bites can sting, they are only intended to serve as a command and make you think twice before making the same mistake.

If your new cat is displaying any of the signals above, think of them as stop signs. Your felion needs more time to decompress, or you may have to work a little longer to earn their trust and friendship. Be patient and always move forward with due caution.

Swats and warning bites can lead to scratches and bleeding. Even small bites from a cat that break the skin can become infected. Although the puncture wounds appear tiny, bacteria from their mouth or claws is deposited deep under the skin. An infection can spread, causing painful redness and swelling. This can happen quickly, often the same day or even within a matter of hours. If left untreated, an infection from a cat bite or scratch can make its way into the bloodstream and become a serious issue, especially for those with diabetes, the elderly, or anyone with immunity issues.

Make sure to properly clean and disinfect any wound, no matter how small. Having been bitten and scratched myself more times than I can count, I normally pinch and squeeze the site several times to push out any bacteria and flush the area with soapy water, but be sure to speak to your doctor if you have any concerns.

CHATTY KITTY CHITTER CHATTER

Felion Overlords are constantly communicating decrees and directives to their human servants, whether we realize it or not. From birth, princes and princesses mew for their queen, but as they grow up, meows are reserved strictly for communicating with humans. While dogs only have about ten vocalizations, cats with an extensive vocabulary are capable of making dozens of distinct sounds including trilling, chirping, growling, and chattering. Not to mention an assortment of meows. These vocalizations express a wide range of moods and emotions. It's pretty amazing when you really stop and think about it. French may be considered the most romantic language, but meowing is the true language of love.

Purrs – Purring is the ultimate expression of contentment and love. The daily routine has been met. The royal belly is full. Life is Bliss. However, cats also purr when they are sick or in pain. It is a self-soothing mechanism, the frequency of which promotes healing.

Chatter/Clicking – Cats often make this sound when bird watching (or in their minds tracking prey). "Hey, hey-hey. Hey birds, who wants to play a game? I bet you can't fly into my mouth."

Growls – The Overlord may be angry, in pain, or simply wants to be left alone. These low, guttural warnings are intended to frighten off threats. They could also be a precursor to aggression. "Do I look like I'm in the mood for you?"

Hisses – The Overlord feels threatened and you're too close for their comfort. Hissing is a fear/threat escalation. "Back off, Motherscruffer!" You are not granted an audience with Your Highness, do not approach the throne. You're on the Hiss List.

Spit – This sounds similar to a hiss, but is shorter in duration, more like a forceful four-letter expletive. In our kingdom, a spit is usually accompanied by a full-claw swipe or a threatening lunge; the First Strike. This is a DEFCON 2 reaction, and kitty is ready to go to war. "I'm about to go medieval on your fluff."

Meows – Cats produce a variety of meows, and each one can mean something different depending on pitch, length, and repetition. Over time, you'll be able to recognize what each meow means. Dialects can vary from kingdom to kingdom, but as a servant who speaks fluent felion, I'll do my best to provide the most accurate translations.

- *Greeting* – Chirpy, coo-like. (trills) "Hi, there. Hello. Long time no see, so give me some attention."

- *Happiness* – High-pitched, short meows. "You're the bestest mom. I'm the bestest, prettiest, kittiest kitty."

- *Playful* – Short, rapid, high-pitched Prrrt! (chirruping) "Would you like to play with me?"

- *Silent Meow* – Polite attention seeking. Voiceless meows, usually coupled with Paws for Pause, are an irresistible attention grabber. "Um . . . Hi, remember me? Notice how extra cute I am? Don't you wanna pet me?"

- *Confused* – With a dragged emphasis on the "ow," this meow really sounds like a question. "Where did that red dot go? This is trippy."

- *Emphatic Attention Seeking* – Rapid succession in conjunction with boops, paw nudging and/or baptisms. "Hey bro, let's hang out and have some fun, man. Look at me, look at me. I'm your buddy. Come on, you can totally pet my head. Scratch my ears. It's your choice. I'm fine with either."

- *Lonely* – Tragically long and dramatic meows. "Mom? Hello? Lonely, lonely, lonely. It'd be really nice if someone paid attention to me. Lonely, Lonely. Lonely."

- *Surprised* – Loud, long, and sharp. "Did you have to sneak up on my like that?"

- *Indignant* – Loud, short and sharp. "I don't have any idea what you are talking about. I swear, it was like that before I got here."

- *Hungry* – "Oh please, dear sir, spare me a morsel, for I have never once eaten in my whole life."

- *Demanding* – "What part of 'Meow' don't you understand?"

- *Derision* – This almost sounds like a meow-sneeze. "What do you mean 'no?' You can't tell me what to do. You're not my real dad!"

- *Complaint* – "Well, well, well. You're late with food service again. I think it's time we have a talk about your unacceptable tardiness."

- *Whine* – "But Mooooooooom! I don't waaaannnnaaaa . . ."

- *Pain* – "DUDE! What the fluff? Watch where I put my tail, Big Foot."

- *Fear* – Low, rambling repetitions which can change in pitch and length, sounding like "O no-no-no-no. O no-nooo!"

- *Distress/Plea for Help* – Loud, long, and distressed yeowl. Depending on the context, this can either be high or low in pitch. "I think someone should take me to the vet." Or "Get away. Leave me alone."

- *Challenging* – Angry meows mixed with grumbles. "Come at me, bro."

- *Courting a Mate* – "I'm too sexy for my fur. Too sexy for my fur. So sexy, I purr."

As I've stated previously, dialects can vary from kingdom to kingdom, or even from felion to felion. Some cats, like my Shinobi, are very vocal, and others, like Puff Daddy, rarely meow, if at all. Whether Your Highness is an outspoken Overlord or a silent sultan, by paying close attention, in no time you will be able to translate their entire lexicon of verbal and nonverbal communication. Not only will this help you become a better servant, but it will also deepen your bond with Your Majesty.

THE ROYAL FAMILY

"I LOVE CATS BECAUSE I ENJOY MY HOME; AND LITTLE BY LITTLE, THEY BECOME ITS VISIBLE SOUL."

—Jean Cocteau

BONDING WITH YOUR MAJESTY

We all aspire to bask in the favor of our Overlord and be rewarded with their friendship. We want our sovereign to love us as much as we do them, but cats can be selective about whom they show favoritism. It can be disappointing when the kitty you adore doesn't appear to reciprocate your affection. First and foremost, you must establish a good rapport and prove that you are worthy of such an honor. Bonding with your felion can take time, and you must put in work. Trust is the foundation to building a relationship.

The Royal Attendant – Out of twenty cats, it's safe to say that at least sixteen prefer my wife's companionship over mine. I can't blame them; if I were a cat, I would too. Not only is she sweet and beautiful, Catherine is very attentive to their wants and needs, fulfilling the role as primary caregiver. I'm just the clumsy second stringer who always manages to drop a food bowl, sending it scattering to the four winds. Cathy has a very calming presence and infinite patience. Whenever we have a new arrival, she will take time to sit with the Duke or Duchess during mealtimes, putting our guest at ease with gentle petting and polite dinner conversation.

If someone else in your home holds the position of Head Servant, ask them to take a step back so you can step in and fill the role of The Steward/Seneschal. Serving your Overlord meals, cleaning the sandcastle, and providing entertainment will help prove your loyalty and dedication to The Crown.

Like Clockwork – Being the facilitator of a dependable royal routine is another layer of building a bond with your Overlord. To some people, doing the same things at the same time each day can sound monotonous, but felions have a castle to rule and require a steadfast attendant to make it run like clockwork. Routine offers them a sense of stability and predictability, helping them to feel secure in their leadership. Repetitiveness is also one way cats learn, and those positive associations will be directly connected to you, so it's in your benefit to always be on time. An established routine of dependable service and daily worship will put your ruler at ease when you clock out for non-felion activities. I know, it sounds a lot like having a job, doesn't it? Welcome to Cat World; it's the best job you'll ever have.

Just Sayin' – Despite the rumors, talking to your cats doesn't mean you're weird. I talk to my cats all the time. Okay, maybe I'm not the best example, but trust me, verbal communication is an important aspect of bonding. Maybe they need a pep talk. Maybe you need a friendly ear. Either way the Overlord will be comforted by your voice. While they won't understand what you're saying, felion wisdom will recognize intention through your reverent tone. Feel free to use terms like "Your Majesty" or "My Queen." When asking for permission, always add "by your leave." Butter them up, and they may even grace you with an answer.

Cat Speak – No matter what languages you speak, none will be more important than becoming fluent in Cat. Pay close attention to your new cat's body language and verbal cues. Heed all stop signs. Let your new ruler decide when they're ready to bond.

The Cold Shoulder – Has the new Overlord not responded favorably to your overtures of friendship? Tired of being ignored? I know the frustration. It's time to turn the tables and get their attention. Giving your new cat the cold shoulder could make them warm up to you. Exert all of your willpower to withstand their felion charm and instead play hard to get. Hands off. Resist the urge to worship them. No muss, no fuss. Don't even give them the benefit of a side eye. This non-interaction allows for choice and will make the cat feel secure enough to make first contact. Cats hate to be ignored and relish the challenge of converting a reluctant human into an adoring member of their felion congregation.

The Kitty Olympics – Games and interactive play are other ways to help build a strong bond. Felions need to burn off energy and satisfy their primal instinct for hunting, so provide toys that let them act out their natural impulses. Interactive toys like feather wands, laser pointers, and cat fishing poles can be fun for both of you. No matter what kind of activity your monarch dictates, sharing the experience and becoming a part of it will undoubtedly bring the two of you closer together.

Ever since she was a kitten, my Akiko loved to walk around in wide circles as a form of entertaining herself. When I am in the kitchen, she will happily gallop around me, including me in whatever game she thinks she is playing. For my part, I will sing her glory hymns and proudly cheer her on. It's dizzyingly adorable how much enjoyment she takes from our derpy little game. This may sound utterly ridiculous, or ridiculously cute, or maybe both, but earlier this morning as I was working on this book—and the reason I'm including it here—Akiko was in the kitchen, and I heard loud, sad mews. My little tuxedo gal is not a very vocal kitty, more of a silent meower, so I got up to go see what the fuss was all about. Upon seeing me enter the kitchen, Akiko immediately perked up. Her tail raised and she gleefully started circling me in a cheerful trot. That's how we spent the next ten minutes. Her mews had just been letting me know she missed my company.

MAKING FRIENDS WITH RELUCTANT RULERS

Less social Overlords are at a great disadvantage when hoping for a kingdom to rule. The Shy Ones often want to be overlooked, as they are reluctant to take their place among humans. No Overlord should have to spend their life cowering under the throne rather than ruling on top of it. As a loyal servant, you can help your hermit king realize their greatness and come out of their shell.

The Inner Sanctum – Introvert Overlords will require more time to adapt to new places and relationships. An insecure cat may panic and attempt to flee on approach. It's kind of hard to bond with your Queen if you have to go on safari throughout the kingdom to find her. At this point, the Throne Room (see page 60) will need to serve as the Overlord's private world within the castle until the seeds of socialization take root. Then, even when the rest of the kingdom is bustling with activity, your felion will always have a refuge from the hullabaloo. However, this doesn't mean that Your Majesty should be condemned to live in solitude—leaving the Throne Room on their terms is fine. There is great work to be done.

The Inner Sanctum is not merely a safe space; it is a lion's den where confidence is built and lifelong friendships are born. Offer your service and daily overtures of friendship. Even if your good will is refused, your persistent presence in the sanctuary will eventually have a positive impact on your cat. Predictability leads to trust.

When attempting bonding rituals, it is important to block off any potential hiding spots within the inner sanctum that are inaccessible to you. Cats can make Hide-n-Seek challenging even in a small room, so allow them no access to the shadow world of dust bunnies. At the same time, make sure there is a cat cave available where kitty can retreat should they become overwhelmed. Encourage Your Majesty to claim ownership of everything in the sanctum. Ownership inspires confidence. Confidence begets bravery. Courage overcomes fear.

The Love Shack – Often, I utilize a large, covered crate as a cocoon of socialization for shy guests of Hotel Mancuso. This is a good option if kitty castle is short on space but high in population. The more chaotic the kingdom, the more anxious a new felion will be. Book your kitty for a staycation in The Love Shack. Splurge for a luxury suite, large enough to comfortably house a litter box, hidey-hole, as well as an area for complimentary room service. The Love Shack should have plenty of hanging

Eight-week-old Inu's intake photo for Hotel Mancuso.

After five days in The Love Shack, she's looking forward to attention.

danglers, scratchers, and a rotation of treat puzzles to entice activity. Most of all, provide frequent positive interactions to initiate trust. Cater to their ego. By utilizing a combination of trust building and bonding rituals, your reluctant ruler will soon feel the magic spark of love, perhaps for the first time in their life. Well done, servant. Your Majesty is ready for the next step up the royal ladder.

Dependable Service – Remember the royal routine. Keep the basics of the cat's life as predictable as possible. As previously discussed, a solid schedule will help put your anxious felion at ease.

Show Reverence – Always speak in a calm, soothing voice. When making eye contact, do not stare at their grandeur, but rather slightly bow your head in reverence to The Crown and blink slowly to show that you are not a usurper. By moving slowly and predictably your nervous Purvis is less likely to be startled. Humble and respectful servants are the most successful in earning a seat on the High Council.

Bribery – Sometimes, you may just have to buy yourself some good will, and the way to a felion's heart is through their stomach. As passed down from rescuer to rescuer, I now share this key advice with you: Use baby food as high value enticement for trust and social interaction. More than any other treat, this Catsgiving delicacy won over a vast majority of the shy or anxious kitties boarding at Hotel Mancuso. Baby food is a valuable indulgence that has opened many doors to felion trust and friendship. Surely, someone who presents such a worthy offering can't be all bad.

When proposing baby food as a yummy incentive, be sure to use only all meat, chicken, turkey, or beef, no fruits or vegetables. Start with a small portion on a plate, as the trick is to always leave them wanting more. Serve the Overlord close to their hidey-hole and give them some room to consider your enticing offering. Once cats realize how much they love the taste of your generous gift, the door to a good relationship has been unlocked. But do not rush the process; you must earn trust slowly and prove you are a devout servant before they'll let you inside.

After the Overlord has approved of your offering, begin to serve the bowl farther from the safe space, or advance to a spoon. After your felion feels comfortable being spoon fed, upgrade from the spoon to your finger. In no time this little trick should have Your Highness eating out of your hand. Remember, only use this Catsgiving treat when it's directly involved with human-felion social interaction. Some gentle petting while they dine will help a cat associate their delicious snack with loving contact.

The Hunger Games – Training is a great way for you to have some quality one-on-one time to work on deepening your relationship and communication skills. Food motivates a lot of Great Ones, but others are hungry for your affection. Once you find the preferred incentive and reward, there are various ways to train Your Majesty with easily recognizable sounds or hand motions. Consider this simplified Cat-mathical equation: Action + Sound = Food. Food = Good. Food + Human = Good. Human = Good.

Create a positive association between a sound, gesture, or word with a reward. Clickers are a commonly employed training tool for both dogs and cats, but you're free to get creative and improvise. However, it's important that whatever sound, gesture, or combination of both that you utilize be unmistakable to avoid felion confusion. To prevent frustration on both sides, if your cat takes longer to make this connection, lower the bar to the ladder of success. For example, if you're attempting to elicit a high-five, you can first offer the reward when Your Highness sniffs your hand. Sure, this wasn't quite the answer you were hoping for, but kitty should be rewarded points for showing their work. As the tutor, you must build the Overlord's confidence with each session and encourage them to solve the equation. And when the Overlord finally makes the connection between their reward and the desired behavior is something they will remember. It becomes a kingdom decree; one Your Majesty will use to manipulate your heart at will.

Using clicker training, Mitsurugi quickly learned how to give high-fives. Eventually, he swapped out the clicker for finger-snaps and treats were traded in favor of devoted worship. Eager to flaunt his superior intelligence, Mitsurugi is also able to lie down upon verbal request, and even meow when prodded with a certain look. His Majesty thoroughly enjoyed our personal training sessions. These Hunger Games are the main reason he and I have formed a deep bond. It has made him a better leader and communicator. Following our success, I began implementing clicker training as social protocol with any reluctant guests of Hotel Mancuso.

Bend The Knee – Even if you're shorter than my wife, you still tower over your felion. For an anxious cat the thought of interacting with a kaiju is intimidating. In the wild, cats are not at the top of the food chain, which might contribute to why they feel very vulnerable when you have the high ground. The lower you are to the ground, the less threatening you are. If you're bonding with a timid kitty, get down as low as you can and allow them to approach you first. This can make all the difference.

When I walk around the house, some of my shy cats act like I'm Godzilla. *Run! Hide! It's coming this way!* Panicked tails scurry under couches and seek refuge on the castle's towers. However, when I'm seated or lying down, Petey, Puff Daddy, and Karma will be much more likely to approach me and look for affection. If this is the way they feel the most comfortable interacting with me, so be it.

The High Ground – It's a good idea to provide some vertical space for your cat to utilize, especially if you have bad knees. Besides, you have to be upright sometimes. Your highness should have an elevated throne upon which they can perch and look down on you, the way nature intended. Ceding the high ground is great confidence builder.

Manifest Destiny – Slowly expand access to the castle, allowing them to fully own one room before introducing them to the next. Make a point to hold worship service with your cat daily, preferably multiple times a day, for about fifteen to twenty minutes each session. Once Your Highness is comfortable interacting with you within their inner sanctum, start conducting worship and play sessions in other castle chambers as well. If your monarch is reluctant, utilize treats to your benefit in each room. Some timid felions need more trust and confidence building than others, and as the Head Servant, you will help them to achieve a great reign. Be patient and take the process one small step at a time; you have the rest of your lives to get to know and love one another.

CAT TALES: Ilythia

A pretty, medium-haired tuxedo, Ilythia, became a guest at Hotel Mancuso in November of 2020 after spending several months in the Newark shelter during the Covid lockdown. Pregnant, she had been brought in to the shelter as a stray where she gave birth. When the kittens were old enough to be safely separated from their mother, they were placed with another rescue, leaving the four-year-old queen lonely and confused behind the kennel bars. Frightened and alone, Ilythia didn't make a good impression on anyone who interacted with her, spending much of her time hiding in her litterbox, trying to console herself. While it was obvious she wasn't a friendly cat, she wasn't feral either. Surely in the right setting she could thrive; someone just had to give her that chance. It would be unfair to judge her based solely on her shelter performance. However, that is the sad reality for many of the cats that end up at shelters around the country. They never get the chance to show people their best side. Cathy and I offered to give Ilythia that opportunity. With an unknown history and very little information to go on, we weren't sure if she would even be friendly and sociable, but we knew she deserved the chance. Aware that this could be a formidable challenge, we set our expectations low from the beginning.

Compared to her shelter kennel, the large crate in my office was a penthouse, but Ilythia was in no mood to thank me for the upgrade. With a quick hiss, she immediately disappeared, taking refuge in the crate's hidey-hole. No matter how nice the set-up, it still felt like being behind bars, alone in a new, strange place.

Over the next few days, I tried to assess Ilythia's behavior, but she refused to come out for any interaction whatsoever. The least she could do was politely laugh at my jokes, but my standup routine fell on flat ears. Peeking in, I could see two yellow eyes looking back at me and hear her low, grumbling complaints. When the time was right, I decided to bribe her. Gerber chicken was on the menu. Cathy and I made sure we had plenty of this delicacy available for such a need.

Putting a dab on a plate, I slid my offering right in front of her hidey-hole. It didn't take Ilythia long to cautiously poke her head out. When she saw I was safely across the room, she took a little taste, then another. After she licked the plate clean, her head popped back into her hidey-hole, not unlike a turtle. Again, I peeped into her sanctuary. No growls. No hisses. That was the first sign of hope that she would come out of her shell.

A few minutes later, I tempted her felion palate with another taste. This time I set the plate farther away from her. With little hesitation, Ilythia crossed the crate and eagerly gobbled the treat. She even made

After months languishing in a shelter, Ilythia transformed from a shrinking violet to a confident queen.

those adorable "nom-nom-nom" sounds. It was actually the first time I was able to get a complete look at her. Throughout the remainder of the night, I offered several more portions of baby food as I sat a little closer. Each time, she was less and less hesitant, even when I moved the offering to the front of the crate, a mere foot away from me. By the end of the night, we even exchanged slow blinks.

The next day Ilythia was licking baby food off a spoon. Two more spoons, then she accepted a single finger, a gentle touch. We repeated these sessions several times throughout the day and into the night. Soon, she was no longer hiding in her cubby but sitting on top of it. Within two days, she was licking the food off my fingers and allowing me to pet her as much as I wanted while she ate her new favorite treat.

Of course, there was still plenty of work ahead of us. Some flowers take longer to bloom than others. Ilythia spent the next five months at Hotel Mancuso. During that time, she built confidence, learned to trust people, and made friendships with other felions. Her true personality was quite agreeable. By April, Ilythia decided she was ready to move into a new castle and chose a purrfect family who were touched by her story and very familiar with felion servitude. 🐾

THE RULES OF ENGAGEMENT: CATS AND KIDS

Introductions between kitty and kiddies will vary depending on the age of the children. To the Overlord, young children are likely to be frightening due to their unpredictable behavior. At such a young age, a toddler may see the cat merely as just another plushy, stuffed animal in their menagerie of toys. Unfortunately, young children may play too rough or handle a fragile kitten the wrong way, leading to serious injury. On the other hand, kittens have particularly sharp teeth and claws, which can accidentally injure delicate young children, even in play. Heartier and more tolerant, adult cats are best suited to rule over young children, especially preschool age.

If your kids are old enough to understand what's going on and follow instructions, you can explain the rules of Cat World. Have children to approach slowly and reverently rather than scooping their new furry Overlord up in their arms right away. Instead, allow them an audience with The Crown under supervision and only for short periods of time.

Show And Tell – As the head servant, it is your sworn duty to help children understand and properly worship Your Highness. For very young children, teach them by example. Show them where and how to worship by gently petting the cat on their head, chin, neck, and back. Make sure to avoid the belly trap and any other spots Your Highness may not approve.

Royal Chaperon – Supervise all interactions, as both kids and cats can be unpredictable. The younger the child, the more closely they should be watched. If the Overlord seems distressed, get the child to back away and allow the cat more time to get comfortable.

Silence Is Golden – Children can often be obnoxiously loud, which, like myself, felions find unappealing and nerve wracking. Encourage children to always be quiet and patient in the presence of royalty, and model this behavior for them. Your new felion will acclimate faster and healthier in a quiet, peaceful castle.

Kid-Free Zone – Allow the Overlord access to a kid-free zone. Cats prefer to escape rather than engage in conflict with young children. If Your Highness has a safe and comfortable perch where they can watch the castle activity without having to be in the center of it, they'll feel much less stressed. Other felions may take to the sanctuary of their hidey-hole to avoid interacting with children. Although your kids may just be curious, do not allow children to stare at the cat in their hiding place. It's not proper kitty etiquette and the Overlord will feel threatened.

Student Internship – Give the children treats to place on the floor as a peace offering. Involve children in basic care activities for the Overlord, like grooming, feeding, and shovel duty. Of course, if your kid is young, these activities must always be supervised. This instructive internship will educate a youngster on how to grow into an exceptional servant. Perhaps make a quiet game out of it, or invent service badges for young acolytes to earn as they climb the ranks in the kingdom.

Handle With Care – Kings, queens, princes, and princesses all need to be handled with care. Do not allow the children to pull the cat's tail, ears, legs, or whiskers. Remind children that cats are not stuffed toys but living animals, and they should always be treated delicately. Also prevent kids from grabbing, squeezing, or carrying felions like footballs—cats can become injured or scared, which is dangerous for everyone involved.

Proper Play – Make sure your child knows how to safely engage in kitty play with the proper toys. Cat toys belong to the Overlord; to avoid frustration and confusion, they should only be used when interacting with them. Do not allow your child to use their hands as cat toys. Instruct your kids that human hands are only for petting or giving tasty treats, otherwise Your Majesty may inadvertently teach them a painful lesson.

Cat-Lingual – Teach children to be cat-lingual from an early age. The sooner they learn to read and respect Your Majesty's body language, the better their relationship will be.

No Papurrazzi – Let's face it, kids are obsessed with social media these days. And what better way to accumulate tons of online reactions than posting videos or photos of the Overlord? Although clearly the most photogenic of all species on the planet, not every cat approves of the paparazzi chasing them through the kingdom or forcing them into awkward positions in an attempt to garner online attention. If your felion is not into voguing for the camera and evades photo shoots, it's important to respect their wish for privacy. While viral cucumber pranks and the like may seem funny to your kids, practical jokes don't go over well in Cat World. No amount of social media views, likes, or shares is worth frightening or annoying Your Highness.

FUTURE SERVANT: A NEW BABY

So, you're having a baby? First, please allow me to offer you my congratulations on years of sleepless nights, endless diaper changes, and a lifetime of worry. Better you than me. Second, and more importantly, speaking on behalf of cats everywhere, I'd like to inform you that having a baby is not a valid excuse to rehome your cat or surrender them to a shelter. You wouldn't give up your first kid just because you're having a second, nor should you dethrone your Overlord.

Yes, I know I've said that cats hate change, and I realize adding a newborn to your family is an enormous change for everyone in the kingdom. Some felions can get jealous and possibly display stress-related behaviors because they're no longer the center of your attention. With preparation and patience, Your Highness can and will adjust to this new paradigm (much better than I would). The transition may be easier than you think, and it's certainly preferable to the alternative. So, before everyone in the realm is upheaved into chaos, let's see what you can do to make this adjustment less stressful.

Don't Panic – I have received calls and emails from expectant mothers looking to rehome their cat in a panic because they read somewhere about Toxoplasmosis and don't want to risk infecting their baby. A typical phone call sounds about like this: "Oh, my God, I'm so stressed. I can't do this. He has to go. I love Jax, but I just can't have a cat in my house anymore. I can't scoop his litter box—it has infected poop in it—and my husband certainly won't do it. I'm sorry, the baby is my top priority now. You have to take Jax, or I'll have to bring him to a shelter."

According to the Center for Disease Control, "Toxoplasmosis is an infection caused by a microscopic parasite called Toxoplasma gondii. More than 40 million people in the United States carry the Toxoplasma parasite. Toxoplasmosis can cause severe illness in infants infected before birth (when their mothers are newly infected just before or during pregnancy), or in persons with a weakened immune system."[16] Sounds scary, I know, but before you grab the cat carrier and get ready to shuffle Mittens off to a new life, take a few minutes to read on.

While Toxoplasmosis is something to take seriously, it should also be approached in a rational manner. Keeping the Overlord confined to their castle means they are not likely to be infected as long as they don't hunt small animals such as mice or birds. This is yet another reason to avoid serving Your Highness a raw meat diet. Stray cats and kittens that reside in The Great Backyard have a higher chance of being infected. Since the parasite is released in feces, it is highly unlikely for transmission to occur by the simple act of worship. Toxoplasma does not become infectious until one to five days after it is shed in a cat's feces, so make sure to shovel the sandcastle often. The sooner the better! If possible, relegate another servant to handle this task, or wear gloves and a mask, and always wash your hands after you complete this chore.

The CDC asserts that "if you were infected with Toxoplasma at least six months before becoming pregnant your baby is protected by your immunity."[17] If you are pregnant or planning to put a bun in the oven, it's a good idea to schedule a vet visit and have your cat tested for toxoplasmosis. The test checks for antibodies to the parasites. If your cat tests negative, this means he has never been exposed and cannot transmit the disease to you. Eggs will only be shed for two or three weeks after infection, after which time your cat will build up an immunity and the parasite is rendered dormant. If your cat tests positive and is actively shedding, you'll be happy to know there is treatment. It's a little extra money for a big peace of mind.

Desensitization – The best way to help Your Majesty adjust to a new baby is desensitization through a slow transition during the course of pregnancy. If the castle is going to add a nursery, set it up early. Allow the Overlord to get accustomed to any new furniture but not jump or sleep on it. Felion safety inspections must be limited to visual review. If you need to relocate the sandcastle, cat scratchers, or thrones, do so several months prior to bringing home baby, or as early as possible. But do not move them the entire way all at once as this may confuse or upset your monarch and they could file complaints. Follow the path of least resistance, Your Majesty's personal items should be moved incrementally. Depending on how far away you plan to relocate the litter box, this could take a while, but you have many months for the box to reach its final destination, and it will be worth the effort.

A new baby in the home also means plenty of unfamiliar sounds and smells that can cause stress and anxiety for an unprepared felion. Playing a recording of various baby noises such as crying, screaming, and giggling at a low volume during royal feasts or play time will go a long way to help desensitize your cat to life with a hairless noise monster. You'll want to increase the volume gradually until your cat appears to be comfortable with the sounds, as annoying as they may be. Additionally, placing baby products like shampoos, lotions, and powders on your own skin can help Your Highness develop positive associations with the new smells.

Having to care for a baby will undoubtedly bring changes to your schedule, and perhaps someone else will be taking over, at least temporarily, as the head servant. Slowly implement any changes in the daily routine before the baby is born, however it is important that you always set some time aside to worship and pay homage to The Crown.

Clip Those Nails – If you haven't already been doing so, it is now more important than ever to keep your cat's claws from growing too long and sharp. I'll say it again because it can't be overstated: Avoid playing hand games. Hands are for petting. If your cat is used to playing games with your hands, stop this as soon as possible. What was cute when they were kittens can now lead to injury. Even a gentle cat can upset or injure a baby by accident, and you can't really be upset by this behavior if you have encouraged it in the past. Teach your cat that only toys are appropriate for play.

Supervision – The Overlord will be curious of their newest subject. Place a used receiving blanket or piece of infant wear in a quiet area where your felion can inspect it. Don't expect a royal reception, Your Majesty may choose to keep their distance, at least at first, but that is okay. Don't force interaction; allow your Overlord to decide when they are ready to meet their newest subject. However, any interaction needs to be supervised. Make sure the crib and other locations where baby sleeps are off-limits.

Inclusion – The Overlord has been used to having your love and devotion all to themselves prior to the birth of your child. Be sure not to ignore your cat during pregnancy and especially after baby comes home to the castle. Give Your Majesty plenty of worship when baby is in the room.

I'm not trying to give cats a bad rep with babies, insinuating they inherently dislike or can't be trusted around them. In fact, some cats grow attached and become self-appointed protectors of their human siblings. Just be sure they continue to feel your full love and devotion before, during, and after the baby arrives.

. . . .

FUR FACT   Nicholas Dodman, chief animal behavior at the Tufts University School of Veterinary Medicine in Boston, found that cats and humans have practically identical sections in the brain that control emotion.[18]

. . . .

CO-RULERS: OTHER FELIONS

Felions are territorial by nature, even when they live indoors. The Overlords are very protective of their domain and everything in it. After all, they own it. A common mistake servants make is putting cats in a room together and thinking the two strangers will immediately get along and be best buds. If only. Unfortunately, in Cat World, this is often seen as a hostile invasion. Both cats are likely to be frightened, and chaos can erupt in the Throne Room.

As you can imagine, we've done a lot of introductions here. It wasn't always easy, especially in the beginning, Thankfully, our resident cats have gotten very used to meeting new cats, kittens, and even an occasional pup. For the most part, my cats are unfazed by any new guests at Hotel Mancuso. *He brought home another carrier today. Here we go again.*

Now, the process of incorporating a new foster cat into the realm can be a smooth transition. Most of the time.

Let's talk about how you can introduce a new felion into the castle without inadvertently starting a war for the throne.

Time Is on My Side – For both cats this period of adjustment can be an equally stressful time. Take things slow. There's no need to rush; time is on your side. Allowing the more anxious cat to set the pace will yield better results. The Overlords will have the rest of their lives to rule together in peace, but first they must learn not to perceive the other as a rival. Empires aren't built in a day. A gradual introduction process is the foundation to building strong, felion friendships.

The Inner Sanctum – Any time a new cat is brought into the castle, they must remain separated from other cats, not only for decompression, but also a medical isolation period of one week. Much like when you fashioned the Throne Room for your first cat, the Inner Sanctum is the safe space within the castle for the new felion. As before, this will serve as their temporary living quarters and sanctuary, with all the necessities for comfort and confidence building.

Smell It Like It Is – Since the Overlords have a superior sense of smell, utilizing olfactory senses is a good way to help felions get familiar with each other before they ever meet in person. By feeding meals on opposite sides of a closed door, you will encourage each cat to form a positive association with the scent of the other. Additionally, you can allow them to sniff each other's belongings. Use anything with their scent on it, like a bed, blanket, or toy.

Blending In – One tip I have found quite effective is using the same brush on multiple cats as a scent exchange. This eau de toilette will give the new cat the same scent as the other, making it easier to be accepted into the royal family. I'll also snuggle with a foster cat for a while, then interact with my own and vice versa. Since I will be carrying the scent of the other cat, this also helps to form a positive association between the two.

Peek-A-Boo – If both Overlords are tolerant of the other's scent, it's time to let them sneak a peek. With the use of a pet gate, you can allow the cats to see each other for the first time. If you don't have a pet get, you can prop open the entrance to the Inner Sanctum by an inch or two—just enough to peer through the crack. Never force face-to-face introductions. A cat can be unpredictable when they feel threatened or territorial. Depending on their reactions, you can allow them to maintain a sightline during the royal feast or quell any uprising by closing the door to the Inner Sanctum. Repeat this game of peek-a-boo until both cats are showing no signs of stress.

A Castle Without Borders – Once both felions are comfortable with peek-a-boo, remove the pet gate or open the door for brief encounters. It's best to do this when they are most likely to be calm, such as after a royal feast. Keep them under close supervision and make sure to have your arsenal of peacekeeping tools handy to disrupt any physical confrontations. It's better to have a squirt gun and not need it than to need one and not have it. They may quickly get up close and personal or choose not to interact at all. Either is okay; let them set the pace. As the cats become more familiar with each other, allow them longer and longer periods of time in a castle without borders.

Plentiful Resources – Even if your two cats never become best buds, you at least need them to tolerate each other and coexist peacefully, so be sure to have enough of everything (including your attention) to go around. Each felion will have their own favorite spaces of solitude and develop a time-share system for the common areas. In time, they may form a friendship or even become strongly bonded.

Co-existing in the same realm is quite different from having a royal bond of fellowship. I've often been asked if adult cats can really form strong relationships with each other. They absolutely can and often do. Adult felions usually do not bond as quickly as kittens, partly because kittens tend to be friendlier and more playful, especially with their litter mates. As adults, Overlords may become standoffish, with derisive snobbery towards new royalty. Even if cat-cat bonding seems unlikely at first, you could be surprised when you find your dynamic duo sharing the throne.

Here at the Island of Misfit Cats, we have subsets of friendships within the kingdom's ranks. For example, Inu and Pumpkin, two queens who arrived years apart, have formed a special friendship within the fur-brigade. Our Suki is a social butterfly who flutters throughout the castle looking for grooming partners, especially shaggy Shinobi.

At a young age, kittens can be separated from their siblings with no resulting depression or behavioral issues, however cats that have been bonded for a long time is quite a different story. A familial union between royals should not be taken for granted as Overlords are committed to their relationships for life.

CAT TALES: *Love Lost and Found*

D'Morien had a traumatic beginning to his life. As a young kitten then named Sebastion, he was brought to one of the New York Animal Care Centers with a broken leg. Staten Island Hope pulled him from the shelter and sent him to a foster to recover. At this point I had just started reaching out to the rescue's group director, offering to volunteer my videography services. When Cathy and I saw a pathetically adorable photo of this tiny black kitten in a leg cast on Facebook, we instantly fell in love with him. After a brief discussion, we applied to adopt him into our family. Two weeks later, his cast was removed, and he came home with us on December 20, 2013, just in time for Christmas.

Having been through so much already in his short life, D'Morien was understandably a bit shy and apprehensive. However, he almost immediately attached himself to his new big brother, VanDuzer. As I mentioned earlier, VanDuzer had a great disposition; for the last nine months he had doted on his younger sisters, Caramel and Molly, whom we brought home at only eight weeks old. VanDuzer was happy to welcome a new brother, too, and D'Morien soon became his Mini Me, growing more social and confident by the day.

Four years later, when VanDuzer passed away from kidney disease at the age of nine, it was devastating on the entire household. He was the patriarch, the peacemaker, and the official greeter of our pride. All of our cats felt his absence, but none more so than poor D'Morien. He went into

(L) VanDuzer, the felion patriarch. (R) D'Morien, VanDuzer's shadow.

emotional distress, feeling all alone in a house full of cats. It may sound like I'm anthropomorphizing, but his emotional state was obvious. D'Morien withdrew from everything. He would often go into hiding and was no longer interested in socializing, even when we offered his favorite treats. *Come on out, my little man. You love Turkey.* Normally, if I made a sandwich, D'Morien was a professional beggar. He'd sit straight up and look at me like he had never been fed in his entire life. They he'd gently tap my leg, letting out a tiny meow: *Please, Sir, can I have some more?* It worked on me every damn time, and he knew it! Other cats had learned from him and joined his growing chorus. But now? Nothing. The bits of turkey breast I'd drop in front of him went untouched, until one of the other cats came along and vacuumed up the treats. D'Morien couldn't have cared less.

We tried so hard to offer comfort and raise his spirits, but even when we petted and groomed him, D'Morien could not be consoled. Cuddling was out of the question. The twenty-minute belly rubs, which he had always loved (weird, I know) were a thing of the past. D'Morien no longer came up to claim his spot on the bed at night, nor could he be coaxed to play. He had lost weight and completely stopped grooming himself.

Weeks slipped into months as D'Morien remained in mourning. We were at a loss. We had tried everything except medication, which I was reluctant to do. How could I help him? You know, it's ironic: I was so proud of myself for having helped so many other cats, but now I found myself unable to help my own little guy cope with his grief. Talk about humbling.

When things seemed at their lowest, something wonderful happened: Phoebe and Hershel stepped in. Even more unexpected, this duo was an unlikely team with a long-standing rivalry. Two years prior, we had taken in our sassy Phoebe, who was extremely picky and only associated with two other cats: VanDuzer and D'Morien. Shortly after, we began fostering Hershel, our three-legged tuxedo. Hershel, a real cat's cat, had gotten along with everyone . . . except Phoebe. She would scream and swat if he went anywhere near her. For his part, Hershel would sometimes chase her in his cute bunny-hop way, and Phoebe would shriek and hiss as she raced through the house. She'd hide behind a corner and slap him in the head as he passed by. It was almost like the roadrunner and the coyote. You can imagine our surprise when the two of them suddenly began spending time with D'Morien. Together!

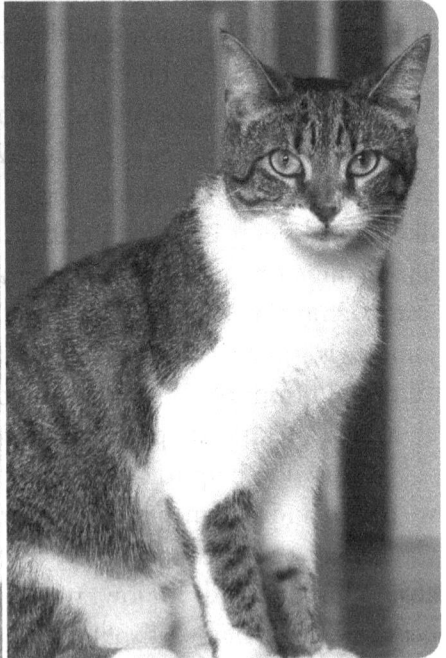

(L) Hershel, our tripod and Phoebe's future husband. (R) Phoebe doesn't know it yet—he's still on her Hiss List.

The two of them accomplished what I had failed to do. D'Morien came out from his mourning spot. Phoebe and Hershel lavished him with head boops, body rubs, and group grooming. He seemed to appreciate the attention, but he still wasn't the same. Although he had finally come out of hiding, his playful happy spark was gone. But at least it was a start, a reason to hope. He just needed a little more time.

Three months later D'Morien fell ill with a URI. He stopped eating, and I had to resort to force-feeding him several times a day. We got him checked out at the vet and started him on antibiotics. After he didn't respond to the first round, the vet prescribed something stronger. For a brief time, I thought he was getting better, but D'Morien suddenly passed away on December 23, 2017—about four years after we brought him home, and eight months after VanDuzer crossed Rainbow Bridge.

If you ask me, I sincerely think D'Morien died from a broken heart. Even as I type this, my eyes blur from tears.

A love triangle. Phoebe and Hershel console heartbroken D'Morien.

"He's happy now. He's with VanDuzer again," Cathy said as we cried together, stroking his fur. "That's where he always wanted to be."

I found solace in her words. Still, part of me couldn't help but think I had failed him. I am still haunted by the guilt.

The lone shining light from that miserable tunnel of darkness is that Phoebe and Hershel had bonded. D'Morien had brought them together, and though he was lost to us, Phoebe and Hershel had found the love of each other. Over time, their bond grew stronger. Today, they are the husband and wife of our tribe. They are inseparable, sleeping, eating, and parading their love through the house.

Yeah, I think it's safe to say that cats can be bonded. ❧

THE FAMILY PET: DOGS

Before getting a new cat or dog, you need to factor in pet personalities. Find animals that have lived with or had positive exposure to other species. Dogs and cats aren't the nemesis they are often portrayed to be. They can live in harmony, but they are very different animals, and caution should be taken when introducing them.

Room To Grow – When a dog arrives, the Overlord may feel threatened—a canine interloper has infiltrated the castle. Likewise, resident dogs are protective, and this new felion ego is clearly not part of the pack. Either animal can become territorially aggressive. Whether felion or canine, the new pet should be sequestered to separate rooms with all their necessities. For the Overlord, this is the Throne Room. For the dog, it is a conversion chamber to induct them into Cat World. Here, in their safe space, they will have plenty of room to grow more confident and relaxed.

Smell-O-Vision – Behind a closed door the pets will not see one another, but they will still be keenly aware of each other's presence. Certainly, they will hear each other's movements and a variety of alien vocalizations: barking, growling hissing, meowing. Most of all, the animals will use their superior sense of smell to pick up information about the four-legged stranger in the next room.

Use Smell-O-Vision in your favor to create positive associations. Like with cat-to-cat scent exchanges, start feeding your felion and canine on opposite sides of the closed door. Introduce objects with the other's scent for a good whiff. They're going to be very curious and likely cautious. If at any time a pet displays aggression, anxiety, or over-excited behavior, immediately remove that animal from the situation. Repeat using this tactic until both the Overlord and their canine subject are at ease during the royal feasts.

On-Site Inspections – Before meeting face to face, the Overlord must first conduct an onsite inspection. A newly crowned monarch will want to survey the castle and take an inventory of all they have inherited. While Your Majesty explores, use the time to grant your dog admittance to the Throne Room. Likewise, if you've brought a new dog home, the Overlord will require access to examine this canine's conversion chamber before fraternizing with their newest subordinate. In the effort of diplomacy, any dog petitioning for residence is granted a castle tour as the Overlord conducts his inspection. After all inspections have received passing grades, it's time to host a peace summit.

Interspecies Introduction – I know, that sounds like the title of a B-rated, sci-fi flick, but it is important to remember that dogs and cats are entirely different species of animals. They have different instincts, motivations, and reactions. Therefore, as the royal translator, you must be able to interpret and react to body language from both species during any peace summit. Consider the following tips for making introductions:

- Enhance your calm. Both dogs and cats will be able to pick up on your anxiety, and that could cause either to have a negative reaction. Put out calm, happy vibes and your pets are more likely to respond in kind.
- In general, even if the dog isn't adversarial, a canine that is eager to make friends with their Overlord tends to get up close and personal without invitation. Such impudence breaks with felion etiquette, often leading to a call to arms. In order to avoid offense to the Crown, keep the dog on a leash and let the Overlord come and

go as they wish. Do not restrain either pet in your arms as injury could result—to you or them—if either pet behaves aggressively.

- Ideally, you want your dog to be aware of the cat but focused on you. Reward with praising and treats every time they display calm behavior around the Overlord. Give your cat treats as well for their positive reactions and interaction with Rover. If the dog becomes tense or obsessed with the cat, end the encounter and schedule another meeting for later.

- Conduct introductions with a dog crate. If your pooch is already crate-trained, even better. With doggo safely confined behind bars, the Overlord can walk freely, scrutinizing their canine subject from a position of power.

- Protect the King. If either pet demonstrates aggression, calmly distract and redirect them. Toss a toy to lure the cat from the room, or call the dog's name and reward their attention. Return the Overlord to the Throne Room, or remove the dog to the conversion chamber.

Tactical Retreat – Safety is paramount. Even after a successful introduction, Your Highness may still feel vulnerable. There will still be awkwardness and social tension as they learn to interact appropriately. You don't want Fido to see cat chasing as a game, because it sure isn't a game for the cat being chased. If cornered, Your Majesty can become aggressive towards the dog or even indirectly towards you. Protect everyone by always leaving an escape route for your cat. Ideally, your living space will have multiple high areas, like shelving or furniture where your cats can easily escape the dog if needed. You can also use pet gates to help keep your dog from chasing your cat, until they become better acquainted.

Spread The Wealth – Remember, when it comes to any type of castle provision, the motto is yours and mine, not yours is mine. Being forced to share resources such as food and water bowls will cause your cat significant stress. Spread the wealth. Make sure there is more than enough of everything to go around. Some dogs and even some cats are prone to resource guarding, even if they otherwise get along. Organize the castle so your pets can easily ignore one another and have space and belongings to call their own. Eventually, the Overlord may choose to share a throne or a toy with a canine subservient, but let that be their choice, if and when they are both comfortable.

While plenty of cats and dogs live harmoniously together and form loving relationships, not every dog is suited for living with a cat. Some dogs, for example, are hardwired with an innate drive to hunt and kill small animals. If your dog hasn't previously been exposed to cats, it's important to have them cat tested before bringing an Overlord into your home. Watch and see how your dog reacts to any strays you may spot on your walks. Does poochie immediately stiffen up and stare intensely? Do they lunge and bark at the cat? You can also test your dog by playing recordings of cat sounds in your home and observing their reaction.

CAT TALES: *Doggone Crazy*

On several occasions, Hotel Mancuso has opened its doors to guests of the canine variety. Of course, we had to be selective so as not to overly upset the royals. For the most part we fostered a few pups and small breed seniors anywhere from a few days to a few weeks. These stays were largely uneventful; the fur-brigade tolerated hosting a dog the best they could. A blind Chihuahua puppy named Rupert even made friends with a few of our kitties during his stay. Then came Wilson, a seventy-pound Treeing Walker Coonhound rescued from a shelter from down south. God helps us.

On July 4th of 2020, Wilson was in desperate need of a foster home. Most of my volunteers had taken the day off to be with family and friends, but as manager, placing pets in foster homes was ultimately my responsibility, even on holidays. Understandably, with everyone prepping for fireworks and barbeques, my calls and texts to open foster homes went unanswered. Social media was a graveyard. The kennels were all closed, so boarding was not even an option. With nowhere else for him to go, I decided to keep him in my home office until he could be moved to a more appropriate foster home. A hunting breed, Wilson had a high prey drive, and keeping him under the same roof as twenty cats, even

Boarding Wilson in a houseful of cats for 10 days. What could go wrong?

temporarily, was going to be a challenge. The situation was far from ideal, but desperate times . . .

The wife's jaw came unhinged when she heard the news. "Um, hello? We have cats." Catherine looked at me like I was crazy. Well, she married me, so she would know.

I showed her his photo. Handsome dog. "Wilson has nowhere else to go. It's only temporary."

Besides, I had devised a plan to keep everyone safe. Cathy and I would work as a team. I was the dog handler, and she was the cat wrangler. Reluctantly, she agreed, but I was threatened with castration should anything go wrong. Fair enough.

When he arrived, I was thankful to find Wilson was completely unbothered by the loud pops of neighborhood bottle rockets and firecrackers—one less thing to worry about. However, his nose detected our cats immediately. I tried to keep his focus on me as I escorted him safely to my office.

Wilson was smart and he needed to be active. We'd go outside multiple times a day to burn off some energy. Unfortunately, going outside wasn't as simple as grabbing the leash and walking out the door. Wifey and I had established a system, and it was important to always follow the plan.

"We're going to go outside for a walk now!" I shouted through my office door.

On the other side, Cathy herded the cats, keeping them away from Wilson's path to the front door. She quickly accounted for the whereabouts of every member of the fur-brigade. "Okay, it's safe to come out now," she would call back.

Of course, my cats were terrified at this huge, gangly beast invading their home. Most of them hid at the sound of his nails clacking on the wood floor. Hearing his approach, they gave Wilson a wide berth. Tails shot under the furniture. Fear turned some to stone. Even Mr. Bitey was smart enough to keep his distance. Some cats were braver than others, daring to watch in plain sight from their wall perches across the room with a *you gotta be fluffing kidding me* look pasted on their faces.

"Come on, buddy. This way." I used my body to block the cats from his sight and keep myself as a barrier between predator and prey. Even if Wilson couldn't see them, he knew they were there; he could smell them, sense them. He pulled hard, eager to follow his instincts. I kept his leash very short, tightly wrapped around my fist, fast-walking through the kitchen and down the stairs.

Once outside, Wilson was eager to fulfill his hunting instinct. During our daily mile-long walks, he would try to follow his keen sense of smell, which meant his nose was always trying to lead me into someone's yard. Even though we regularly worked on leash manners, he would still bark and lunge at squirrels and lawn gnomes alike, pulling and straining against me. Despite all of our walking and playing, Wilson still had plenty of energy to spare. When it was time to come in, Cathy and I would exchange texts while Wilson and I waited on the front stoop for her to clear the path. We followed this routine several times a day for the next week and a half.

Although there was never an incident, those few days were a stressful time, not only for us, but also for Wilson and especially our fur-brigade. It was an imperfect solution to an imperfect situation, but knowing that Wilson's stay would be short, we made it work as best could. Had we not taken proper precautions, the situation could have led to a disaster.

This tale falls under the disclaimer: Do Not Try This at Home. That said, Wilson wasn't a bad dog, just a hunter following his natural instincts. The two of us even bonded during his short stay.

Geo, on the other hand, was an eleven-month-old Chihuahua-mix pup whom I affectionately nicknamed "Chicken Wing" due to a birth defect that caused one of his forelimbs to resemble a furry little flapper. He was a curious pup and just wanted to play with my cats. Even though he wasn't much bigger than many of them, I'd always made sure to keep him on-leash and pay close attention during any interactions. Needless to say, the fur-brigade was much less threatened by Chicken Wing, although not necessarily approving. 🐾

HOLDING COURT: VISITORS

Honored guest or unwelcome trespasser? How will your meowing monarch view social calls from humans who live outside the castle walls? If your felion is an extrovert, they likely will be happy to hold court and accept offerings of friendship from visiting ambassadors. That said, even confident cats can find hosting a get together stressful. Keep in mind that visitors bring disruption and unpredictability. *What is a Michael and how long is it staying?* Untrained humans are clumsy and chaotic barbarians. At best. Face it, your friends are loud, your relatives are obnoxious, and that Michael smells funky. It's understandable why your cat would prefer to nail a "No Visitors Allowed" proclamation to the door.

Fortress Of Solitude – Prior to your guests' arrival, the Overlord should retreat to their Inner Sanctum. As mentioned, this fortress of solitude should provide ample privacy from the chaos of unwanted visitors. A safe space, this room should include all of the necessities, like food, water, toys, and a sandcastle. Introduce a new toy to help keep your cat occupied while ambassadors are present. Make it a point to keep guests out of this safe space. The door can be left ajar in case Your Highness decides to creep out and collect data on a reconnaissance mission.

Forging Alliances – When it comes to foreign policy, many felion Rulers tend to be strict isolationists. To protect their domain, the Overlord will order borders closed and the unwashed masses kept out. However, you can use your position on the High Council to show the benefits of forging alliances with outsiders.

Be selective about whom you allow to enter the castle. The guest list should be kept exclusive. Until such time as the Overlord adopts a general admission policy, limit visits to one or two trusted ambassadors and appointments from envoys on official business. Making smart choices in the company you keep will help in building future alliances. Leave the Sloppy Joes at home; it's best to admit ambassadors you can trust to respect Felion Law.

No Soliciting – Forced interactions rarely end well. Any guest should be instructed not to approach Your Highness without having been summoned. In fact, the best thing one can do is make themselves available for inspection and wait for an audience with The Crown. A petitioner may offer treaties. However, acceptance of said treaties should never be mistaken for consent, approval, or a binding familiarity agreement. Any kind of physical contact between felion and guests must be initiated at the sole discretion of your Overlord.

Visiting Hours – Keep visiting hours consistent. Knowing strangers will depart the realm by a specified time will subconsciously help put your cat at ease. Keep visits short to start, gradually extending hours as the Overlord becomes more accustomed to hosting ambassadors. Avoid having overnight guests whenever possible.

Party Planner – Keep Your Majesty in mind when planning your next gathering. Keep it low key for the high-strung felion. If your cat is not comfortable around company, opt to host an intimate book club as opposed to a rowdy jamboree. Forego the horns and party-poppers or anything that could startle your cat. Plan to start your event after mealtime. With a full belly, the Overlord may just decide to curl up and take a nap. Additionally, anytime you're going to have guests over, ensure that safety protocols are in place to keep your Overlord from escaping the castle in fear.

Take A Chill Pill – If your cat becomes too stressed or aggressive with visitors, have a discussion with your veterinarian about using anti-anxiety medications. Some cats will never enjoy company, no matter what, and you may need intervention to help reduce their anxiety and stress.

8

YOU GOTTA BE KITTEN ME

"THE SMALLEST FELINE IS A MASTERPIECE."

—Leonardo da Vinci

BORN TO RULE: SAVING ORPHANED KITTENS

There are myriad reasons a queen might abandon one or more of her kittens. A mother may reject one with a birth defect or one that becomes sick enough to jeopardize the health of its littermates. If her litter is too large, the queen cannot produce enough milk to feed all of her kittens, so the smallest and weakest will be left behind to go hungry. Young mothers in particular may become overwhelmed and not adequately develop a maternal bond with their offspring.

Not all abandonments are intentional, especially for those cats that reside in The Great Backyard outside of castle walls. Feral and stray Queens also need to leave their nests to hunt, and not every mother makes it back safely. I know of too many instances where a mamma cat got lost, injured, or killed while in search of a meal, leaving her kittens to starve or fall victim to nearby predators. If born indoors, treacherous humans have been known to discard accidental offspring of their unspayed queen. In any case, when it comes to abandoned kittens, their only hope for survival is someone like you.

If you have a big heart, you may suddenly find yourself caring for orphaned kittens you never expected to meet. Maybe you found them in your yard, or in a box next to a pile of street trash. Some people may shrug off such a sight and walk away. Let nature take its course. Not you. You desperately want to help these kittens, but you have no experience. Don't fear, the Celestial Meow has set you on this path, and you just need to believe in yourself.

Caring for newborn kittens can be a frightening proposition, at least it is for me. Whether you are caring for a single kitten or an entire litter, being a surrogate for neonates isn't easy. You'll have to put your heart on the line and take their life in your hands. Stress levels will elevate, and you will definitely miss out on some sleep for a few weeks. The kittens will be completely dependent on you, and you'll worry day and night about your fragile little mew-mews.

Sadly, sometimes you can do everything right and still one or more kittens may not survive. If you're anything like me, losing a kitten will break your heart and make you feel like a failure. It's happened multiple times to Cathy and me, when despite our best efforts, some newborns lived only a few days, sometimes only hours. I remember agonizing over what I must have done wrong. Beating myself up with thoughts I had been too late. *If only I could have helped sooner.* I want to tell you that losing an abandoned kitten under your care is not your fault. Nor should such a tragedy prevent you from trying again. Doing the right thing isn't always easy, but if we can provide a little one with love, even for a short time, it leads to a better end for them than had we not tried at all.

Kia, Kimchi, Kashmir, & Kowasaki were found crying in a cardboard box.

Many will survive, though. And the sense of reward you will feel from raising a newborn kitten is a hundred-fold. You will find yourself marveling at simple accomplishments, like when they start eating without your assistance. Kittens give as much love as they get. As Cat Parent, you will form a special bond with them as they grow. Your home will be filled with life and laughter. Whether you decide to adopt the kitten as your Overlord or let them find another castle to rule, you can sleep with a full heart knowing that you saved a life. Not all heroes wear capes.

FUR FACT   Kittens in the same litter can have more than one father. This is because the female cat releases multiple eggs over the course of a few days when she is in heat.

TO THE RESCUE

Before you rush to scoop up the kittens, step back, watch, and wait. As a single parent, Mom must occasionally leave her babies alone and hope they will be safe. It's likely that she is not far away from the nesting area. She's probably on a quick errand, food shopping. If the queen returns within an hour, it's best to leave them in her capable paws, unless you decide to rescue her as well. If she doesn't, it's time to step up and take them in.

If Mom returns, assess the situation. How safe is the den? Are there nearby threats from predators? Are the kittens going to be warm enough? What if it rains; will the family stay dry? If you're unable to take in the queen and her brood, is there another way you can help them? Perhaps allow the queen and the royal family access to your garage, shed, or porch. You can bring food and water for Mom, so she can stay home with her litter. You can make some improvements to their existing space by providing extra concealment, warmth, and comfort. Start reaching out to local rescues for assistance.

There are situations when time is a luxury you can ill afford, like finding kittens placed in a carrier, cardboard box, or garbage can. If they are left exposed in harsh weather, or near dangers like busy roads or construction, don't hesitate to act. If any of the kittens look sick, have them examined by a veterinarian as soon as possible.

AGE APPROPRIATE

When caring for extremely young catlings it's important to be able to approximate their age. In the span of their adult life, a week is no big deal, but a kitten's first eight weeks are critical for growth and development. Remember, this stage of their life is when they are at their most fragile. Handle with care. A surrogate caregiver must be vigilant and observant to best serve the youngest of royalty. From the number of feedings per day to their developmental milestones, once you reasonably determine the kitten's age, you can know what to expect and make a care plan according to their needs.

Week One – These palm-sized princes and princesses are the newest of newborns. They're adorable, little wiggly-wiggles. At this age, they cannot hear or see; their eyes are closed, and their ears are folded. Unable to walk, the heat-seeking wiggler will manage to crawl a little in search of warmth, milk, and the comfort of their queen. During their first week, the future Overlords do little more than eat, sleep, and poop. And they make it look so cute!

The first 48 hours of a kitten's life are a critical period for obtaining maternal antibodies through nursing. During the first two days, a nursing queen will pass her royal immunity to her kittens through her milk. Whenever possible, newborn kittens should receive their mother's milk, or they will be more vulnerable to sickness. In newborns, you will also notice that the umbilical is still attached. There's no need for concern, leave it alone. The cord will naturally fall off on its own in a few days.

Two Weeks – During the second week of life, kittens will experience a first blurry view of their dominion as their eyes slowly open. This is a gradual process that can take a few days. Never attempt to pry open a kitten's eyes; let them open naturally. As you'll notice, all kittens are born with blue eyes, which will change to their adult eye color as they age. Also, in the second week, their ears begin to unfold, and they start to develop hearing. What better way to be welcomed into the world than to the sounds of your praise and worship!

By their second week, newborns will be more adept at crawling. These kittens will become slightly more active and curious about the world around them. They may even attempt to take their first steps but are not likely to get very far. By now, little princes and princesses will also develop their sense of smell, which is why at Hotel Mancuso we always include items in the nursery suite that will familiarize and comfort the younglings with our scent.

Three Weeks – It's amazing how fast these princes and princesses grow. At three weeks, baby teeth are coming in. With eyes and ears fully open, a kitten's eyesight and hearing will have improved. You will start to notice them responding to noises and movement. Kittens will begin to play and socialize with you as well as their littermates. These tiny puff balls with legs are most likely walking and exploring by now. The brave ones may also take up climbing, especially on you—the great mountain of love. At three weeks, claws have yet to retract so their stabby little knives are always on hand. This is a good time to carefully start getting the little royals used to pawdicures.

They will also likely be going to the bathroom on their own. *Thank God!* You can start litter box training. Simply place kitten in a small litter box and wait for instinct to take over. If they don't evacuate, you'll still need to stimulate them for elimination, but keep at it. They'll catch on.

Four to Five Weeks – Typically within this time period, kittens will start to wean from the bottle and be able to lap up formula and eat soft food. Although they still spend much of their time sleeping, the periods of wakeful activity will become longer and more frequent. By this time the little royals are more graceful on their feet. Now they start to act like true catlings, running, playing, discovering the world around them. The hard work of ruling a kingdom is still a long way off, but even at four weeks the future Overlords are wise enough to realize that when they issue a mewling decree, we are there to serve them. At times, they can be adorably insisting. Thankfully, most of their demands are either for food or attention. If you have multiple siblings, you may see the first cues to their personalities. *Snuggles gives the best hugs. Why so shy, little Petey? Umm . . . where did Catstofur Columbus go?*

THE HEAT IS ON

During their first four weeks, kittens are unable to regulate their own body temperature. In the absence of their queen, these delicate little purries will need you to provide a comfortable heat source. Whenever I go out on a call to rescue abandoned kittens, I make sure to place HOT HANDS hand warmers under the bedding in the carrier until I can get the kittens registered at Hotel Mancuso. If a rescued kitten feels cold, you will need to get them warm as soon as possible. If they're wet, make sure to get them dry quickly. Understandably if you're not a rescuer, you're likely not going to have hand warmers, blankets, or a towel on you when you find your little treasures. You can, however, use what you have at your disposal, like a hat or shirt. You can also give them gentle massages to help promote circulation. At the very least, keep the little ones close to your body to provide them with some heat until you get them home.

When you get the kittens inside, gently place them on a heating pad wrapped in towels. Use the lowest setting and check the temperature often. If you don't have access to a heating pad, you can always heat up a warm water bottle to about 100 degrees and place that under the blankets. Other ideas for a heating source you may have available at home are a clean sock filled with uncooked rice and warmed in the microwave or a latex glove filled with hot water and properly tied. In any case, just remember to keep an eye on the temperature and reheat as needed.

Do not place kittens on a direct source of heat—always use towels or blankets as padding to protect them from being burned. Monitor the temperature of bedding often to keep kittens from being too warm or too cold. If they're newborns, make sure to flip them over from side to side, like little furry pancakes. Bedding should cover the carrier's entire bottom area, but leave enough space for the kittens to escape the heat source if they desire.

Since catlings can't digest when they're cold, do not attempt to feed a chilled kitten; wait until they are thoroughly warmed before nursing.

ON THE MENU

Kittens sleep up to twenty hours a day, but you won't. Set your alarm and sleep light. Depending on their age, newborns will need to be nursed every two to six hours. That's right, even at such a young age, the Overlords rule our lives. The royal babies wake up long enough for us to feed them, make them poop, and adore them. You'll be tired and cranky . . . until you pick one up and they bless you with purrs, mews, and snuggles that melt those feelings away. If you're able to, recruit help. Since Cathy and I are usually on opposite schedules, we take turns and share the responsibility caring for them in shifts. It's only a few weeks, and who doesn't love adorable, fluffy munchkins?

KMR – KITTEN MILK REPLACER

Adequate nutrition is essential for healthy princes and princesses. If not nursing off their queens, neonates should only drink kitten milk replacer as it is specifically formulated with the proper fats, proteins, and carbohydrates that newborns require. Do not feed kittens dairy milk. I repeat, despite the common cliché of cats drinking milk, do not give dairy to your kittens. Same goes for soy and nut milks. Not only do these lack the proper nutrients needed, but they will also cause upset stomach, diarrhea, and dehydration. Kitten milk replacer can be found in almost any pet store. I recommend buying the powdered version; the pre-made liquid cans are only good for two days once opened, and if you only have a single kitten, or a very young litter, much of the can will go to waste.

When mixing a batch of KMR, be sure to follow the package instructions properly. Opened KMR powder should be refrigerated. Formula should be warmed prior to feedings, but never hot. Much like their sleeping area, the temperature needs to be at the Goldilocks temperature. Only make small amounts of replacer at a time, keep leftover KMR refrigerated between feedings, and discard any unused portion after twenty-four hours. If any formula is left at room temperature for one hour, throw it away.

AGE	WEIGHT	AMOUNT PER FEEDING
0–1 Week	1.7oz–5oz	2–6ml every 2 hours
1–2 Weeks	5oz–7oz	6–10ml every 2–3 hours
2–3 Weeks	8oz–12 oz	10–14ml every 3–4 hours
3–4 Weeks	12oz–16oz	14–18ml every 4–5 hours
4–5 Weeks	16oz–19oz	18–22ml every 5–6 hours
5–8 Weeks	20+oz	offer wet food every 6 hours

This feeding schedule is a good guideline, but there is a little room for adjustments if necessary. For example, I've had newborn catlings that wouldn't intake enough formula at the scheduled time, so we modified the nursing schedule to every hour until they started taking in the proper amount per feeding. If you're a little late with a feeding, there's no reason to panic, just feed the kitten at that time and resume your schedule thereafter. If you're more than a little late or you accidentally miss a feeding, don't feed the kitten twice as much; just feed them the normal amount at the next set time and get back on schedule for the rest of the day.

HOMEMADE FORMULA (FOR EMERGENCIES)

Since rescue is unpredictable, my wife and I always made sure to have kitten-care essentials in stock at Hotel Mancuso. What if it's late and the pet stores are closed, or you're simply unable to make it to the store for a few hours? Well, with some items you hopefully have in the kitchen, there is hope.

> 8 ounces homogenized whole milk
> 3 egg yolks
> 1 teaspoon corn oil
> 1 drop liquid pet pediatric vitamins (optional)
> Small pinch of salt
> Mix well and warm 95-100°F before using. Keep refrigerated in
> between feedings.[19]

Keep in mind this homemade concoction is for temporary, emergency use only. As soon as the pet store opens in the morning, buy a can of powdered commercial milk replacer (KMR).

Bottles and Syringes – Until four weeks of age, motherless neonates will need to be bottle fed. Unfortunately, most nipples don't come with pre-made holes, so you'll need to cut one yourself. Avoid holes too big or too small. Formula should drip out when the bottle is held upside down.

Personally, I like to use 1ml syringes for feedings (3ml as they get older). This allows me to see exactly how much a kitten consumes with each feeding. Not to mention the fact that I am a disaster at making a proper sized opening in a nipple. Bottles and nipples, or syringes, should be cleaned and sterilized between uses.

In addition to bottles and syringes, here are some other supplies you will need to care for abandoned neonate kittens:

- *Heat source* – As mentioned, any kittens under five weeks old will need to be kept warm at all times. From a heating pad to hand warmers to re-usable microwavable discs, there are a lot of options from which to choose.

- *Digital Food Scale* – You'll need to monitor daily weight gain to ensure the kittens are growing properly. Write down their weight, feeding schedule and progress each day.

- *Flea Comb* – Because . . . you know. If you don't, keep reading. We're going to talk about fleas more in a few pages.

- *Cuddle Buddy* – We always put a plush toy with the kittens for added comfort. We've upgraded to a stuffed cat with a heartbeat that helps them feel soothed.

- *Kitten Wet Food* – Mix with warm water. If kittens are at least four weeks old, they can start weaning from the bottle and lap up some gruel.

NURSING

When bottle feeding a kitten, it is important to follow felion etiquette by feeding princes and princesses in their natural position—belly down; this is how they would nurse from their queen. Feeding a kitten on their back, like a baby, can result in aspiration. Not only can the little catling accidentally inhale or choke, being fed like a human servant is degrading to felion royalty.

Use one hand to gently hold the kitten's head up in a dignified position. Reverently place the nipple into their mouth; instinctually, kittens will catch on and latch on. Fussy little royals may need a little coaxing before they get the hang of it, and gentle petting can often do the trick. Ear-wiggling is an absolutely adorable indication that the kitten is successfully suckling. Holding the bottle (or syringe) at a 45-degree angle will help keep air from getting into their stomach. Allow the kitten to drink at their own pace until full. They will typically let you know when they've had enough. With a full belly, a catling will often unlatch and push the nipple away, or simply turn their faces. Monitor the measurements on the

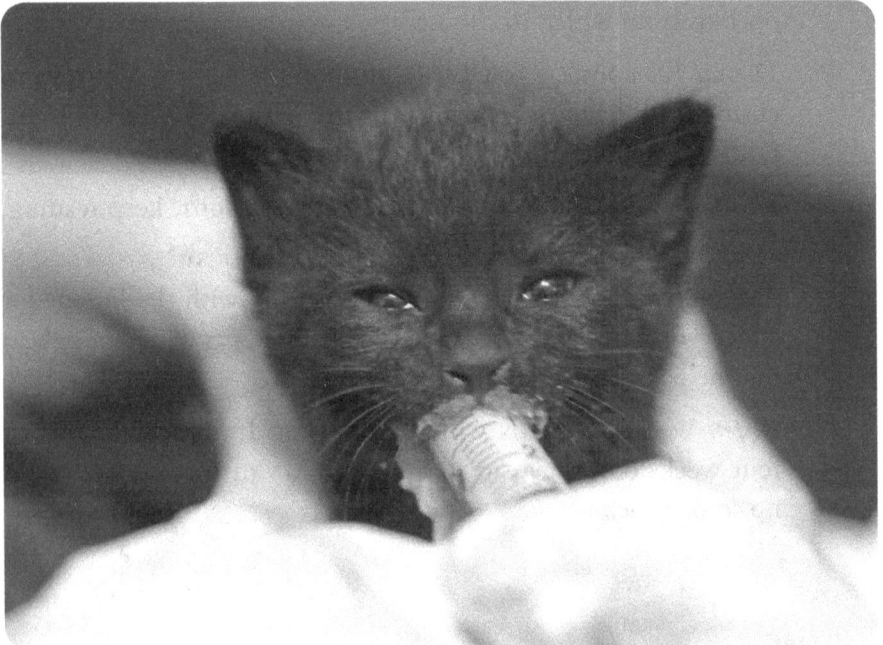

Feeding time for a three-week-old catling.

bottle/syringe to ensure they are drinking enough at each meal. Kittens that are weak or not drinking enough should receive extra feedings. If a kitten is refusing to nurse, don't try to force formula down their throats, see a veterinarian as soon as possible.

Despite being felion royalty, catlings are notoriously messy eaters; clean those lovable, dirty faces with a warm, damp cloth. You should burp a kitten after each feeding by gently patting their sides or back with your fingers. Lastly, before putting them back to sleep, you will need to make sure the kittens pee and poop.

THE PROCESS OF ELIMINATION

Proper bathroom protocol must be followed when caring for neonates. Until they are at least three to four weeks, precious catlings will need to be stimulated after each nursing, or as Wifey is fond of saying, "wipe that tushy." Just be glad you're not their real mom—queens use their tongues! I prefer to use damp paper towels since they provide a rougher texture than tissues, toilet paper, or cotton balls and more closely mimic the feel of Mom's tongue, however any of those options would suffice. To facilitate the process of elimination, gently rub the kitten's genitals; you can either do so in a circular motion, or vertically. This will stimulate newborns to poop and pee. When they are done, clean the area.

Starting at three weeks old, little lords and ladies should start relieving themselves on their own. Provide kitten access to a litter box. We typically improvise by using a small, shallow cardboard box. Place the kitten in the litter box after each feeding. In no time they will start using it on their own. Since the elimination behavior of covering their waste is instinctual, that's all it takes to train your kitten to use their box.

It's important to pay close attention to kitten bowel movements. Keep in mind, it's not normal for your little stinker to have diarrhea and it should be taken seriously. While sometimes diarrhea can be caused by a kitten's sensitive stomach adjusting to the kitten milk replacer, mushy stools can be a symptom of intestinal parasites, or a bacterial or viral infection. A change in poop color from brown to green, black, red, or even pale yellow is a good indicator that veterinary intervention is needed. Neonates dehydrate quickly, which means diarrhea can be fatal, especially if coupled with lethargy, vomiting, and/or loss of appetite. Once a kitten reaches two weeks old, it's imperative to start deworming treatments, even if the kitten appears totally healthy.

If mushy stool is a brown color and your kitten is otherwise acting normally, you could try some of the following at-home remedies.

- Supplement unflavored Pedialyte in their formula instead of water to help keep them hydrated. If needed, you can also add an extra feeding of just Pedialyte. From my personal experience, I have also found unflavored Pedialyte can aid with kitten constipation.
- Try feeding kitten some organic/natural canned pumpkin, NOT pie filling. Pie fillings have sugars and other ingredients that are unhealthy for adult felions, much less tiny catlings.
- Add a pinch of cat probiotics (FortiFlora) to their formula. Probiotics contain good bacteria and promote healthy digestion.

Seek immediate vet attention if diarrhea lasts more than a day or two. Since diarrhea leads to dehydration, kittens can take a turn for the worse and crash quickly, becoming a life-or-death emergency. They younger the kitten, the more fragile they are, so when dealing with kitten diarrhea, time is of the essence.

From feedings to flea baths, if you need a visual aid for neonate care, you can find all sorts of video tutorials online. Some rescues or shelters may even offer classes on kitten care for the community. If you know someone who has cared for neonates before, recruit their help.

PARASITES

The Great Backyard is full of monsters great and small. One of the challenges of taking in strays is dealing with possible parasites. Felions of any age can be infected with internal or external parasites if they have come into contact with a host or even infected poop. Due to their small size and weak immune systems, kittens are at a much higher risk of suffering serious effects from parasites, including death. It is important to eradicate these unwanted invaders from the kingdom as soon as possible. Know thy enemy.

EXTERNAL PARASITES

Fleas – These little blood suckers are a real pest. Their bites cause itchiness and irritation. For adult cats, fleas are a nuisance, but a flea infestation can actually kill a kitten. If the kittens are very young, fleas can suck too much blood and cause them to become anemic. If live fleas, or flea dirt (looks like coffee grounds), are visible, a kitten must be treated as soon as possible. Chemical treatments are DANGEROUS to kittens under eight weeks old, and they must be treated instead with a careful bathing regimen.

Flea Baths are standard protocol for kittens that board at Hotel Mancuso. Our tiniest guests receive the very best spa treatment our competent staff has to offer, including a thorough bubble bath, fur brushing, and a soothing air-dry followed with a warm, snuggling towel massage courtesy of their foster mom. All this luxury is accompanied by my live a cappella performances of "Die, Fleas, Die" and "Clean, Clean, Kitty-Kitty, Pretty, Pretty Kitty-Kitty." Oh, the unhappy mews I receive, as if those ungrateful little munchkins are being subjected medieval torture. Everyone's a critic.

Dawn (blue) liquid dish detergent is easy on the kitten's skin and nontoxic if accidentally ingested. In a sink or bucket, lather the kitten with Dawn and warm water. Be careful not to completely submerge the kitten.

Gently comb out the fleas using a flea comb, rinsing it often in a separate bowl of soapy water as you work. Once you have thoroughly removed the fleas, give that whiny kitty a quick rinse with warm water and immediately towel dry. Remember, kittens under eight weeks old cannot regulate their body temperature, so it's important to always keep them warm. Additionally, you can use a hairdryer set on LOW at a safe distance of two feet. Flea baths may need to be repeated once a day for several days to be fully effective.

Lice – Adult lice are flat, six-legged insects that crawl about on your kitty. Nits (eggs) look like small, white ovals and are attached to shafts of fur. Lice can be passed from one cat to another through direct contact or contact with contaminated objects, such as grooming utensils or bedding. On a good note, cat lice do not move from cats to humans, so no need to worry about these creepers looking to set up shop in your own hair. For kittens under eight weeks, use the same process described above for flea removal. If you're a crooner like me, feel free to change any of your song lyrics to fit the occasion. "Die lice, die. You're so gross to have around. Bye, bye, bye. Here's some soap to make you drown."

Ticks – These eight-legged creeps are commonly found in high grass-lands and wooded areas. Ticks will borough their head into the kitten's skin and latch on. They are typically between 1mm-1cm in size, growing larger and fatter as they dine on their host. If you find a tick on your cat, pluck those suckers out with tweezers as soon as possible.

Ear Mites – These nasty micro-munchers live inside the ear. Imagine having Snap, Krackle, and Pop inside your ear canal all day long. That has to be worse than my singing! Symptoms include:

- Inflamed outer ear, sometimes scabby
- Ears flat against their head
- Excessive buildup of earwax and debris that resembles coffee grounds
- A foul smell emanating from the inner ear
- Excessive scratching, sometimes to the point of mutilation
- Head shaking (like trying to dislodge something)

Left untreated, ear mites can lead to infection and result in damage or complete loss of hearing. A veterinarian can confirm any suspicion of ear mites by looking in your cat's ear with an otoscope or viewing a sample of the buildup under a microscope. If your kitten is younger than eight weeks old, a few drops of baby oil in the ear several times a day for a month is a safe way to smother the mites. Consult with a veterinarian for an effective treatment. Thankfully, ear mites are easily treatable, and many of the same preventives used against fleas and ticks also prevent ear mites.

Ringworm – Despite its name, ringworm is not a worm at all but rather a fungal infection. I usually refer to ringworm as "cathlete's foot" since it is basically the same fungus. Ringworm will cause round patches of missing fur, especially around the face and ears. It also makes cats uncomfortable with itchy, scaly, and irritated skin.

Lime-sulfur Dip baths are an effective way to treat a cat or kitten suffering with a bout of ringworm. Dips should be done twice a week with 8oz of solution diluted into one gallon of warm water. Dip the entire kitten or cat up to the shoulders and massage the solution into the fur. Or, using a spray bottle, disperse the solution onto the fur and massage it in. Use a washcloth for the head, face, ears, and nose. Do not allow the solution to get into eyes, ears, nose, or mouth. Do NOT rinse the solution, let it air dry! Yes, the dipped kitten is going to smell like rotten eggs for a little while, but you can always hold your nose while giving them cuddles.

Infected hairs and spores will fall off your kitty and get spread around the kingdom, so a thorough castle-cleaning regimen including daily vacuuming, sweeping, and mopping should be kept up during and after treatment. Use a 1:10 bleach solution (1 part bleach to 10 parts water) every day on any surface that allows bleach cleaning. The bleach solution should sit for a minimum of ten minutes before wiping it off. After interacting with animals infected with ringworm, immediately wash your hands thoroughly and change clothing so as not to inadvertently spread spores around the house. Wash all bedding and clothing in very hot water with color safe bleach. The easiest way to decontaminate is to keep your kitty confined to a limited space with nonporous surfaces. At Hotel Mancuso, we utilize our bathroom for this purpose.

One of the more frustrating aspects of ringworm is that it can take up to three weeks after exposure for your kitty to show symptoms. Of course, proper hygiene protocols will limit the spread, but ringworm is contagious to people and other pets. If you find a spot on yourself, it's easily treatable with an antifungal cream. If you're worried about your kids or other pets, limit and supervise their exposure. Thankfully, ringworm is usually self-limiting, meaning that even if untreated it will resolve on its own in a few months.

Try not to get too stressed about it. Although, I'm not going to lie, the first time we had to deal with ringworm was pretty stressful, especially since it took over two weeks for our foster kittens to show any symptoms. If you think treating a single kitten sounds difficult, I bet you can imagine the challenges of treating a kitten and eight adult cats at the same time. The kingdom was in upheaval. Daily complaints were filed, and the fur-brigade protested against medical treatment. Even our super chill VanDuzer was stressed. After that ordeal, Cathy and I swore off fostering ringworm kittens. Until the next time a ringworm kitty was in need. At least then we were better prepared. Like anything else, we got better with repetition. We learned to keep our other cats safe from infection and now, although an inconvenience, we no longer feel a sense of dread when it comes to dealing with ringworm. It is what it is. I've lost count of how many infected kittens Cathy and I have fostered over the years. If your new kitten or cat ends up with ringworm, don't worry, you'll get through it. It's not the end of the world, I promise.

INTERNAL PARASITES

Like external parasites, these nasty suckers rob cats and kittens of valuable nutrients, however they have a devious advantage, hiding in a kitty like a Trojan Horse. Whether microscopic protozoans like giardia or visible organisms like roundworms and tapeworms, internal parasites attack felions from the inside, often setting up a siege in the in the digestive tract. Out of sight, out of mind, they feed; they grow; they replicate. Once infected with internal ninjas, a kitten's health becomes a ticking time bomb. Unlike adult monarchs, princes and princesses do not have the constitution to survive a sustained battle without human intervention.

For many young kittens, prevention, detection and medication are the best defenses against the enemy within. It's important to be able to quickly identify the symptoms of a parasitic infection:

* Diarrhea
* Dehydration
* Excess Gas
* Vomiting
* Sudden weight loss
* Lethargy
* Poor appetite
* Abdominal swelling (also known as Worm Belly).

Royal younglings experiencing any of the symptoms above should be seen by a veterinarian as soon as possible. Some internal parasites can be eradicated with over-the-counter medications like Pyrantel Pamoate, however unless diagnosed by a veterinarian it could be difficult to tell which type of foe to treat. Keep in mind that depending on when a prince or princess was exposed to a parasite, a kitten may initially test negative while in foster care or in a shelter. If proper sanitization precautions are not strictly followed during treatments, kittens can also reinfect themselves. Undetectable larvae may linger stubbornly, biding time until they can mount a new offensive. Your catling may require additional rounds of medicine to completely eliminate a resilient parasitic infection, lest the survivors multiply in number once more. In a war where time is of the essence, quick treatment gives fragile kittens the best chance of survival and recovery.

Deworming

A lot of nasty little parasites can adversely affect the health of kittens, particularly those born in the wilderness of The Great Backyard. Whether showing symptoms or not, all catlings will need to be dewormed out of an abundance of caution. Even royal offspring born in castles should receive proper deworming treatments. Mom could have picked up a freeloader from her mate or even an accidental transmission from someone's clothes or shoes. Queen Mother may not even have any symptoms, but she can easily pass an infection to her offspring.

Catlings should receive their first dose of dewormer at two weeks old, with bi-weekly follow up doses until they reach the age of eight weeks, even if they seem perfectly fine. Be sure to follow veterinarian's directions regarding dosage and scheduling of deworming treatments.

Fecal Test

Through the miracle of modern science this microscopic test can detect any parasites present in royal poop. Depending on length of time since exposure, a kitten may test negative while in a foster castle or in a shelter, only to later test positive. Hotel Mancuso has hosted several kittens that required multiple rounds of treatments to be fully cleared from their micro-intruders. Luckily, if your catlings positive for any parasite, your veterinarian can prescribe the proper anti-parasitic medication as well as antibiotics. During treatments, you'll need to disinfect the kitten's area, thrones and bedding, as well as change the sandcastle daily (not just scooping the box.) After the treatment, your vet may suggest a retest.

TESTING/VACCINES

To help ensure good health, little royals need to be tested for contagious, cat-specific viruses. This is particularly important if other felions currently reside within the castle walls, or if you plan to take Your Highness on outdoor adventures. Both can potentially expose healthy cats and/or kittens to serious illness.

Vaccines save lives. They are a medical miracle bestowed upon modern science by the Celestial Meow. I can't stress their importance enough, as in my work I have witnessed the tragic outcome of unvaccinated felions. On behalf of Cat World, I implore you to get your kitten all vaccines and boosters on schedule.

SNAP® Test – This is a rapid blood test to check for FIV (Feline Immunodeficiency Virus) and FeLV (Feline Leukemia Virus).

FVRCP Vaccine – Catlings are highly susceptible to contagious illnesses like feline viral rhinotracheitis, calicivirus, and panleukopenia (the equivalent of parvo for cats.) These illnesses can be severe in the unvaccinated. For example, Panleukopenia has a 90% fatality rate. Yes, it's that deadly! Don't allow a tragedy to befall your kingdom when it can be easily averted.

Kittens should receive the initial dose of FVRCP vaccine at four weeks old. To maximize protection, they should receive bi-weekly boosters until they are four months old. Once grown, your cat only needs an FVRCP booster every three years, or at the recommendation of your veterinarian.

The rescue organizations I've worked with provide a minimum of two FVRCP vaccines prior to adoption. I would expect that any reputable rescue, shelter, or breeder would do the same. Nevertheless, it's in your best interest and that of your new Overlord to always confirm their medical history. As the royal chronicler, obtain a copy of their current medical records to preserve for posterity.

Rabies Vaccine – Rabies is a virus primarily spread through saliva/ bites. It's most commonly found in wild animals like skunks, foxes, bats, and raccoons but can spread to any mammal. For cats, rabies is always fatal, since most states require an infected animal to be euthanized. Even felions that are merely suspected of being infected can face euthanasia, especially if have bitten or scratched; the only test for rabies involves decapitation and examining the brain.

Kittens need get the rabies vaccine at twelve to sixteen weeks old. Like with the FVRCP vaccine, rescues and shelters will inoculate any kitten old enough to receive the vaccine prior to adoption. Should you adopt a kitten younger than 12 weeks, you will be responsible for ensuring that they receive the shot from your vet.

Boosters are usually given every three to five years, depending on the vaccine received. I know I recommended that Your Majesty always remain in the castle, so why should you need to keep up with their vaccinations? Accidents can happen. The Overlord may escape the castle one day. Anything can happen in the Great Backyard. By being current on their rabies vaccine, Your Highness will be protected from contracting the virus should they come in contact with an infected wild animal. Also, in New York as well a majority of other states, it's the law.

Now that we've passed all the icky critters and medical necessities, it's safe to let your little princess make new friends and explore the entirety of her kingdom. Long may she reign.

'TIS THE SEASON: ADOPTING KITTENS

I know, caring for an abandoned neonate is a lot to take on. Maybe you're thinking: Chris, bless people like you and Wifey, but I really can't take in any orphaned kittens. I'd gladly adopt a rescue kitten, though. Rest assured, there are many kittens out there that would be eager to claim the throne in your castle. Although little lords and ladies are looking to adopt a human almost any time of year, kitten season usually starts in April and lasts through October. This is when shelters and rescues become overrun with litters of tiny Overlords in search of a castle to rule. The earliest a kitten can adopt a family is eight weeks old, although some rescues offer pre-adoptions. This is a contract that will commit your service and castle to a future Overlord. Until such time the prince or princess has reached the age of ascension and can take rule of a kingdom, they will remain in the care of the Servants of Rescue. To increase your chances of finding your perfect match, I'd advise starting a serious search for any early births or pre-adoptions by May.

By and large, kittens in shelters or rescues find castles much quicker than the adult cats there. Partly due to an emotional response—with their big eyes and soft mews, these sweet little fluff balls are irresistibly appealing. I can't think of anything more adorable than a loving, playful kitten. Cuteness aside, many people or families want the opportunity to raise a kitten because they feel it will create a deeper bond. Others want to have a cat that grows up around children or other pets.

HOME SWEET HOME

It's a good idea to keep kittens confined to a small, kitten-proofed area, especially if the catling is left unsupervised for any amount of time. Otherwise, you may return to find the castle in apocalyptic disarray. The young Overlords are filled with curiosity and playful mischief. With their tiny size, kittens are the ultimate champions of Hide-and-Seek, so limiting the places they can get into will work in your favor and keep them safe. Consider setting up a midsize to large crate to use for overnight and times when you are not available to keep them under close supervision. Since your little lord or lady may not like being locked in a dungeon inside their own castle, it's important they do not think of it as captivity. Make their crate a mini-Throne Room so they feel at home. This should be the site where all royal feasts are served. Add a royal privy, bedding, access to water, and some toys, all of which will help buy their silence while you visit dreamland.

SOCIALIZATION

Being adorable comes naturally to our little lords and ladies, but running a kingdom inhabited by people or other animals can be overwhelming at first. Kittens that receive insufficient exposure to and contact with people during their first two months may develop fears leading to timidity. This young age is when you want to help your kitten develop into a confident, social felion. That's not to say an adult cat won't be receptive to or benefit from behavior modifications. My wife and I have had many successes helping adult cats build trust and confidence. They simply require more time, effort, and patience on your part to overcome their anxiety.

As soon as possible, start exposing your kitten to a variety of social situations in a positive way to decrease the likelihood of fearful behavior. However, this doesn't mean forcing your kitten to endure stressful situations. That will only make things worse. Always provide your little Overlord with choices, allowing them to control what happens in their environment. Once you stroke their ego and earn their trust, you will have the love of a felion ruler for life.

Furry princes and princesses need a minimum of two hours playtime broken up into ten or fifteen minutes sessions throughout the day. Handle kittens often, even if only for brief periods at a time. I mean, really, who doesn't want kitten snuggles? Start good habits early, like regularly trimming their claws, brushing their teeth, and proper play. Use positive reinforcement and treats to encourage ownership, socialization, and boundaries. Teaching your young Overlord that new experiences don't have to be scary will help them rule with confidence.

DOUBLE THE PLEASURE

If you're thinking of adding a kitten to your family, I urge you to consider getting two. Two princes, two princesses, or one of each. They don't necessarily have to be littermates, as long as they are around the same age. Nevertheless, it's always nice to take in siblings if possible. Serving two kitten Overlords isn't any more difficult than serving just one, and in some ways it's actually easier. Yes, it will cost a bit more, but if you ask me, the benefits of having two kittens far outweigh any drawbacks.

The Buddy System – Having one of their own around will help a kitten grow into a better cat. Felion playmates will teach each other when level of play is too rough to be acceptable. Through playful interactions, they will fulfill each other's need to hunt, stalk, and explore. As they grow, kittens with a friend their own age will continue to have a more active lifestyle and will be less likely to become overweight.

If left alone, a curious kitten can be destructive, but two kittens tend to keep each other occupied and out of trouble, as much as kittens can be expected to stay out of trouble, that is. Having a co-ruler at their side will also help prevent them from developing separation anxiety. They'll be too busy playing and enjoying each other's companionship to become lonely or bored.

Pawsitive Influence – Both kittens will learn how to behave socially. Raising two Royals means your cats will pick up on behavior cues from each other. Kittens learn, in part, by observation. If one kitten is timid, or more of a cat's cat, having a social kitty around will help give them the extra confidence they need when dealing with new people or situations.

I have often seen how a companion can positively influence kittens that are shy or anxious. Many times in rescue we have placed a shy kitten in a foster home with a more sociable one. It's wonderful to watch a timid kitten develop confidence and live up to their full felion potential. Even if the shyer of the two never becomes as bold or social as the other, the royal bond between the is irreplaceable.

Second That Emotion – Growing up together reduces stress levels in kittens when changes occur in the castle. They serve as each other's constant source of comfort, which results in fewer unwanted behaviors. Overall, having a lifelong companion improves the young Overlords' emotional health.

Three's Company – If you already have an Overlord, especially a senior, they may be none too thrilled about having a rambunctious little catling invading their kingdom. A kitten will want to play with the resident cat, whereas the Overlord may have neither the energy nor the inclination to be bothered. This unwanted attention can be a source of stress for the adult. Having a second kitten will give your adult Overlord the option to decide whether they want to join the party or simply be a spectator of the games.

Additionally, when the two kittens are busy playing together, you can take advantage of a great opportunity to worship your resident Overlord with one-on-one time. They will appreciate the extra time not being disturbed or overshadowed by an adorable little prince or princess. This will go a long way toward eliminating any resentment and will pave the way to a harmonious coexistence.

KIT-TEENS

Because adolescents no longer look like tiny fluff balls and more closely resemble adults, they often take a backseat to newborns when servants add a kitten to their family. Older kittens are still young enough to be adorable and fun, though old enough to not be so fragile.

Monarchs between five and eleven months are still growing and require more calories. They should be fed three times a day and remain on a kitten diet until they reach at least ten months. Also, most kittens five months or older should be fully vaccinated and spayed/neutered. At this stage kittens are losing their baby teeth and play bites will start to hurt, so if you haven't already been doing so, now would be the time stop any aggressive play. Your kitten might get especially 'chewy' if the eruption of their adult teeth is causing them discomfort. Keep some teething toys on hand, and redirect your kitten to them whenever they chomp down on something they shouldn't.

It is important to set boundaries for older kittens and correct any unwanted behaviors. Keep your Columbus in check. These youngsters are more confident in their abilities, and their thirst for adventure will take them to great heights as they expand their territory from scaling your entertainment center to surfing on your counters and tables.

These adolescent months will be full of energy and curiosity. It is a time when your kitten's personality will be reinforced by their environment. Since they are just starting to mature into the Overlords they will become, you can help encourage the best in behavior and personality as you enter a lifetime of new experiences.

CAT TALES: *Smitten with Kittens*

Whenever I'm doing adoption-screening calls, I always try to ensure a good match based on personal preferences, expectations, and the personality of the Overlord. These conversations are an opportunity to get to understand someone's lifestyle, experience, and level of knowledge regarding care. Most people new to cats are eager to hear my insights and consider my advice. For my part, I enjoy educating people with commandments from the felion gospel. The better I can prepare someone for their inevitable subjugation, the happier the Overlords will be.

If you're working with an adoption counselor, don't be afraid to ask questions or seek advice. Be honest, not only with the adoption counselor, but also with yourself. Just saying what you think a rescue wants to hear is a disservice to yourself and your potential new cat, especially if the cat in question needs more than you can provide in terms of time, patience, or willingness to work through challenges. The more we know, the better we can assist. Take recommendations seriously, whether general information or a suggestion of which Overlord may be your perfect ruler. The kitty of your dreams may not necessarily be the one you've been dreaming about. They have the ability to steal our hearts right out from under our noses. Allow yourself to feel that connection.

Portions of the following emails have been edited for content and redacted for privacy.

Good morning Christopher,

Thank you for your communication. I had the pleasure of receiving an email from Laura, Minnie's foster mom. As much as I loved learning about our little Minnie, I did have some reservations about her age. I want a young kitten (2 months or slightly older) She's probably used to "Minnie". I want to name my kitten and don't want to confuse her. Also, my kitten will be an "only child" and I fear by this time Minnie has grown used to her foster brothers and sisters and I don't want her to miss them.

I am hoping to adopt a younger baby, like Whiskers for instance, or Grace Kelly. I can't stand their cuteness. I want to kiss them all over. So those are avenues for us to explore. I am not closed to a male, but a female would be my preference. Please let me know how to proceed with meeting these kitties.

Thank you so much for your help, and please note your organization is welcome to come to my home and inspect the premises for safety. Just so you know, my new kitten will be the luckiest, most spoiled kitten in the world.

~ Tina

After reading this email, I sighed with disappointment. Having previously spoken to this woman during the screening process, and based on everything I knew, Minnie would be a match. I just had to convince the adopter to be open to it. I picked up the phone, not really sure what I was going to say, but I knew I had to advocate for sweet Minnie. The woman was very pleasant, but reiterated her position and concerns. Restricting herself to a short adoption window of 8-9 weeks was going to limit her options. Not to mention kitten season wouldn't start for several months, and (thankfully) young kittens were scarce during the winter. Over the next 45 minutes, the adopter and I spoke amicably. As a proud Cat Dad, I can talk about cats all day. I scrolled through relevant facts and relayed my own experiences with cats and kittens, trying to assuage her doubts. Finally, I said, "Don't worry, you're approved to adopt a kitten with us no matter what. You're under no obligation to Minnie, but I really think you should meet her in person. Just give her a chance; I think you might be surprised. If you decide Minnie is not right for you, I will personally work with you to find a more suitable match."

I could tell she appreciated the offer. While she remained skeptical, I had at least persuaded the woman to meet Minnie with an open mind. That was all I asked. She had nothing to lose and everything to gain.

Several days later, Minnie's foster mom reached out and informed me that the adopter kept her word and met with Minnie. I was not at all shocked to hear that it was love at first purr. Upon introduction, Minnie made quite the impression. The young tabby went right up and jumped in the woman's lap—something she had not done previously with any other prospective adopter. The two fussed over each other the entire time before Minnie curled up on her for a nap. Her person had been chosen. She adopted Minnie without a second thought. Amazing!

A week later, I received a grateful follow up email.

Hello Christopher,

    Just wanted to take a moment to thank you from the bottom of my heart for helping to bring Minnie and I together. She loves being Olivia and has been adjusting so well.

    I am especially thankful to you, Christopher. As you may recall, my initial position was that I wanted a younger kitten, and you recommended I meet Minnie anyway. She has been an absolute delight. She kneads on me. Her favorite place to sleep is on my neck, and while she's there she nibbles my ear. I'm just loving this new life and have promised my Olivia that I will always be there for her.

    Warmest regards to you and yours.

    ~ Tina

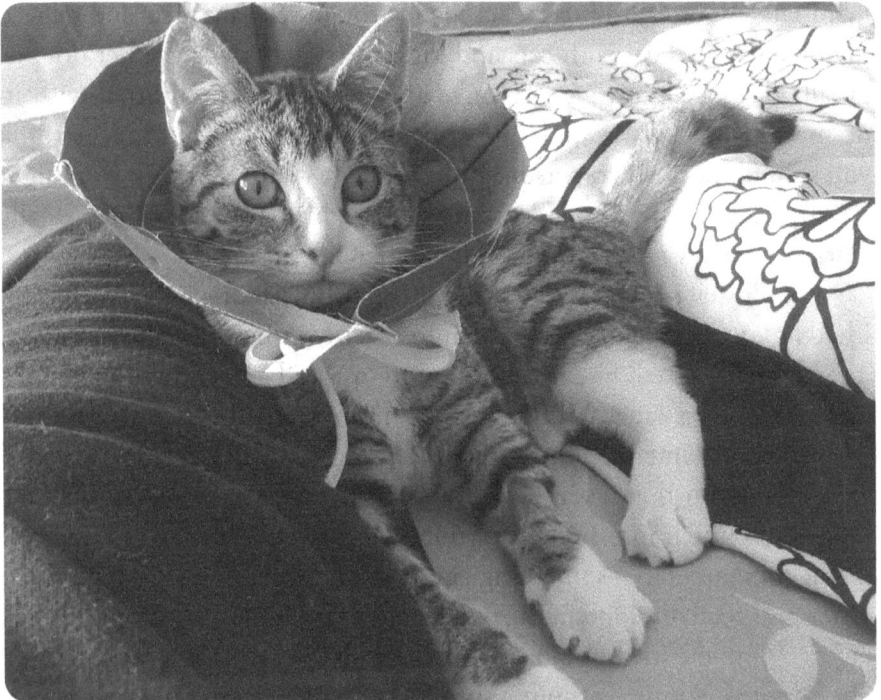

Olivia (aka Minnie) queen of her own castle.

9

SPECIAL KNEADS CATS

THE STAFF AT HOTEL MANCUSO has always been softhearted when it comes to cats with disabilities, medical conditions, or even those simply deemed "less adoptable" due to minor physical imperfections such as a missing eye or a severed tail. Among our VIP guests, the hotel has hosted blind, deaf, geriatric, diabetic, tripods, and even a kitten with hind-leg paralysis. Some of our special guests have successfully petitioned for permanent residence at the Island of Misfit Cats. As far as we're concerned, our Overlords are imperfectly perfect.

The decision to add a special needs kitty to your family should be made with serious consideration. Depending on the level of extra care required, serving these Overlords can be demanding in regard to your time, finances, and emotions, but we happen to think it's worth it. As reward for your faithful service to the crown, your cup will overfloweth with love and purrs. You will advance in the ranks and have an honored place in Cat World, reserved for an elite few. From minor impairments to severe conditions, it takes an extraordinary person to care for a handi-cat. As you read, not all cats in this section will need extraordinary amounts of specialized care, but all these cats are special and need someone to care.

CEREBELLAR HYPOPLASIA: WIGGLES AND WOBBLES AND FLOPPIES, OH MY!

Here at The Island of Misfit Cats, seven of our current felion residents have mild to moderate Cerebellar Hypoplasia, and several more have boarded at Hotel Mancuso through the years. Our first endeavor into caring for special needs cats started with a four-week-old shelter kitten with moderate Carebellar Hypoplasia: Sara Bella. Cathy and I offered to foster-to adopt Sara Bella with Staten Island Hope Animal Rescue. We renamed our new little princess Khalessi and bent the knee promising to be faithful servants. Khalessi was only with us for three weeks before tragically passing away from panleukopenia, but during that short time with us, Cathy and I found ourselves inspired by her determination, and she touched our hearts deeply. After her passing, we promised to honor her memory by continuing to help other cats with special needs. While we love all cats, the wiggles, the wobbles, and the floppies always have a special place in our hearts.

Catherine holding our little CH princess, Khalessi.

Cerebellar Hypoplasia is commonly referred to as "Wobbles Syndrome" or abbreviated to "CH" by people more familiar with the disorder. It's basically the equivalent of Cerebral Palsy in humans. The disorder occurs in utero and causes lack of control of basic motor functions due to an undeveloped cerebellum.

Signs and symptoms of CH are usually noticed within the first few weeks of development. Typical causes of CH are as follows:

- Genetic predisposition
- Nutritional deficiency
- Pregnant mother who contracts distemper
- Viral or bacterial infections
- Vaccinating a pregnant mother
- Poisoning
- Injury/trauma to the fetus

Queens instinctively know when something is wrong with their offspring. When a mother senses that one of her kittens is defective or has a poor chance of survival, she may abandon or even kill that kitten. In 2015, my moderate CH cat, Bonk, was born to a feral mom. After about two weeks, his mother stopped nursing him and actively tried to smother him by sitting on him. Sadly, she had succeeded in doing so to his littermate.

Cats with CH will display one or more symptoms depending on the severity of their condition.

Wiggles – I refer to cats affected mildly with Cerebellar Hypoplasia as Wiggles. They may display some head bobbing and body tremors, especially when they become nervous or excited. Typically, a wide stance can be noted even when sitting, as their front limbs may be splayed for balance. Mild CHers are predisposed to be much clumsier than your average kitty. They will present a tipsy gait when walking, not unlike my twenty-something self on a Friday night! Wiggles will likely experience some trouble with jumping and landing, but despite their gait, mild CH Overlords are high functioning and require very little or no extra care at all.

Wobbles – Moderate CH cats present some of the same indicators as their mild counterparts, but their symptoms are much more prevalent. Tremors and bobbing are more pronounced, often frequent or constant, except during sleep. When feasting they may have to peck at their food like a bird. Walking is usually a challenge for the Wobbles; getting from point A to point B is rarely as easy as a straight line. Movements appear more spasmodic as they struggle to control their muscles, and they may need to alter their trajectory numerous times. Moderate CH tend to fall over often, but they always get up and move forward, undeterred. Like any felion, Wobble cats enjoy a good hunt; the fact that they must work harder to be successful makes victory that much sweeter. Activities like jumping are beyond their capability, but Wobbles can become quite adept at climbing. These little Overlords are determined to conquer stairs and furniture in order to ascend to the throne.

Floppies – Overlords affected by severe Cerebellar Hypoplasia are much more reliant on their servants. They are unable to walk or even properly stand up, simply lacking any coordination to do so. However, that doesn't mean floppies can't get to where they want to go; nothing will stop these determined felions. They will crawl or flip-flop to reach their destination. These Special Ones may require some help eating and using a litter box. I have spoken to several servants who informed me that their Overlords will generally clue them in with specific vocalizing to indicate hunger or a need to relieve themselves. Being observant and recognizing this behavior will help keep you in sync with your ruler and avoid unwanted accidents.

As mentioned, wiggles often do not require any special care, but anyone deliberating service to a wobble and floppy Overlord should consider the following:

- As part of their nature, all felions prefer the high ground. CH cats are no different, they just require a little vertical assistance. Purchase or fashion sturdy ramps and stairs leading up to their favorite spots. Wobbles and Floppies can become expert climbers.
- Keeping your Overlord safe should always be at the top of your to-do list. Use pillows or cushions for safe landings whenever

your Wobble or Floppy is elevated. Pad sharp corners, or anything else that could cause an injury if bumped.

- Ergonomic bowls for feedings can make it easier for Your Majesty to enjoy their feasts. Additionally, it is more difficult for Tippy to topple the bowl and make a royal mess.
- While there is no cure for Cerebellar Hypoplasia, the use of specially made walkers, acupuncture, and hydrotherapy have proven effective in firming up muscles as well as improving coordination and mobility in moderate and severe cats.
- All royalty deserves the red carpet treatment. More importantly, carpeting, rugs, and runners should be placed around the castle, especially on staircases. Gripping the material with their claws will aid stability.
- While wobbles and floppies are able to use a sandcastle on their own, it is not without its obstacles. Most standard litter boxes have an entry point that may be difficult to navigate. You can purchase a low entry litter box or modify your own by cutting a significantly lower entrance. Also consider a covered box, or at least one with high sides that cats can lean against for support.
- Occasional or regular bathing may be required. My wobbles—Tsunami, Dizzy, Faith, and Magoo—cannot stand or sit to alleviate themselves. They lay down in the litter to do their business. Occasionally, one of them may roll over onto their own mess and require our famous spa treatment. As diligently as we clean the royal privy, sometimes accidents are simply unavoidable. If insufficiently clean to their high standards, our queens have been known to leave puddles or nuggets in protest.

Wiggles, wobbles, and floppies can live in relative harmony with other pets; Cerebellar Hypoplasia is not contagious, so there is no worry about an outbreak in the kingdom. Cats afflicted with Cerebellar Hypoplasia are accident prone and may sufferer an occasional chipped tooth, but CH is not indicative of other diseases or underlying health conditions— it does not shorten an Overlord's reign. CH is a non-progressive syndrome, meaning it will not get worse, but neither will it get better. It is what is. Kittens may seem to improve as they grow into adults, but in reality, they are only strengthening their muscles and learning to adapt to their limitations.

Despite their apparent struggles, monarchs with CH are not in any pain due to their condition. In fact, they do not know they are different from any other felion. They enjoy playtime and cuddles and love their servants. While some people may think these cats lack any quality of life, quite the opposite is true. With proper care, any CH cat can rule a kingdom as nobly as any Overlord and have a very good quality of life. Because they are so dependent, wobbles and floppies often form a special bond with their caretaker. They really do make great snugglers!

TRIPODS: STANDING ON THEIR OWN THREE LEGS

Cats with only three legs are referred to as tripods or sometimes "Tri-pawds." Few Overlords are born with this birth defect; most Tripods have lost a leg to amputation caused by infection or traumatic injury. Unfortunately, like the others in this section, they are usually considered "less adoptable" or "defective" and are often overlooked in shelters and rescues.

Having fostered numerous tripods, prospective servants have often asked if these cats can enjoy a normal life. They can indeed. In fact, most tripod cats adapt just fine. After recovering from their surgery, they don't require any more vet care than a four-legged cat. Sure, tripods may not run as fast or jump as high as other cats, but they're not discouraged.

While tripods don't require much in the way of special care, there are certain limitations for them as well as some minor considerations for lifestyle adjustments.

Independence – As a faithful servant, you may have the urge to constantly pick or put down your three-legged monarch. Resist doing so, because they need to use those muscles regularly. At times, Your Highness may struggle, but do not intervene unless absolutely necessary. Be patient and supportive, but try not to be overprotective; you could inadvertently be hampering your felion's adaptation to life on three legs.

Weight Management – Be careful not to allow your Your Majesty to become a felion Henry VIII. Extra weight will only make life harder on their remaining legs, which could lead to further mobility problems, especially as they age. To prevent overeating, I recommend scheduled feasts as opposed to access to food all the time.

Activity – Make sure Your Highness stays active to keep in shape. Holding the Kitty Olympics regularly is important to maintaining muscle tone. Tripods tend to be more prone to Osteoarthritis, and strong muscles will help support their back and leg joints. Keep in mind that they may tire more easily, so allow breaks for your gold medal winner as needed.

Litter Box – As you can imagine, using the litter box properly can be a bit challenging for tripods. Therefore, you should provide a sandcastle that is higher and wider than normal, for added stability. A wide box allows a tripod more room to turn around and Your Majesty can lean against high sides for extra support if needed. Additionally, if the Overlord is struggling on the way in and out, you can provide an entrance ramp or simply cut out a lower doorway so they may come and go more gracefully.

Jumping – Although cats always land on their feet, a monarch with a missing front leg may have trouble with stability when jumping down from up high. Placing cushions around will aid with safe landings. A cat with a missing hind leg may not be able to jump very high, so consider purchasing pet stairs or ramps for easier access to windowsills where Your Majesty can enjoy some CatTV.

VISUALLY IMPAIRED CATS: LOVE IS BLIND

As I mentioned in previous chapters, an Overlord's eyesight is far superior to humans. Their night vision is six times better than ours, and their peripheral includes a much wider field of vision. For feral and stray cats outside the sanctuary of a castle, loss of sight is a death sentence. In a well-designed castle, however, it is merely an inconvenience. Sightless felions adapt surprisingly well to their limitations. In fact, cats are so good at adapting that if their loss of sight happens gradually over time, it may take months before you even realize Your Highness has gone completely blind.

Honestly, blind cats don't require a lot of special care, but they do need some extra attention and prevention to help live safely and peacefully. Any blind Overlord settling into a new castle is going to need time to adjust to the floor plan of a sightless world. Consider the following tips and modifications:

- No matter how the kingdom is arranged, the Overlord will learn to adeptly navigate the landscape without missing a step. Blind cats memorize their surroundings with a mental map. They will use their sense of smell to find sandcastle as well as food and water. They will use their keen hearing to pinpoint your location and trot over for some worship. Avoid moving furniture, unless necessary. Changing the layout of the castle can be disconcerting to your Overlord until they reconfigure their internal blueprint.

- Clear their path. Floor clutter can confuse, frustrate, and potentially cause the Overlord to injure themselves. If you have children, please make sure they put their toys away.

- Use cushions to pad table and chair legs, sharp corners, or anything else that could cause an injury if bumped.

- Consider using rugs, runners, or mats as guides or markers. Tactile differentiations can help a blind cat learn where they are in relation to where they are going. For example, they can easily determine if they are in the kitchen by the sensation of tile under their paws compared to the hardwood floor in the Throne Room.

- If you pick up your blind Overlord, always return them to that same location when putting them down, otherwise they can become disoriented. Or at the very least, place them down somewhere they will find very familiar, like their sandcastle or feeding area.

- All felions enjoy the warmth of sunbathing or whiffing the cool breeze blowing in from the Great Backyard. Block access to any balcony or open window, as Your Highness may be drawn to these unsafe places. Always keep blind cats away from candles or open flames.

- Cats can sniff out water. Maybe your Overlord is feeling adventurous, wanting to try a drink from a different source. Remember to keep the toilet seat down at all times. Not only should your felion absolutely not drink from the toilet, but a blind cat can also misjudge a jump and end up in the water. The fall could cause severe injuries or panic, either of which could lead to drowning.

- Restrict access to stairways, at least at the beginning. If you live in a multi-level castle, allow Your Majesty to get familiar with one floor at a time. Don't worry; eventually, your brave blind felion will be able to conquer stairs, but they will need time to safely build up to that task.

- When it comes to the conquest of staircases, going up is nearly effortless for your fearless but sightless felion. Climbing down, however, is a more dangerous journey. In the beginning, you must act as your Overlord's guide through the darkness. Tap each step as they proceed so your cat can pinpoint the distance to the next one with some quick, cat math computations. Comfort them, encourage them, and be ready to save your Overlord from a nasty tumble. One miscalculation could cause Your Majesty to fall down the staircase and suffer injuries. Until you are comfortable in their confidence, only allow access while you're present.

- A servant must worship the Overlord not only in deed, but also in praise. Talk to your felion often. Speaking lets them know you are near. Your Majesty often finds comfort in your voice and just knowing where you are. Etiquette dictates that for a blind Overlord one must formally announce arrival and departure when entering or leaving a room. To prevent blind cats from becoming startled or defensive, always speak first before you worship the Overlord with petting, especially if they are sleeping.

- If you have other pets, it's a good idea to make them wear a collar and bell. This will alert your blind felion that another cat or a dog is near. If you have small children, you can tie a bell on their shoe as an early warning system.

- For enrichment and mental stimulation, use toys that engage other senses. Toys stuffed with catnip will entice the Overlord's sense of smell. Make the most of their hearing by providing toys that crinkle, jingle, and chirp. You can even create your own interactive play mat, incorporating various textures and scents.

CAT TALES: *A New Hope*

Only a few weeks old, Chloe was found in Brooklyn with two of her siblings. Hearing their cries, a woman was horrified to find three kittens inside a trashcan. It broke her heart to see them like that, so she took them into the safety of her home to care for them. However, there was a problem: Chloe had a severe double eye infection. The woman took the kittens to a vet where she was given eye ointment and antibiotics. She was told to separate Chloe from her siblings to prevent them from also getting sick. The woman became overwhelmed and reached out for help on Facebook; she desperately needed someone to take Chloe and give her the care she needed. A rescue friend tagged me in the post, and of course Cathy and I had to step up.

I contacted the woman and arranged to take Chloe. I really appreciated how the woman's adult daughter exercised caution by asking to view our apartment. This request may have offended some people, but it only proved to me that the family truly cared about Chloe. They didn't want to trust her to just anyone. It also made me feel better about the woman caring for Chloe's siblings. Not to mention I totally hated driving to Brooklyn, especially during rush hour! If she was willing to travel to Staten Island, so much the better. It also gave us plenty of time for Cathy to prepare Hotel Mancuso's isolation suite for our newest guest, and for me to make a trip to the store for supplies.

The daughter arrived around 8:00 pm with Chloe. Cathy went downstairs to greet her and show her inside. As she came up the stairs and laid eyes on our living room, the young woman let out an audible sigh. A look of relief swept across her face. She marveled at all of our cat condos, cat shelves, and toys. She laughed as our fluffy tabby, Shinobi, sauntered up and confidently introduced himself with an amicable meow.

I'm no veterinarian, but I had seen enough of these situations to know that poor little Chloe would likely loose both eyes. Even if her eyes could be saved, her vision would end up fully or partially impaired by corneal scarring.

We provided the young woman with the tour, showed her our bathroom isolation suite. The soft sounds of Beethoven were already playing

Chloe, healed and happy after her eye-removal surgery.

on the radio. Since Chloe was so small, we set up a medium sized crate. We bought her a plush cuddle buddy, a new bed, and kitty blankets. On one side we set up a feeding spot and on the other a tiny cardboard litter box. For enrichment, we got Chloe a crinkle-mat, rattle-mice, balls, and a feathery jingle toy that I hung from the top of her crate.

"Don't worry," Cathy said as she placed the blind kitten in the crate. "We'll take good care of little Chloe."

I took the time to speak with the daughter about medical options, acclimation, and socialization. Once Chloe was ready and able, she would be moved to an even larger crate in the living room. I promised that when she was healthy, I would find Chloe a loving home.

"I can't tell you how happy I am," the young woman said before leaving Chloe in our hands.

We continued Chloe's eye medication regime, but her condition worsened. She had to have surgery to remove both eyes. After her surgery, I posted her photo on Facebook. Of course, there was a multitude of support and well wishes for our latest foster kitten, but not surprising, a few comments suggested she should have been put to sleep—that a blind kitten couldn't possibly have any quality of life. The really sad part is that these heartless comments weren't from random trolls; they were from people I knew, and they actually believed what they were saying.

Unfortunately, no amount of reasoning or debate could persuade their views. But we all know different, don't we?

That same night, on that same post, a woman named Stacey was drawn to Chloe. She was already expressing interest in adoption. At only four weeks old, it would be at least a month before the adorable, blind calico would be ready to be crowned a Queen. Stacey would have time to think about it.

Day by day, I'd received messages from Stacey inquiring about Chloe. I sent her photos or short videos of Chloe's development and antics. Over the weeks we chatted about caring for a blind kitten and how to help Chloe adapt to a new home. Honestly, I was a little surprised that Stacey never lost interest. When she finally came from upstate to officially adopt Chloe, I knew this wasn't an impulsive decision. Stacey would give Chloe a great home and a great life. She was renamed Hope and had a felion brother named Obi-wan. A year later, Stacey added Luke, another blind kitty, to her family. The Force is strong with them. 🐾

DEAF CATS: LISTENING WITH THEIR HEARTS

Living in a silent kingdom can be lonely for an Overlord, but with the right servant it doesn't have to be. Deafness is not only a congenital birth defect, but it can also be caused by trauma, untreated parasites, medical issues, or age-related degeneration. All cats will lose some hearing in their senior years; some eventually become completely deaf. Since felions adapt so well, though, especially when the loss occurs over a period of time, it can be hard to tell that their hearing is declining. Perhaps Archduke Fluffykins is no longer afraid of the vacuum, or maybe he no longer takes notice when you enter the room. Lord Tigger may seem to sleep longer and deeper, or startle more easily. Your Pretty Princess may become more chatty or her meows more demanding.

. . . .

FUR FACT   If a solid white cat has one blue eye, there's a 40% chance it will be deaf. That percentage increases to between 60% and 80% if the all-white cat has two blue eyes.

. . . .

If you suspect that Your Highness is deaf, you can test hearing by calling their name, jingling a set of keys, or a loud clap when their back is turned. Even if they don't turn around, you should notice their ears reflexively twitching or swiveling in response to the sound. Of course, it's always best to get a proper diagnosis from your veterinarian.

Normally, Overlords have amazing hearing, much better than humans or dogs. So, how would they fare without it? If Your Majesty is (or becomes) deaf, you will need to use some extra caution around the kingdom and modify your methods of communication. Consider the following:

- In the absence of their sensitive hearing, deaf Overlords rely much more on sight for observation. With a little repetition and reinforcement, Your Majesty can easily learn to respond to hand signals or other visual cues.
- Deaf cats can be easily startled, especially during slumber. If sleeping, gently tap their throne or the area near them. When awake, always approach The Crown with deference so they can see you coming. Upon entering a room where our deaf Baby Girl was hanging out, I would flick the lights as a cue to my entrance. During one of her many royal naps, I would stomp so she could feel the vibrations of my approach and wake up without being startled.
- Deliver a consistent signal to indicate your intention to pick up Your Highness. Without proper communication you leave yourself open to getting accidentally nipped or scratched by a very unruly monarch. Before attempting to pick up my Baby Girl, I would present my hand for inspection. After a blessing, I would follow up with a few pets before lifting.
- Always keep alerted to the whereabouts of The Crown by having your royal wear a bell on their collar. You'll always know when they're on the move, and you'll be able to discern their general location in the kingdom. This will lessen the chance of any human or furry family member terrifying the Overlord with a surprise encounter.
- Like all felions, deaf cats need mental stimulation, affection, and physical activity. Provide toys and activities that will engage their

other senses. Remember, they are still cats and enjoy the thrill of the "kill." Entice their noses to explore by creating a treat-filled scavenger hunt around the castle.

• Deaf cats are unaware of their volume, usually resulting in ear-splitting meows. This can become an ordeal, particularly in the middle of the night. To help end those midnight edicts, start by getting Your Majesty on a bedtime routine, preparing them for sleep. A late night snack or rigorous play session before you turn in can work wonders in helping your monarch catnap until morning.

• Unfortunately, your Overlord cannot hear you sing their praises. In the absence of lengthy homilies to boost their ego, extra worship services like brushing and petting can soothe stress or anxiety. As a senior cat, Baby Girl would often become stressed by some of the more active felions of the fur-brigade. This may sound a little silly, but to help calm her nerves, I would often purr when snuggling her. Obviously, she couldn't hear me, but she was able to feel the comforting vibrations and responded positively by purring in kind.

• It should go without saying that your deaf cat should always remain in the castle. Their disability makes them much more vulnerable to predators and traffic accidents in the Great Backyard.

Depending on their personality, deaf cats can jointly rule a castle with other felions. It may even be beneficial. Not only will the Overlord be less inclined to suffer from loneliness, they also will look to their counterpart for cues and reactions. Since cats speak to each other with body language, a lack of hearing should not affect their relationship.

FIV+ CATS: POSITIVELY ADOPTABLE

When potential servants hear that an Overlord is infected with FIV, they are either confused by the term or think they know what it means and freak out. Cat AIDS! A potential servant will almost always lose interest in devoting their service to an infected Overlord, causing FIV+ cats to get a bum rap. But most people simply don't understand enough about this condition. In all honesty, before becoming a Servant of Rescue, I didn't know what FIV was either, and I sure didn't want it spreading through our castle. Thankfully, I've overcome that fear through knowledge and understanding. You can, too. Let's explore what being FIV+ really means for an Overlord, as well as for those who serve them.

Feline Immunodeficiency Virus (FIV) is in fact similar to human immunodeficiency virus (HIV), but referring to it as Cat AIDS is misleading to say the least. AIDS is an advanced stage of HIV where a patient's health is typically in severe decline. You may be thinking that an FIV cat is guaranteed to have a short lifespan. This is not necessarily so. I know of a loyal servant whose FIV+ Overlord lived to be almost twelve. Despite being FIV +, in the right castle and with faithful servants, a felion can enjoy a long, healthy reign. The Asymptomatic Phase of this disease could possibly last for years. Luckily, monarchs can live normal lifespans without ever developing related symptoms.

While FIV is transmissible, it is a species-specific disease and cannot be contracted by humans or dogs, only other felions. The virus doesn't easily pass from cat to cat. It is primarily spread via saliva in instances such as a deep bite wound. Of course, unneutered males tend to be more aggressive and are more apt to spread the disease. Queens can sometimes pass the infection on to their offspring, but it is not as common as you might think. That being said, her kittens may temporarily test positive for up to six months due to the presence of maternal antibodies in their system. These antibodies will disappear around six months of age, and subsequent tests will likely be negative for infection. This false-positive places an unfortunate stigma on the little catlings and through no fault of their own, they are not usually granted a kingdom until they re-test negative. Sadly, some FIV+ kittens in high kill shelters will never even get that chance.

Not long ago it was believed that FIV+ cats could not and should not live with uninfected felions. This meant they would either be destined to rule alone or only share their kingdom with other FIV+ felions. However, with more knowledge of the disease and how it is spread, opinions have evolved over time. Most now agree that it is possible for positive and negative felions to cohabit a castle. Since cats do not get infected with FIV from grooming, normal play, or sharing the same sandcastle, bowls, or toys, the risk of transmission between household Overlords that rule in harmony is very low. But if discord pervades the domain, war may breakout, and when a peace pact is broken, bloody battles can spread the infection.

Serving an FIV+ felion comes with challenges and additional financial costs, as they require a moderate amount of special care. Because of their lower immune response, they are extremely susceptible to all other diseases. Infected Overlords get ill more easily and severely, and they take longer to recover. With proper care and caution, however, Your Highness can have an excellent quality of life and a long reign. Let's discuss how you can keep your FIV+ cat healthy:

- Anxiety and stress can make FIV+ cats more susceptible to health issues. Try to keep the kingdom as low stress as possible. Stick to the routine, engage in regular worship, and provide plenty of stimulation, all these undertakings will support the comfort and security felions need to stay healthy.
- Feed Your Majesty a healthy, high quality diet. Consult with a veterinarian on recommending balanced nutrition to suit your cat's particular requirements. Adjust their diet as needed. Consider buying a water fountain to encourage your felion to stay hydrated.
- A weakened immune system means the Overlord is very susceptible to illness and infection, so keeping up to date on all their core vaccinations is essential. Vitamin supplements and immune boosters may also give your kitty an edge in prevention.
- Always keep the Overlord contained within the castle to shield them from the many infectious diseases and parasites found in the Great Backyard. Consider using parasitic preventatives out of an abundance of caution. Parasites will deplete your cat's body of essential nutrients.
- You must be consistent in scheduling the Overlord's bi-annual veterinary check-ups, even if they aren't presenting any symptoms. Running a complete blood work-up and urine analysis should be an annual event.
- Later in life (hopefully much later) Your Majesty may enter the Progressive Phase, leaving them even more vulnerable to

secondary illness and opportunistic infections. Cats may develop chronic or recurrent infections. Once a felion becomes severely afflicted with multiple illnesses, their chance of survival is greatly diminished.

- Be alert to subtle changes in your royal's health. A vet must address any sudden behavior change or sign of illness as soon as possible. The Overlord may require stronger treatments and multiple courses of antibiotics, so the sooner they receive treatment, the better off they'll be.

All this being said, there is no guarantee your FIV+ felion won't get sick. Indeed, the virus may progress, and in that case, you'll need to be able to serve as Head Nurse. But the same can be true of seemingly healthy cats with unknown congenital conditions. At any age, cats suffer from kidney disease, diabetes, or a myriad of other illnesses. Unfortunately, we've had our share of healthy Overlords whose reign ended much too soon. We also willingly signed on to serve a few Rulers who were on borrowed time, like Gurami, a nineteen-year-old Siamese suffering with kidney disease, and a very ill six-week-old Catrick. Our hearts broke each and every time we lost one of our fur-brigade or foster felions, but we don't regret for one second loving any of them during the brief times we had together.

Every cat deserves the chance to run a Kingdom. Now that you know what FIV is and how to best attend to an FIV+ Overlord, you can better assess whether or not you're fit to serve as a hero to these pawistively lovable rulers

DIABETIC CATS: LOVE IS SWEETER THAN SUGAR

Having been recently diagnosed with prediabetes myself, and having previously fostered two diabetic cats, I'd like to help demystify the disease for all would-be servants. Odds are that at least a few of you will have to deal with this condition at some point. Even if you're currently in the service of a healthy monarch in their felion prime, there is a chance your cat may develop diabetes later in life. I know the prospect of sticking Your Majesty with needles twice daily and finding that tiny vein in their ear to prick them yet again while collecting a blood sample is a chilling thought. Overwhelmed servants have panicked, exiling their Overlord from the kingdom.

Exiled to a shelter, your dethroned monarch will sit frightened and alone, surrounded by strangers, praying to the Celestial Meow for your return. Relatively few diabetic cats will find a new kingdom to rule, but many will not. Surrendered cats with diabetes are at a much greater risk of dying, either from a hunger strike, unmanaged glucose levels, an illness picked up at the shelter, or euthanasia. Unfortunately, the reigns of many Great Ones have ended with such a sad fate. I mean, if children get sick, do parents just drop the kid off at an orphanage? No, of course not, so why do that to a beloved felion? Granted, caring for a diabetic cat can be stressful at times, but don't psyche yourself out. In the battle against felion diabetes, we don't have to be helpless spectators. You have been ordained by the Celestial Meow; have faith in its wisdom and in yourself.

Knowledge is our first line of defense. Recognizing the causes and symptoms of diabetes will allow us to take preventative action against the disease, or promptly respond if and when the enemy draws its sword against the Overlord. Cats suffer almost exclusively from Type II diabetes, aka adult-onset diabetes. As they age cats can also develop insulin resistance. Common risk factors for the development of feline diabetes include:

- *The Chonk Factor* – Overweight cats are more common than ever before, largely because many are fed a diet high in carbohydrates. As strict carnivores, carbs are just empty calories, completely unnecessary in felion nutrition. If obese, your royal chonk is at greater risk of developing type 2 diabetes during their lifetime, although it is possible for the disease to affect a cat of any age and weight.

- *Lazy Days* – Cats that are less active, and don't engage in daily exercise are more prone to develop diabetes as they age.

- *In the Blood* – As with humans, some felions have a genetic predisposition to develop glucose intolerance. Unfortunately, there is often no way to know the medical history of Your Majesty's royal bloodline.

- *Medications* – Medical treatments such as steroids cause insulin resistance in cats, especially if these medications are used long term.

- *Other Diseases* – Pancreatitis damages the ability of the pancreas to produce the hormone insulin and regulate a cat's glucose level.

If you make yourself aware of symptoms, you will be able to act more quickly at the onset and prevent your cat's diabetes from going unchecked and getting out of control, which could lead to further complications, hospitalization, and death. If you notice any of the symptoms below, please schedule an appointment with your veterinarian. Common symptoms of diabetes include:

- *Sprung a Leak?* – You notice that Your Highness is making more frequent trips to the royal privy. Or maybe your felion has been having regular accidents outside the sandcastle. No, your cat hasn't sprung a leak, but the kidneys attempt to remove excess glucose from the body through urine. Increased urination can mean possible dehydration.

- *Aquaholic* – Because of their increased urination you may notice your cat drinking much more than usual as they try to rehydrate their bodies.

- *Feed Me* – Your Highness may always appear hungry and constantly demand food despite having been recently fed. *Yes, I've had breakfast, but what about second breakfast?* Insulin resistance prevents their bodies from sufficiently using the fuel supplied in their diet.

- *Extreme Makeover* – If your royal looks as if they've started taking Ozempic, this could definitely be a symptom of diabetes. Maybe the Overlord was overweight and could stand to drop a pound of two. However, if you haven't lessened their caloric intake, or added more exercise to the daily routine, sudden weight loss is never a good sign. Nor will this extreme makeover stop until the underlying cause is being managed. Despite a voracious appetite, the body begins to break down proteins and fat stores, which leads to weight loss and muscle atrophy.

- *Wardrobe Change* – Aside from sudden weight loss, Your Majesty's attractive coat may have lost its luster, appearing oily and full of dandruff.

- *Lethargy* – Your cat may seem lazy, losing interest in royal cativities like playing and grooming. Your Grace may also appear graceless. They may be weak and unbalanced when they walk.

Keep in mind that these symptoms are not exclusive to diabetes and may be indicative of another illness, so following up with your vet is important to rule out other issues before you decide to start treatment on your own.

Treatment and Management – Following a diagnosis, your vet will help you plan the management and treatment of your cat's diabetes, which can take some getting used to for both of you. Management will be a lifelong process that requires diligent servitude on your part, but if done properly, some cats may even go into a state of remission where insulin injections are no longer necessary. Caring for a diabetic cat includes:

- *Just A Drop* – Monitoring blood-glucose levels is a daily ritual which is be done in the castle and typically involves pricking the inside of your cat's ear with a lancet, collecting a drop of blood on a test strip, and using a glucometer. This can be tricky at first, but it just takes some practice. If you're too anxious or having a hard time with ear-pricks, glucose levels can also be monitored by urine test strips, although this method is less accurate than blood tests.

- *Menu Changes* – Your vet will likely switch your cat to a high-protein, low-carbohydrate diet. Since getting an accurate test result is critical to glucose management, royal feasts will be served on a strict schedule rather than allowing Your Majesty to feed at their pleasure and leisure.

- *Gym Membership* – As the royal health coach, you'll be tasked with making sure your meowing monarch gets daily exercise. Sign them up for a membership at the castle gym. An active reign, combined with a proper diet can help them lose weight in a safe and healthy way. Not only will they stay in shape, but I'm sure your felion will appreciate the extra play sessions, too.

- *Health Tracking* – As the royal chronicler, it is your scared duty to keep a daily log of your Overlord's diet, activity, glucose test results, daily insulin dose, and weekly body weight. Note water intake as well as their volume and frequency of urination. Accurate records will help you recognize any changes from their regular pattern, which should be brought to your vet's attention.

- *Give It Your Best Shot* – This is a lot less scary than it sounds once you've done it a few times. Injections are generally given under the skin by the neck and shoulders; the needle is really thin and doesn't cause your cat any pain. These injections are given twice a day, 12 hours apart, at the same times each day. Insulin is typically started at a low dose and will be gradually increased based on response.

Never give your cat a double dose of insulin. If you've missed a dose or are not sure if Your Majesty received the full shot, just wait until the next injection is due and administer the normal amount. As PetMD states, "One of the most serious risks and potential complications of managing a diabetic cat at home is the risk of hypoglycemia (low blood sugar). This can happen to any pet being managed for diabetes at home, even if you give them the appropriate dose (or less than the appropriate dose) prescribed by the veterinarian. For this reason, it's important that you strictly follow your veterinarian's instructions and schedule for feeding and giving insulin, and that you never administer a full dose of insulin to your pet if they are not eating."[20]

Hypoglycemia, also referred to as low blood sugar, is potentially life-threatening and should be treated as an emergency. Signs of hypoglycemia in cats:

- Weakness or lethargy
- Disorientation
- Vomiting
- Diarrhea

- Not eating
- Trembling
- Seizure

If you see any of these signs, give Your Highness a sugary treat (corn syrup, maple syrup, honey) in an effort to help raise their blood sugar. Do not wait. Usher them to an emergency pet hospital as soon as possible. If your felion is having seizures, try rubbing syrup on their gums, but be cautious of inadvertent biting or you may need to visit the hospital as well.

Unfortunately, I have seen too many humans unnecessarily dethrone their beloved monarch for having been diagnosed with diabetes, but it is a completely manageable disease, and when you learn the ins and outs, you'll be a pro in no time. There is also a plethora of information and resources available online. Diabetic Cats in Need (dcin.dreamhosters. com) and Felinediabetes.com® both offer a wealth of knowledge and support, including possible financial assistance.

Caring for a diabetic cat can seem like a lot to handle, especially at first, but soon it will become a matter of routine. If you truly love Your Majesty, the extra care is well worth the effort. A diabetic cat whose blood sugar and insulin levels are well regulated can live a normal lifespan, and their love is sweeter than sugar.

CAT TALES: *Save Meow*

Meow Meow, a handsome, seven-year-old, brown and white tabby was brought to the Staten Island shelter with dangerously high insulin levels. Due to this, he was scheduled for euthanasia if placement was not immediately found for him. Being the Assistant Director for Staten Island Hope Animal Rescue at the time, I had the unenviable daily chore of placing kill-listed shelter cats. Typically, when cats are kill-listed, rescues have several days to work on finding fosters. However, given the seriousness of Meow Meow's condition, this was not a typical situation. He was time stamped for 6:00 pm. By the time I had even received the email about Meow Meow, it was already late in the afternoon. I had two hours to work a miracle. Chain smoking half a pack of menthols down to the filter, I furiously networked him on social media and emailed or called all my foster contacts. Anxiously reading through the online comments, many people offered their thoughts and prayers, but no one offered to save Meow Meow.

Another cigarette. A lighter sparked. So did an idea. What about me? I'm someone. I can save him!

I had no prior experience with diabetic cats, but after a phone call to a fellow rescuer at Diabetic Cats in Need, Cathy and I decided to be Meow Meow's miracle. DBCIN graciously offered not only guidance, but also to expedite a diabetic care package for Meow Meow, which included a blood glucose monitor, test strips, insulin needles, and more. With the clock still running, I had one more call to make: to our veterinarian. Aadobe Animal Hospital closed at 5:30 pm, but Dr. Singh told me if I could make it there by six, he would wait for me. Bless that man.

As Cathy went about setting up a space for our last-minute guest, I reached out to my shelter contact to let her know I was on the way. Luckily, the shelter is minutes from my house, so by 5:00 pm I was at SIACC with a cat carrier in hand. I barely got a chance to look at Meow Meow before loading him up in my van and racing against a river of taillights better known as rush hour traffic on the Staten Island Expressway. The Rescue Gods were with me, and I managed to get to Aadobe Animal Hospital at 5:48 pm where Dr. Singh greeted me with a tired smile.

In the exam room was the first opportunity I had to get an up-close look at Hotel Mancuso's newest guest. I introduced myself as the concierge while Doc read the medical paperwork from the shelter. Meow Meow blessed my hand with his nose. As Dr. Singh examined him and tested a few drops of blood, he dealt with the situation in a noble silence. Meow Meow's blood glucose was edging over 460.

"His sugar is very high. We have to get it down with insulin shots twice a day," Doc said. "Are you comfortable with that?"

I'd pushed any self-doubt aside. "Yeah, I can do that, Doc."

He nodded his approval and patted me on the arm. Doctor Singh knew our affinity for the Special Ones and always went above and beyond during visits. He walked me through the management plan, and we scheduled a reevaluation in three days. Knowing that Doc was

Meow Meow, our first diabetic VIP at Hotel Mancuso.

supportive of the rescue and would be on hand to answer questions and offer advice helped give me confidence.

While there was initial anxiety, caring for a diabetic cat became a routine. Despite my often clumsy efforts to draw a dot of blood, Meow Meow tolerated the lancet pokes better than I anticipated. Maybe the fact that I always ended up accidentally pricking myself made him feel a bit better about it. Lucky for us, not only did Cathy and I have each other as we kept watchful care of Meow Meow's health, we also had a support system to help. I was able to reach out to my contact at Diabetic Cats in Need with any questions, as well as to my friend and fellow felion acolyte, Kimbra, who had managed diabetes with her Overlord for years. ❧

CATS WITH PARALYSIS: THEIR WILL, YOUR HANDS

Those unenlightened by the wisdom of the Celestial Meow may assume it is impossible for a paralyzed cat to have a good quality of life. But I can testify to paralyzed cats enjoying happy and otherwise healthy lives. In fact, one such tabby queen by the name of Gracelyn is a permanent resident of the Island of Misfit Cats. A paralyzed felion is totally capable of ruling a kingdom. And if you're lucky, your house could become their castle. But first, let's discuss how paralysis will affect Your Majesty and your role as Hand of the King (or Queen.)

Paralysis is the loss of movement and feeling in parts of the body. There are three types of paralysis in cats: Paraplegia affects the hind limbs only; Hemiplegia affects one side of the body; and Quadriplegia affects all four limbs, which means they have no mobility whatsoever. Paralysis can either be temporary or permanent depending on the cause and prognosis. It's important to have Your Highness examined by a vet for an accurate diagnosis and possible treatment options. Some causes of paralysis in cats:

- Congenital spinal malformation
- Traumatic injury
- A stroke or embolism
- Infection in bones or spinal tissue
- Inflammation of nerves surrounding the spine
- Tick-bite paralysis
- Tumors in the spine or brain

It should go without saying that Your Majesty will require specialized care, particularly if he or she has no mobility. Unable to stand or sit up, hemiplegic and quadriplegic cats remain in a lying down position. Unlike floppies, which have limited mobility, cats affected with hemiplegia and quadriplegia will not have the ability to move on their own, requiring around the clock nursing and supportive care. Depending on the diagnosis, you may be tasked with administering daily medications, physical therapies, bathing, and assisting The Crown during mealtimes as well as elimination. To commit to this level of servitude, you'll need to learn some new skills. If the condition is determined to be permanent, have a serious conversation with your veterinarian on your Overlord's specific needs and how to ensure that under proper care Your Majesty can have the best possible reign.

Around The Clock – An immobilized Overlord will require a comfortable throne that offers support for joints. Add extra pillows under their neck and limbs to reduce pressure. Spending too much time in the same position can result in bedsores. If Your Highness is unable to turn over or change positions easily, you will need to reposition them opposite side every few hours to prevent the development of skin ulcerations. Keep a close eye on your paraplegic felion; they can injure themselves and not realize it. Dragging limbs across the castle floor can result in sores, scrapes, and other injuries, especially around areas with less padding like the elbows, ankles, and hips. Consider padding vulnerable areas to protect Your Majesty from an avoidable trip to the vet.

Bathroom Etiquette – One of the first things to consider is that Overlords, like our Gracelyn, may suffer from functional incontinence. Unable to relieve themselves, or at least having no control over it, these monarchs will require assistance to perform their royal duties. In these cases, a servant will need to express the cat's bladder multiple times a day. Each time, the bladder should be completely emptied to prevent urinary tract infection. This can take a few tries and be a little tricky because the bladder isn't stationary and can easily slip out of your grip. Your veterinarian will be happy to show you the proper method. The process will take some practice and getting used to, for both you and your Overlord. I have often encountered some whining and fussiness, not just from my wife, but also from Gracelyn (this joke is likely to get me in trouble, I hope it was worth it). Do your best to speak words or comfort or praise your felion in song to ease their anxiety during the process.

You may also need to help your Number One go number two. It's important that you ensure your felion drink enough water to aid with regular bowel movements; this will make it easier on you both. Defecation involves gently massaging the anus with a wet, warm cloth or paper towel to stimulate elimination—just like neonatal kittens. Cats typically defecate once a day, but I always try to make Gracelyn evacuate her bowels every twelve hours. Since she has no control over defecation, when scooting across the floor she can sometimes leave a trail of bite-size Hershey bars in her wake. She's lucky she's so damn cute. So, if your Overlord only poops once a day, it's not a cause for alarm . . . just don't be surprised if you find a few gross gifts on the floor.

It's equally important not to skip genital hygiene, even if Your Highness can relieve themselves on their own. This is especially important for hemiplegic and quadriplegic cats, or if your paraplegic wears specially made cat diapers. Cleaning will prevent urine and fecal scalding as well as infection. Don't forget to dry them afterwards. Additionally, some topical creams can aid in healing and prevention.

Royal Spa Treatment – The Overlord will require regular grooming and bathing as they cannot properly do so on their own. Gently brush their coat daily to prevent any tangles or knots and to remove any solid bits of dirt or waste matter from the royal coat. If they have long fur, I'd suggest having it clipped to a more manageable length. Grooming sessions help your felion with looking and feeling their best, and most Overlords enjoy this type of worship by their servants as part of daily worship. Additionally, perform pawdicures on a bi-weekly basis as part of your grooming routine.

Unfortunately, many felions do not enjoy bathing as much as they do a brushing, which often makes this task difficult. So, be prepared for some crying, definitely from Your Majesty and possibly yourself. Be mindful of the water temperature. Use the Goldilocks approach: not too hot and not too cold; make sure it's just the right amount of lukewarm. Use a mild cleansing agent, like unscented pet shampoo, and always remember to fully rinse them. Never, under any circumstances, completely submerge your cat; keep water away from their faces. To clean their heads and faces, simply use a damp cloth to gently wipe them. When bathing is complete, thoroughly dry your kitty with a clean towel. Of course, singing is optional during bath time, but Your Highness will likely find comfort in the sound of your voice. So even if you're not a fan of sea shanties, at least be sure to regale them with felion praises.

The Royal Chariot – Paraplegic cats may require or at least benefit from using a wheelchair to help them get around. These can be expensive, but if you're handy, there are budget friendly designs available for constructing an assistive mobility device. You can select from various schematics, many of which are customizable to your cat's specific needs. An alternative to a wheelchair is sometimes referred to as a drag-bag, which protects Your Majesty's legs and stomach from friction abrasions while they scoot around. There are also specially made cat diapers with a hard shell that prevent your incontinent kitty have having accidents all over the floor. Any of these options will likely take time for Your Majesty to become comfortable using.

Physical Therapy – If your felion is recuperating from an illness or trauma, physical therapy is necessary to help your Overlord regain mobility. In the event of a permanent condition, these activities can at least prevent muscle atrophy. Consult with your veterinarian to develop a physical therapy program for your Overlord. Types of therapy include:

- Acupuncture
- Hydrotherapy
- Massage/Scratching
- Passive range of motion
- Resistance
- Stimulating the paws

Uplifting Hearts and Minds – Always be sure to give Your Majesty plenty of appropriate worship. It is vital for their psychological wellbeing and to prevent depression, whether their condition is temporary or permanent. Routinely move them to different areas of the castle for a change of scenery, especially locations with a lot of activity. Arrange for your Overlord to safely spectate from windows. You can use a sling or baby harness to carry them around throughout the castle so they can supervise your daily chores. Consider using a royal carriage to escort them on a thrilling adventure into the Great Backyard.

When our deaf Baby Girl suffered from a stroke at twelve years old, she was rendered temporarily hemiplegic, unable to use her left side. We kept her in a large crate so she couldn't be disturbed or stressed by the troublemakers of the fur-brigade, but the crate was in a common area in the castle so she could safely view the daily kitty Olympics or simply watch some Cat TV. As part of our supportive care regimen, we'd put pillows under her and flip her over every few hours. We'd reposition her for different views and take her out for cuddle sessions so she wouldn't feel alone, and she'd also be able sit atop her favorite thrones like the couch, the bed or even a lap. Cathy would sit with Baby Girl during royal feasts in case any assistance was needed. We would gently groom her and slowly move her legs, not only to help prevent muscle atrophy, but also as a form of social contact. We weren't sure how long her condition would last, nor how much our deaf queen would recover, but we had committed to serve her for better or worse. Thankfully, after several weeks, she eventually recovered about 90% of her mobility, although she moved a bit slower and preferred to climb rather than jump from then on.

CAT TALES: *Graced with Gracelyn*

In 2019, not long after I started my new job as the Foster/Adoption Manager for Louie's Legacy, I received a text message from one of my former coworkers at the shelter who asked the rescue to take a seven-week-old kitten in danger of being euthanized. Gracelyn was severely injured when she was accidentally caught in a closing door. Spinal damage left her unable to walk, but rather than taking her directly to a vet, her humans did nothing for three days, finally deciding to surrender her to the shelter. Unfortunately, Gracelyn's medical needs and long-term care were beyond the capability of the shelter staff. If rescue placement couldn't be found, this helpless kitten would be at risk for "humane euthanasia." Knowing my soft heart for special needs cats, my former coworkers immediately contacted me with a plea for assistance. At the time, we didn't know the extent of her injuries or if she would ever recover. After consulting with the Medical/Intake Manager of Louie's Legacy, she agreed to take Gracelyn into rescue.

It's no small commitment for a rescue to take on such a medical case. Veterinary exams and treatments can add up fast, costing hundreds or even thousands of dollars. Honestly, in cases such as this, rescues rarely ever recoup the medical costs through an adoption fee or crowd funding campaign, and most simply can't afford to take on the financial burden. The same holds true for shelters around the country. With so many homeless animals in need, they can't invest limited financial resources in a single animal, and sadly many of these medical cases end up being euthanized. I was so grateful that Louie's Legacy was able to step up and step in.

After a short stay with a temp foster, Gracelyn ended up at Hotel Mancuso. Because of course she did. At first, caring for a paralyzed kitten seemed like a daunting task, but our experience dealing with other special needs cats gave Cathy and me the confidence to accept the extra responsibility. After several visits, the vet informed us that her hind legs would be permanently paralyzed. Although we were saddened to learn she would not recover any rear limb mobility, we were relieved to know the littlest dust mop was not in any pain from her condition. As a kitten, she was playful, cuddly, and happy.

Despite hope and treatment, Gracelyn remained incontinent, meaning we needed to manually express her bladder and help her to defecate daily, not to mention regular grooming and the occasional, much-disliked baths. The level of care was consuming, but eventually what started out as a big deal became more mundane and routine. What once took nearly a half hour to bathe, dry and groom Gracelyn was cut in half. Inevitably, we grew so attached to her, and she fit in so well at The Island of Misfit Cats, that she officially adopted us a few months later.

Today, Gracelyn is quite the spunky mamma's girl who likes her all-fur fam and tolerates me, the Chief Elimination Officer. Yeah, I'm on doody duty. Cathy tends to spoil her Gracie, and the furry little diva loves every second of it.

Gracelyn is resilient, and her easy adaptation to life without rear mobility is inspiring. Gracelyn is good at communicating what she wants,

Gracelyn's favorite spot is at the foot of our bed. She climbs up there by herself!

for example, but she also has an independent streak. Like any other cat, she is curious and playful. She will climb up the cat trees using just her front legs so she can stare out one of the windows and enjoy her Cat TV. The littlest dust mop zips around the house like a speedster. We marvel at how quick she is despite her disability. Seriously, when it's bathroom time, I can't even catch her before she escapes under the bed. ❧

ELDER-FELIONS: THE LOVE OF AN OLD FRIEND

They are the wise elders of Cat World, although kitten-hood is well in the past, senior cats live for today. Keep in mind that even young, healthy felions age, and as seniors, they may develop medical issues that require extra care. Like us, as cat's age, they can be prone to a myriad of medical illnesses or age-related health conditions. Your Majesty may begin to encounter age-related changes around ten years and are most susceptible by the time they are twelve. While all senior cats will experience a gradual decline in hearing and vision, some eventually lose their hearing or eyesight entirely. Aged, overweight cats are prone to develop diabetes. Age-related issues like arthritis can limit mobility. Pain and illness can also lead to undesirable behaviors, like litter box accidents.

To help your elder felion best enjoy their golden years, consider these suggestions:

The Doctor Is In – As Your Highness enters their golden years, make sure they stay healthy. Once a cat has reached the age of nine, annual wellness exams should become mandatory, whether or not the Overlord agrees that they are necessary. As they age, a cat's immune system is less effective, making them more susceptible to disease. Remember, even elder felions are ninja-stealthy at hiding illness. By the time you notice minor symptoms, those hints could betray a more serious condition. Maintaining good health is an investment in a longer, happier future.

Do Not Disturb – Cancel their three o'clock kitchen inspection and pencil in extra naptime. Elder cats are less active and less prone to micro-management. As Head Servant, the Overlord trusts you to duly govern the kingdom in their name. Keep the bowls full, keep the sandcastle empty, and keep calm. A kingdom that is low stress will keep the Great One happy, even on days when they're not feeling their best.

Accessibility – Many elder cats are affected with mobility issues. They can't jump as high. They can't move as fast. And they just can't get around the way the used to. Provide easy access to the things seniors enjoy and need. In a multi-level castle your elderly monarch should have access to food, water, and litter boxes on every floor. If the kingdom is restricted to a single level, provide additional bowls and sandcastles in other rooms.

- Make using the litter box easier by getting one that is low entry. If you're crafty, you can even modify an old box to make it more accessible.
- Create steps, ramps, or purchase pet stairs that allow Your Highness to safely reach the highlife they enjoy, like the bed, couch, or windows.
- Nightlights help older cats with poor vision navigate the castle chambers in the dark.

Spa Day – Whether due to limited flexibility, the result of an illness, or an oversight in time management, aged Overlords may require frequent aid with grooming. Daily brushing leads to a healthier coat and promotes blood circulation. Unkempt fur can develop into painful matting. Litter can clump and become lodged between a cat's toe-beans, causing discomfort. Felions who groom themselves less efficiently may become as dirty and stinky as a dog. Treat your senior to a spa day. Pampered with special treats, gentle massages, grooming, bathing, and trimming, the Overlord will know you care enough to help them always look their best.

You Time – Familial relationships are everything. Since elderly monarchs are more reliant on their servant, they can often become clingy. Adapting to change gets more difficult over time, so Your Majesty will seek comfort in the familiar. Senior cats may need more attention or emotional support as they age. Extra snuggles? Sign me up!

Hesitant about adopting a senior cat? Well, don't be. There are many reasons to offer an elder cat a retirement castle. Seniors have been around for a while and know what it means to rule a kingdom. They have had families, and a well-adjusted senior will have an easier time with settling in to a new castle. They need less supervision and require less activity. Plus, in general, older cats are much more mellow than younger cats. Grateful for their servants, many of them become very affectionate. They are better at communicating, and they really seem to appreciate your service—good help is hard to find, you know! Kittens and young cats are not only more active, but also more inclined to cause accidents, whereas laid-back seniors tend to be easier to care for than their younger counterparts, making them great companions for elderly people. Elder Overlords are also great cats for people new to Cat World because their terms of service are lenient. Seniors can still have plenty of happy years ahead of them, and even the old grumps have lots of love left to give.

CAT TALES: *My Hiro*

He sat quietly on a small blanket, staring at me through the kennel bars in the SIACC cat adoption room. I was at the shelter on my weekly visit to snap photographs of cats in need. Although the majority of kennels were occupied, there wasn't much for me to do. I was happy to see so many I'M ADOPTED or I'M PLACED WITH A RESCUE tags on the cages. I greeted all the cats and kittens as I worked my way towards the orange tabby on the opposite side of the room. He visibly perked up at my approach.

"Hey, bud. Nice to meet you"—I read his kennel card—"Voyager."

His tail went up and he issued a silent meow, rubbing his body against the bars as he paced back and forth. Voyager was fourteen years old, a week prior he had been brought in to the shelter as a stray. Given his friendly disposition, it was obvious Voyager had once ruled a kingdom, but for an unknown reason he had either been sent into exile or had left of his own accord. There was no telling how long he had been surviving on his own. Clearly, life in The Great Backyard had not been kind to the old cat. He was a pitiful sight: Thin as a rail at only five pounds, and his fur has lost its luster. Not to mention he was dealing with some gastrointestinal issues and his cage smelled ripe enough to make eyes cross. That being said, he seemed quite spry for a senior cat.

Unlocking his kennel and opening the door, I let him sniff my hand. He leaned in for petting. Of course, I was more than happy to oblige. We became fast friends. He patiently sat still for the camera. After I had a few quality photos of him, I put my camera aside for some extra one-on-one time; he looked like he could use it. Voyager was very appreciative of affection, constantly offering head-boops and rubbing his cheeks on my arm.

When it was time for me to go, I was reluctant to leave him. The old cat watched me intently from across the room as I packed my gear. Voyager pleaded with his eyes for me to take him home.

"I'm sorry, I can't." I said. "I already have a full house. Don't worry, someone is going to fall in love with you."

Someone already had.

Voyager reached through the bars with his paw. He was really laying it on thick. I crossed the room to give him a proper goodbye. I opened the kennel one last time. "Okay, I'll make you a deal," I whispered. "If you're not placed by the time I come in next week, I'll take you on a voyage with me to the Island of Misfit Cats. Would you like that?"

He didn't look convinced, but I meant it.

After saying goodbye to my new friend, I popped into one of the offices to talk to my former coworker about him. "If Voyager . . . you know . . . gets listed, let me know and I'll adopt him." Of course, I'd have to get Cathy on board, but I honestly couldn't imagine her saying no.

That night I posted the old cat's photos to the Lost and Found Pets of Staten Island Facebook group, hoping someone would claim him or decide to give him a home. I kept an eye on the comments, hoping for Voyager's happy ending. Over the next few days, his photos were shared and reposted, but no one recognized him.

A week later, on November 2nd, I got the call. Having come down with an upper respiratory infection, Voyager was going to be placed on the euthanasia list. Although shelter colds are treatable, they are highly contagious, and to prevent an outbreak, which can put a strain on funding, sick dogs and cats can be put to sleep. He would have three days to

Hiro's freedom photo. Home sweet home, as promised, buddy.

be adopted or find placement with a rescue. All it took was a phone call. As promised, Voyager came home to live with us that same day. Hence forth, he would be known as Hiro.

The sweet, old tabby made quite an impression on Cathy. They bonded instantly. With a proper diet, he gained a healthy weight. Adding some fish oil to his food did wonders for his coat, which was now soft and lush. Even at fourteen years old, Hiro was quite spry, and after two weeks in isolation he was eager to explore the rest of his new castle. He settled into kingdom life quickly, with minimum static. For the most part, the fur-brigade (except Mr. Bitey) gave Hiro his space. There were a few minor skirmishes, but no escalations. Hiro didn't need to run the castle, nor was he a pushover. He was more than willing to share space to keep the peace. Often content with a spot on a lap or the sofa, he took turns, patiently waiting for a window seat on one of the cat trees. Eventually, he was on everyone's good side.

As the years passed, Hiro has gotten slower. Now, at almost eighteen, he has lost some vision due to cataracts. A year and a half ago, he was diagnosed with kidney disease, which is being managed with medication and a special diet. Even as I write this book, when he wakes from one of his many naps, he will still scratch on my office door to be let in for a safety inspection. Five minutes later, feeling satisfied, he will scratch to be let out. No sooner than I let him out, Hiro is scratching at the door again. He may be old, but he's still a cat.

10

BREAKING BAD

FAKE MEWS

Despite what you think or may have heard, there's no such thing as a Bad Cat. Not my Mr. Bitey nor my mystery wall-sprayer, and certainly not your own monarch. Maybe you're thinking: *Wrong! You don't know my cat.* But I'm going to interrupt that thought with a simple truth: There are no alternative facts in Cat World. Any such notion is a MewAnon conspiracy theory, or perhaps dog sanctioned propaganda. Either way, it's just fake mews.

Overlords are always true to themselves. A cat's sense of right and wrong is without guile as they are governed by their own instincts. "Life, liberty and the pursuit of happiness" are not just words in our Declaration of Independence; they are enshrined in the Cat Code and define how all felions live their lives. Cats despise drama of any kind, and they will respond to any person, thing, or situation that challenges their comfort. What you may perceive as spite or malice is really a simple form of communication in Cat World. Well, maybe it's not always so simple, unless imbued with knowledge by the Celestial Meow.

Felions don't understand our rules of conduct. *Why wouldn't I scratch such a perfect couch? Why shouldn't I spray my scent there, how else will a new cat know to keep off my property? Of course I lashed out at you; I'm sick, for Meow's sake!*

Think of unwanted behaviors as Your Majesty filing a formal complaint. They know that when they're happy, we will be too. As their protector and servant, we are charged with addressing the issue, finding an amicable solution, and restoring order throughout the kingdom. They trust us to figure out the logistics, as such menial duties are below them. The Overlords let us know when we have succeeded in our quest and all is right with the world again.

THE PROBLEM: LITTER BOX ISSUES

Get ready; I'm about to devote even more pages to cat pee and poop. Are you excited or what? Before you go thinking that I have some kind of sick obsession with this topic, let me assure you that house soiling is one of the leading reasons why cats are surrendered. That makes it a very important issue. In fact, when I put out an open call for FAQs on social media, litter box issues are one of the most common responses. Unfortunately, we've had our share of these problems here, with both fosters and our own fur-brigade. I can relate to the struggle and aggravation of trying to find a solution.

When monarchs void outside of the royal privy seemingly on spite, they're simply communicating to us that something is wrong. Litter box issues can stem from medical conditions, behavioral issues, or both. If Your Majesty starts leaving presents for you outside of their sandcastle, it's time to schedule an appointment with your vet. This needs to be the first thing you do, not the last. Trust me—urinary blockages, urinary tract infections, bladder stones, kidney failure, and even diabetes can cause your kitty to skip their box as a cry (sometimes literally) for help. These issues require immediate attention by a vet.

Urinary Blockage – I am placing this issue at the top of the list, not because it's the most common, but because it's the deadliest. I know from experience with my own cats that a urethral obstruction is a painful and life-threatening condition. This blockage will not resolve on its own; it requires immediate medical intervention. Symptoms include:

- Vocalization in the litter box
- Repeated attempts and straining to pass urine
- Meowing in pain
- Blood in urine
- Decreased appetite

- Vomiting
- Abdomen may be tender to the touch.
- Lethargy
- Hiding
- Weakness and mental dullness

If you have a male that has an "accident" outside the litter box, watch him carefully to see if he makes frequent trips to his box. Check the litter to see if he urinated or if there is any blood. Observe him for any of the symptoms above.

Urinary Tract or Bladder Infection – A UTI is a bacterial infection of the bladder and urinary tract. We've had a few of those at Hotel Mancuso, mostly with females. Some VIPs came from castles where their servants had exiled an Overlord from the kingdom for frequent peeing outside the royal privy. The vet can easily diagnosis this issue with a urinalysis, which they are usually able to do on site. Most UTIs are easily treatable with medicine, but it is important to get your felion started with a prescription of antibiotics as soon as possible.

Again, I really want to stress the importance of taking your cat to a vet if they are not using their litter box. At the very least, you can rule out a medical problem and focus on other possibilities for this behavior.

CAT TALES: *Hershel's Emergency*

"Chris! Chris!" Cathy called from the kitchen. There was panic in her voice. "Chris, wake up!"

I bounced from the bed like my legs were made of springs. My body was on autopilot, striding out of the room as my brain tried to catch up from my pillow. Turning into the kitchen, I froze; this wasn't a dream. It was Hershel, our tripod. He was lying on his side, pitifully wailing in pain. I was suddenly wide-awake, coffee not required.

We were in the van in less than ten minutes, the engine racing almost as fast as my heart. Cathy's beautiful eyes were wet, her face full of worry and sadness as Hershel groaned. She turned, looked into the carrier, and offered him soothing words of comfort. "I know. I'm sorry. It's gonna be okay, Hershey. You'll be better soon." She hoped, but she wasn't sure. "We love you. We love you so very much."

Morning rush-hour traffic impeded our travel. I honked, weaved, and spat out a slew of curses to every vehicle that shared the expressway with us. In my growing frustration I probably even coined a few new, colorful insults. Come on, Catdammit! Get out of my fluffin' way!

I veered off an exit ramp only to be thwarted by the never-ending construction of Staten Island streets. *Stop. Wait.* One hardhat worked a Jackhammer while fifteen supervisors stared blankly into a hole. *Stop. Wait.* An orange flag waved. *Go, go, go!*

After a frantic drive that seemed to last forever, we finally pulled up to Aadobe Animal Hospital. Hershel was taken in immediately. Dr. Singh instantly confirmed his blockage and went to work. The adrenaline from the drive had worn off, sinking me into a quicksand of worry. Cathy and I sat together in the waiting room, holding hands and praying for our boy.

When Doc finally emerged from the back room later, his face was serious, and his tone was solemn. Hershel was alive, but he would need to spend the next two days at the vet hospital under observation with a guarded prognosis. He had a fifty-fifty chance of survival. We were reluctant to leave, but there was nothing else we could do for him here. Hershel was in the very capable hands of Dr. Singh and his staff. They would call us with any change in his condition.

At home, Phoebe, Hershel's wife, paced in distress. They were almost always together, rubbing faces, giving each other confidence and companionship. She meowed, calling out to him. It was a lonely sound. When Hershel did not appear at her side, Phoebe searched from room to room, looking for him in all of their favorite hangout spots. Of all our cats, Hershel is the only one she likes. At all. Catherine and I could do nothing but worry and blame ourselves with should've, could've, would've.

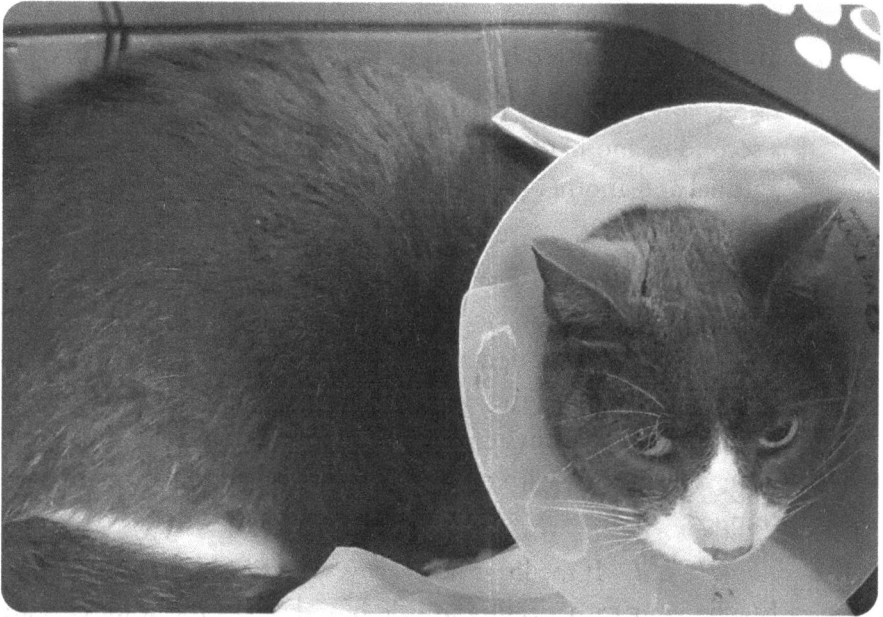

Hershel on his way home after three days at Aadobe Animal hospital.

Thankfully, Hershel pulled through. Relief swept over us like a warm hug. Soon, he and Phoebe were happily strutting around the living room, their heads virtually glued together. The vet prescribed a special diet, and now we make sure to add extra water to his wet food daily. Still, we remain vigilant, always keeping a close eye on the litter box habits of him and the other boys. 🐾

Litter Box Aversion – The most obvious reason for a cat mess on the floor, or anywhere other than their sandcastle, is a dirty box. As I've stressed earlier, cats hate a dirty litterbox. I don't need to rehash those images of that public bathroom, do I? If you're not scooping frequently enough or haven't given the box a thorough cleaning and complete refill in a while, that could be the problem. Then again, no matter how clean you keep King Claw's sandcastle, there may be other reasons. Here's what you should consider:

- *More Or Less* – If you have less than a two-inch layer on the bottom, Your Highness is going to have a hard time burying their treasure, and not enough urine is being absorbed. If the box is over filled with litter, it could feel unstable beneath their paws.

- *Plus One* – If you only have one litter box in the castle, try adding a second in another location. Some cats prefer one box to serve as a urinal and another for their smellier business. Can't say I blame them either.

- *Relocation* – Even in Cat World, when it comes to real estate, it's all about location, location, location. Where is the box in your home? Is it hidden away or hard to get to? Is it in a high traffic area? Is it in the basement next to any loud machinery like a dryer? Try moving the box to a more appealing location, somewhere quiet, with privacy, but also where the cat won't feel trapped.

- *Flip The Lid* – If the litter box is covered, try taking the hood off. Maybe your cat is feeling a little boxed in. In the wild, cats are always on alert for predators, and since relieving themselves is a vulnerable time, some cats prefer a quick escape and may find a covered box to be a little claustrophobic. Conversely, if the box is uncovered, try getting a box with a hood as your royal may be looking for some privacy.

- *Unplug* – If you have a robot litter box and your cat has ever watched *The Matrix* or *The Terminator*, they may fear a robot uprising. Even if you don't think their concern is legitimate, humor them, and try switching to a standard box that will never have the ability to travel back in time and try to kill Sarah Connor with a phased plasma rifle in the 40 Watt range.

- *Swap Out* – As I mentioned earlier, there are a variety of litter types and brands to choose from. Felion royalty can be finicky. Your cat may have sensitive paws and not like the granular feel of sandy litter. The clumping kind can stick in between their toe beans. Maybe Your Highness prefer pellets, or litter made from shells. If the litter is scented, maybe they don't appreciate the smell; try an unscented kind. With so many choices, you may need to endure a bit of trial and error to find the right fit.

- *Come Hither* – If your kitty enjoys catnip, rub some on the sides of the box or sprinkle a little inside. There are some attractants on the market with good reviews, but I can't personally attest to any product. If you're looking for something all natural, try a bit or research for safe herbs or scents that the Overlord may find more alluring.

Negative Association – Consider that something may have happened to upset Your Majesty while she was using the litter box. If your cat had a blockage, UTI, or even painful defecation, that association may still cause them to avoid the litter box, even if their health has returned to normal. If this is the case, you'll need to bring back a positive association. Try any of the suggestions above or other ideas you might have or find online. As with all things cat, a negative litter box association will take time and patience to resolve. Whatever you do, please do not force your cat into the litter box. This will not help, and you could inadvertently create a negative association or make an existing one even worse. Don't give your kitty any reason to fear the litter box.

Stress – Stress can cause litter box problems. Overlords can be stressed by things their servants may not think of as traumatic, but remember, as rulers of the kingdom, felions like to be in control. Moving, changes in routine, large gatherings, and even adding a new family member can make Your Majesty feel anxious. Cats don't deal with stress particularly well, and poo or puddle protests can be filed around the castle as a formal complaint. Once you learn the trigger of felion displeasure, you can take steps to help reduce the stress, which will make solving the problem easier. In all of these situations, you will need to clean previous soiled spots with an enzymatic cleaner. Block off access to that area, or use something that smells like citrus to make it less appealing. Do not scare your cat—this will only worsen the problem. Try to get them into a positive association with their litter box.

Turf War – If there are multiple royals in the kingdom, one may guard the sandcastles and prevent the other cats from using them. Aggression doesn't always manifest as an all-out war. Even if a felion bully isn't physically confronting the other cats in the litter box, they could be intimidating the other with looks or subtle body posture. These gestures can be almost imperceptible to servants not fluent in Cat Speak. Any royal conflict in a kingdom can create enough stress to cause litter-box problems (see Territorial Aggression, page 212).

THE PROBLEM: SPRAYING/MARKING

Although it's easy to confuse the two, marking is different from a litter box issue. Rather than finding a puddle or a pile outside the sandcastle, a servant will find streaks of pungent urine dripping down walls or other vertical surfaces. When a felion sprays a small amount of urine on a vertical surface, they are trying to communicate a territorial dispute through smell. An Overlord that sprays is marking their territory. However, they will still use their litter box as normal, although at times there can be crossover between the two, such as with a royal who is stalked by another felion while using the sandcastle. Urine marking may happen because your cat feels anxious, stressed, or is just sending a scent message to others as a warning, and it is especially common in multi-cat kingdoms. Think of it like social media for cats—they're posting passive aggressive comments to their wall. As aggravating as this behavior may be to us, it is preferable to physical confrontations between cats.

In castles with a single Overlord, spraying is less common, but it can happen due to stressors like moving, strangers in the kingdom, or any upsetting change in their royal routine. Unneutered males and intact females mark when trying to attract a mate. Getting your kitty sterilized will eliminate those urges.

Your Majesty may also get upset when they see a strange felion lurking outside the castle walls, especially if that cat begins spraying nearby. The outside felion is viewed as a usurper and this can cause territorial spraying inside the castle. In such cases, block any view your cat might have of the outdoor cat. Additionally, you may need to clean any outside portions of your castle where the offending felion might have sprayed.

Tips for dealing with a spraying cat:

- Do not punish your cat or rub their nose in the pee. You have no authority over The Crown! It is not helpful, and you're only succeeding in terrifying your poor, misunderstood cat.
- Clean soiled areas using mild-fragrance soap. Strong-smelling cleaners could cause your felion to mark again. Urine contains ammonia, so cleaning with ammonia can likewise attract Your Majesty to leave their calling card in that same spot.
- Make soiled areas inaccessible. A royal blockade will keep Your Highness from marking the same area over and over.
- Spray scents like citrus or vinegar on surfaces as a deterrent. Noble noses will be offended by these unappealing aromas and your felion will avoid these spots. Keep in mind, the scents will fade and need to be reapplied to remain effective.
- Set up motion-activated air-sprays around the perimeter. These devices will expel a hiss of air whenever Your Majesty gets into proximity of their preferred spraying spot.
- Keep items that smell foreign to The Crown out of reach to discourage sprays of disapproval.
- If you serve a single ruler, anxiety reduction is key to preventing future markings. Be observant and attentive. Once you figure out what is triggering their response, take steps to manage their stress and work out a program aimed at desensitizing and counterconditioning.
- In a multi-cat kingdom, spread out resources around the castle. Make sure each Overlord has access to their own things, like thrones, scratching posts, and toys. If you only have one litter box, get at least one other.
- You may need to separate your royals by carving the castle into individual territories. Closed doors can serve as boundaries between the feuding monarchs. After a week or two of isolation from one another, you can always try reintroductions.
- Overlords can get jealous. Set aside time daily for each of your cats to enjoy your worship so they feel equally loved. Playing with individual cats in different chambers of the castle can sometimes reduce conflict.

THE PROBLEM: DESTRUCTIVE SCRATCHING

Destructive scratching can be a nightmare, especially if Kitty Kruger is shredding your couch worse than an Elm Street teen. You've nicely asked Your Majesty to stop. You've tried to appeal to their sense of reason. You've even caught them in the act, only for the Overlord to stare at you while their murder mittens are tearing your drapes to ribbons.

A cat has a natural instinct to scratch, which serves multiple purposes. It spreads their scent, provides a convenient way to dispense of worn claw sheaths, and allows felions to stretch their muscles. Scratching is something you cannot stop. What you can do, however, is redirect their need to scratch toward something more appropriate.

A Better Choice – Make sure you have appropriate scratching posts and scratchers. (see Itching the Scratch, page 58) Do not force your cat's paws onto the scratcher to "teach" them, because the only thing that may end up being scratched is you. Instead, rub some catnip or other attractant on it. I'll brush my Overlords and rub their fur onto the new scratcher so it will have a scent of familiarity. Do not throw away a favorite scratching post when it becomes unsightly. Felions prefer shredded and torn objects because they can really get their claws into the material. Used posts will also appeal to Your Highness because they smell and look familiar.

Can't Touch This – Block your cat's access to an un-scratchable item, or if that's not possible, make the object less appealing by using double-sided tape, or cover it with plastic or sandpaper. Place the approved cat tree/scratcher next to these objects. Once Your Majesty is fully utilizing the approved scratcher, you can remove boundaries or blockages.

Clips or Tips – The shorter the claws, the less damage they can do. If you're having trouble with giving Your Highness regular pawdicures, consider using nail caps. They are a humane alternative to declawing your felion. Nail caps are soft coverings that are glued on to your cat's nails. They are great for keeping excessive scratchers, like cats with skin conditions or allergies, from injuring themselves. If you're concerned about claw marks in your expensive furniture, nail caps could be a useful solution to consider. They typically last between four to six weeks, at which time they will need to be removed, the claw trimmed, and a new set of tips properly glued on. Remember, a cat's claws will continue to grow beneath the caps, so don't leave them on longer than recommended or they can become painful and unpleasant.

Swing And a Miss – As previously mentioned, the rules of Cat World are vastly different than ours. The Overlord does not understand why something as natural as scratching is wrong, nor do they recognize your authority to enforce your will on them. With punishment, you're not going to prevent kitty from scratching, you will only succeed in making sure Your Highness learns not to get caught in the act. Your best bet is to come to an amicable arrangement that satisfies their urges while keeping your furniture safe from claws.

Not an Option – Do not declaw. It may seem like an easy solution to curb the scratching issue for good, but you may only be creating worse problems. Declawing is a painful surgery, putting your cat at risk of developing an infection or lameness in their paws. With this type of surgery, a cat's claw is not simply removed but parts of their digits are amputated as well. The process has been described to me as comparable to humans having all of their top knuckles removed. A declawed cat can suffer pain for the duration of their lives, and because of it their temperament can be adversely affected.

THE PROBLEM: CAT AGGRESSION

There are several types of aggression in cats, and a range of causes. Here at Hotel Mancuso, we've been through them all: playful bites that go too far, accidental scratches meant for someone else, and warring factions battling for the throne. We've witnessed our share of screaming chases, ambush attacks, and friendly fire.

Play Aggression – Your feet have been stalked, swiped at, and pounced on. Your forearms have a complex tattoo of scratches. Play aggression isn't a malicious attack; it's merely rough play, including stalking, chasing, biting, ambushing, swatting, grasping, and bunny-kicks. These types of rough and tumble play are common among catlings and young felions. Despite their playful intentions, some of their games can cause injury to people, especially young children.

Having hand-raised single orphaned kittens, I can tell you that one of the biggest contributors to play aggression is the lack of socialization with other kittens. When catlings are very young, they learn the limits of going too far from littermates or even their mother. In our capacity as a surrogate family to a single kitten, we would not only help them become social but also teach them how to play appropriately. Cathy would utter a high-pitched squeak when a prince or princess began to get overly rambunctious. For my part, I would issue a soft, short hiss to help curb their behavior, much like I've seen queens do. Both methods achieved the desired result. The catling would stop, looking confused, then we would redirect their focus to some type of toy.

Never play with your cat using your hands. Did I mention that already? Multiple times, you say? There's a good reason I have always discouraged fosters and new servants from using their hands, feet, or any body part to play with Overlords. Sure, it's adorable when kittens are itty, bitty harmless balls of fluff, but that type of play only teaches them that hands (or feet) are playthings, too. Of course, this becomes a problem as they get older and playful bites and scratches can actually cause injury. As early as possible, teach your cat that you are off limits for rough play. Your hands are for petting.

- *This, Not That* – Attract your cat's focus with teasers, wand toys, a stuffed animal to kick, anything but your hands or other parts of your body. Interactive play, like making them chase a teaser around the castle, will burn energy and help satisfy Your Majesty's instinct to hunt. And you'll have more fun, too. If they are intent on trying to grab you in a kicking paw-clutch, redirect their actions onto a plush toy. They can battle their evil, archenemy until their predatory heart is content, while keeping you safe from little fangs and claws.

- *Game Over* – Ignore them. Get up and walk away. Don't speak or interact at all for 10-20 minutes. If they seek out your attention, make sure you don't engage until they have had enough time to calm down. Each time Your Majesty tries to play with you inappropriately, simply remove yourself from the situation. Make it routine. The Crown may not understand specifically what they are doing wrong, but if you disappear every time they try to go five rounds of Kicky-Scratchy-Bitey with you, they will soon make the association.

- *Play Pal* – A single Overlord spending long hours alone in the castle without opportunities to play can be frustrated and full of energy. You'll need to make sure to give them plenty of extra play with appropriate toys. If your meowing monarch has more energy than you can handle, consider adding a new royal playmate to the kingdom. As I mentioned, with The Buddy System, co-rulers will not only keep each other occupied, they will help establish boundaries of acceptable Kitty Kung-Fu during play sessions.

- *Don't Punish Your Cat* – As with destructive scratching, aggressive behaviors should never lead to physical punishment, which is always counter-productive. You could inadvertently make matters worse by inducing anxiety, leading to even more unwanted behaviors.

- *Well Done* – Praise good behavior, and reward your felion with treats. By adding positive reinforcement to the routine, you will help them learn the desired behavior and associate it with your positive reaction. Well done! The Overlord has taught you well, Grasshopper.

Redirected Aggression – If you think Your Majesty is attacking out of the blue, think again. Redirected aggression occurs when an Overlord gets royally worked up but can't get at the source of their angst. Instead, they lash out at the nearest person or other pet. Although you are not the intended target of claws and fangs, and it's merely a reactive instinct, the attacks could be dangerous or damaging as the cat is not just pulling punches.

Unfortunately, there can be a delay of minutes or even hours with redirected aggression. If this is the case with your felion, you'll need to observe them and attempt to determine the trigger of this behavior.

- *What's Up, Doc?* – Schedule an appointment with you vet for a health check. This is one of those unanticipated expenses we spoke about earlier. If your cat's health is the cause of aggressive behavior, none of the tips I am providing will be a benefit or solve the problem. If Your Highness has a clean bill of health, your veterinarian may also be able to make some recommendations.

- *Cancel The Show* – Sometimes Cat TV can be the source. Staring at birds or small prey through a window can set off their hunting instinct, and they become frustrated when they aren't able to act on those ninja impulses. Or perhaps there is another cat lurking outside and your felion may feel the need to protect their territory. If this is the cause, restrict access to the window.

- *Fear Factors* – Perhaps Your Highness is being frightened or harassed by a person or other pet in the kingdom. Is your doggie trying to play with your felion, or could the two royals be having a dispute over property or territory? Are the kids or someone else intentionally scaring the Overlord or making some other effort to create a viral cat video on social media?

   Cats don't have a sense of humor, especially when they feel threatened. If your dog is the instigator, you'll have a better chance at training him. If another royal is the instigator, you can try re-introduction or time-outs. If it's a person harassing The Crown, you should inform them of the felion gospel and tell them to stop.

- *Keep Out of the Strike Zone* – If you try to break up a cat-fight with your hands or any other part of your body, you're going to have a bad time. Although you can't let two felions duke it out, you'll need to break them up in a hands-off fashion. Loud clapping, shaking a jar of change, or even using a spray bottle will break up the fight from a safe distance. If those options fail, you can toss a blanket over the aggressor. After the felions are completely separated, allow each to decompress in their own room for at least a day before they possibly meet again.

- *Blending In* – Much like their wild brethren, felions have a strong territorial sense. The Overlords mark and identify ownership by scent. While imperceptible to humans, the scent of a strange cat on clothing could trigger a negative reaction in your felion. The scent of an unfamiliar monarch is the smell of betrayal. Even if Your Majesty doesn't view you as a Benedict Arnold, they may feel compelled to defend their castle. If you or someone else has been interacting with another cat, don't approach the resident Overlord as you may find yourself a target of their misdirected ire. Before trying to interact with your cat, wash up to remove the stench of disloyalty from your face and hands. Try to make Your Highness feel as non-threatened as possible by using familiar scents and letting them come to you when they are ready.

- *A Quiet Place* – Hearing loud or high-pitched noises can trigger your felion to go into attack mode. Since cats are hardwired to prey on mice and small animals, their hearing is tuned to pick up frequencies beyond our ability to hear. Be mindful about where you locate the sandcastle and their favorite throne; if they are near any type of electronic or mechanical device, move these objects to a less stressful location. Likewise, sudden explosions of sound, such as fireworks or thunder, can cause anxiety and fear. Unfortunately, some cats from abusive backgrounds may also find loud noises triggering past trauma. Allow plenty of quiet places for your cat to hide, and add some treats or their favorite object to enhance their calm. There is also music specifically composed for cats. These tunes were designed by animal behavior specialists to appeal to a cat's ear and brain. Don't you just love science?

- *Armor Up* – To calm The Crown during storms, fireworks, or some other cacophonous event, you can use a kitty compression shirt, which acts as sort of a security blanket, to keep cats feeling safe. An anxiety shirt or vest wraps around Your Highness much like a swaddling blanket for an infant. The gentle pressure from these types of garments can offer temporary comfort to an anxious felion, but they are not intended for long term wear. Keep in mind not every felion is willing to be outfitted, even when it's for their own benefit, especially if they have already been triggered. Never try to get Your Majesty to suit up in emotional armor if they are communicating any of the Stop Signs.

Aggression Between Two Cats – Can't we all just get along? Aggression between Co-rulers is frustrating for everyone in the kingdom, whether they are directly involved in the dispute or not. Unfortunately, Overlords don't resolve differences through palace summits. Without human intervention, they will fight it out, and such aggression will only result in casualties as it escalates to full-on war. In the quest for peace, humans must play a vital role.

- *Who Dis? Non-Recognition Aggression* – This is a type of misdirected aggression towards a familiar cat. Overlords that live together develop a group scent, and it's how they identify one another. If one of your felions takes a trip to the vet, they are going to smell quite different when they return home. Their fur will have picked up new, unfamiliar scents at the vet's office, causing their furry brother or sister to mistake an ally for an invader upon return to the kingdom. And they will defend their territory.

  To prevent this, consider taking both of Overlords to any appointment. However, it is understandable that a group outing may not be easily, much less realistic, especially for royal who have an aversion to travel. In that case, take the other cat's blanket. Do not take the blanket into the vet's office. Leave it in your car (or inside a plastic bag), and once you leave the office, put the blanket in the pet carrier so your cat with the appointment can pick up the family scent on the trip home. Another option to diffuse non-recognition aggression would be to separate the felions with a time out. Should that fail, complete reintroductions may be necessary to rectify the problem. If one cat has a prolonged stay at the animal hospital, ask to have them bathed before discharge, or visit a groomer before going home, to wash away the unfamiliar smells. In addition, it's a great idea to rub kitty down with a towel that your other cat has been sleeping on, and use the communal brush to add back the group scent to their fur.

- *Royal Rivals: Territorial Aggression* – Some Overlords are not very big on the idea of sharing, especially a ruler who may not have been exposed to other pets. When a new felion comes into their territory, Your Highness can become defensive or aggressive.

Likewise, the instigator could be your new kit on the block, looking to dethrone the resident Overlord of the manor. Like Connor MacLeod in a felion version of *Highlander*: There can be only one!

A territorial dispute between felions could be a conflict over space or resources, such as sandcastles, thrones, access or food and water bowls. However, this doesn't mean that warring factions are incapable of a peaceful coexistence. You will need to serve as the royal arbiter, supervising a truce with fair and just terms, as well as facilitating enforcement measures.

- *Spay/Neuter* – With high levels of testosterone, intact males are particularly prone to aggressive behavior. Once neutered, testosterone levels will drop within several weeks and reduce many aggressive tendencies.

- *Know Their Roles* – In order to resolve aggression issues, you'll need to figure out which felion is the aggressor. Become fluent in Cat Speak. Since a cat's body language can be subtle, antagonistic gestures often go unnoticed to humans. You may be surprised to learn that the hissing cat is the one being intimidated. Hisses are only employed as a defensive tactic from a cat that is feeling threatened.

- *Allocate and Relocate* – Divide and separate resources. As omniscient as the Overlords believe themselves to be, they can't be everywhere at once. Reduce competition between felions by providing multiple, identical food bowls, thrones, sandcastles and toys in different areas of the castle. If you reside in a small castle, place these items on opposite sides of the room and put up visual barricades allowing each cat to have a little space and privacy from the other.

- *For Whom the Bell Tolls* – Put a bell on the aggressor as an early warning system. This could help avoid sneak attacks and give other cats a heads-up as to the location and movements of their antagonist. With a variety of resources spread throughout the kingdom, other felions will be able to make strategic choices to avoid conflict.

- *Break It Up* – Interrupt staring contests and growling matches before they escalate into a battle royal of teeth and claws. Placing a large object like a pillow or piece of cardboard between your feuding felions will break their line of sight, ending the showdown before Quickdraw McClaw can take a swipe. Never let cats fight it out. Felion disputes are never resolved that way, and one or both cats can wind up with serious, or in extreme cases, fatal wounds. To avoid personal injury to yourself, never try to break up a fight with your hands. If the cats are actively engaged in mortal combat, stop the aggression from a safe distance with a loud clap, throwing a blanket over them, or a few well-aimed sprays from a water bottle.

- *Trading Places* – You may want to confine cats to separate rooms for several days or more and start an exchange program. Remember, the goal is for the felions to become desensitized to each other's presence. You can exchange beds, blankets, toys, or even have the felions switch rooms before you try reintroductions.

- *The Space Program* – Félicette was the first cat in space, but the Overlord doesn't need to hop aboard a rocket to escape from a royal rival. Even if you live in a one-room castle, you can make the most of limited space by adding perches on the walls. Build upward. Convert the top of the old china cabinet or entertainment center into a kitty skyscraper with rooftop access. This will create some available prime real estate. Having access to vertical spaces will allow your cats more room to spread out as they prefer.

- *The Art of Distraction* – Try spending more time with the aggressor. This may sound counterintuitive, but the extra attention could reduce jealousy and stress. Your worship and service are valuable kingdom resources. Unwarranted jealousy or not, one thing you can be certain of is that an Overlord would prefer extra time being doted on by a loyal servant over focusing on a felion feud. Additionally, rubbing a bit of tuna juice on the cats' bodies and heads is a great diversion tactic. Since grooming is a self-soothing behavior, the cats become so preoccupied that they're less likely to be bothered by one another. If a truce is reached, the former rivals may even start to groom each other.

- *Burn, Baby, Burn* – When felions get bored, they can hunt or attack one another for amusement. While this is entertaining for the aggressor, for the victim, it's terrifying. While it could be argued that this is a form of play aggression, it's not a two-player game. Keep cats busy with plenty of toys and interactive playtime, especially the bully. Help them satisfy their need to burn off energy and hunt in a less caustic manner. The more rigorous the play session, the better. A tired felion is less likely to fight. If you're able and the cats are willing, have both royals join an interactive play session with you. By getting them to interact together in play, you can help facilitate bonding. Successfully implementing the Kitty Olympics will make both cats winners.

- *Love Is in the Air* – Try pheromone sprays. A chemical spray alone likely isn't going to resolve the issue, but these sprays are a useful tool in your arsenal and can play a role in helping to create a calmer atmosphere throughout the realm. However, keep in mind that these types of sprays don't work instantly. They may take weeks to actually have an effect.

- *Reinforce the Treaty* – Reward your royals with treats when you see them interacting in a friendly manner. Keep in mind, the peace treaty could be fragile in the beginning so it's important to reinforce the terms of the truce for as long as necessary. Employ the above tactics should the kingdom's harmony ever be broken.

- *Never Surrender* – Whatever you do, don't wave the white flag. Unfortunately, there are no easy, long-term solutions. Behavior modification doesn't happen overnight. Setbacks can and likely will happen, and you may need to rethink your strategy. Finding the right combination of measures takes trial and error. Set achievable objectives over a longer period of time. Take comfort in every small victory as each is a step in the direction of peace.

CAT TALES: *War & Peace*

You recall Mr. Bitey from earlier in this book, don't you? He had been residing in my office for several weeks, and we had made a lot of progress in our relationship. Eventually, I had the unenviable task of introducing the gray devil to all of his new brothers and sisters. When the time came, Mr. Bitey swaggered out of my office and shortly thereafter began his reign of terror. He was the schoolyard bully, sauntering around, taking random swipes, even going after our defenseless special needs cats if they got in his way.

Hershel, our good-natured tripod, hobbled up to greet Mr. Bitey, who locked eyes and growled. With an angry yowl, Phoebe sprung forward and bapped Mr. Bitey right in the hisser. Shuttup! Nobody growls at my man! The situation escalated quickly. I was quick draw on the water bottle, like the sheriff in an old Western. "Break it up. Break it up. There's nothing to see here."

Most of my cats were terrified of this hostile takeover. Petey and Puff Daddy would skedaddle as Mr. Bitey entered the room, but some of our sassy gals like Phoebe and Moon weren't going to roll over so easily. At times, they would even go on the offensive by striking first. A chorus of hisses followed Mr. Bitey throughout the house, like walking through a snake pit. The feisty cat made enemies on every front and had frequent clashes.

Soon, however, Mr. Bitey turned his focus on a single foe. He seemed to shift to the prison strategy of taking down the biggest inmate to rule the roost. His opponent? Mitsurugi: A jet-black, mini-panther who outweighed him by five pounds, almost double his size. Mitsurugi is by far the largest of the fur-brigade, and after the benevolent patriarch, VanDuzer, passed away, he picked up the mantle as top cat. Although he wasn't as popular as his predecessor, Mitsurugi became the unchallenged leader of the biggest household clique.

It was all out war. Black vs. Gray. The battle for dominance of the Island of Misfit Cats had begun. Mr. Bitey was a one-cat army, and although Mitsurugi was clearly much larger than his enemy, he's kind of a big baby. It was a tumultuous time. Breakfast, dinner, late nights, it

Mitsurugi vs Mr. Bitey. The Felion Civil War of 2018.

didn't matter—a battle could break out at any time and often did. There were daily stare downs, showdowns, and growling matches. Hunting. Stalking. Ambush attacks. We had a few scuffles where fur went flying as the two cats rolled in a blurry ball of fury, not unlike a cartoon fight. At times Cathy would shake a can of coins like a maraca, sending the opponents dancing back to their corners.

Dive bombs.

Cats shrieking.

Collateral damage.

Claws out, time out.

I began to feel like a prison warden, and to be honest, none of the usual tips worked. Neither Mitsurugi nor Mr. Bitey were going to back down any time soon. There had to be a solution. I just hadn't found it yet. I asked seasoned veteran rescuers for their advice. Despite everything I tried, these two adversaries would mix it up almost daily in a flurry of swatting paws. The cats were stressed. Cathy was completely frustrated with our new, gray hellion. I had to think outside the box to find a solution. Mr. Bitey may have been my problem child, but after all we had been through together, I was not about to give up on him.

I found something they both liked more than anything else: my attention. Mitsurugi has always been attached to me, and Mr. Bitey and

Mr. Bitey lost this round, but he isn't out for the count.

I were forming an equally strong bond. I finally decided, if I wanted to end this civil war with some kind of truce, that I'd have to put myself in the middle. Literally.

"You're crazy!" Cathy exclaimed, after I told her my plan.

"Ya know, there's a fine line because crazy and genius." More often than not, Wifey is right, but I had already made up my mind. "To beat a cat, you have to be crazy like a cat. Meow!"

Cathy rolled her eyes. "And I know which side of the line you're on."

At that point, I'm pretty sure I heard at least one of my cats trying to pass off their derisive laughter as a sneeze, but no one ever fessed up to my suspicion.

"Honey, please," she said, "you're going to get bit again."

"Not if I bite them first." I gave my wife a playful hiss. She was not nearly as amused by this as I was.

My mad scheme was put into action. First, I would start by sitting with Mr. Bitey on the couch and petting him. He would be lulled into relaxation. Then, I would snap my fingers for Mitsurugi—he will almost always accept an invitation for petting. Sitting between them, I would simultaneously give them equal attention. Within a few minutes, I would move slightly, allowing them to see each other. It was a risk. The first time they realized the other was there, they simultaneously hissed, hopped off the couch, and fled in opposite directions. I could have ended up with scratches or even a bite as a result of redirected aggression. The fact that I didn't, in my mind, was at least a mild success.

I did this with them over and over, establishing a routine. There were a few stares, a few growls, but each time I would distract the aggressor by saying his name. When he looked at me, I would reward him, either with a treat or an ear scratch, then I would reward the other one the exact same way. If that didn't work, I would stop the session and not pet either one until we tried it again later. This routine went on for months, but week by week there was progress.

Mitsurugi and Mr. Bitey are still not what I would consider best buds, but they can co-exist relatively peacefully. When I'm on the couch petting one, there's a pretty good chance the other will join in, and they're both happy, getting equal attention. The truce is holding up rather well, and peace has been restored. 🐾

Overstimulation (Petting-Induced Aggression) – Have you ever been worshipping Your Majesty when suddenly they turn to bap the fluff out of you like a smiting from the Almighty? Or maybe they suddenly chomp at your hand like Pac-Man? Overstimulation is the probable cause for this seemingly unprovoked behavior. Like redirected aggression, overstimulation aggression is more of a reaction than a deliberate attack. Even for cats that apparently enjoy petting, the repetitiveness of the action can cause an overload in your Overlord. Consider the following:

- *Rule Out Medical Issues* – As always, a veterinary appointment should be at the top of your list when looking to find the root of a problem. Neurological conditions, skin sensitivity, arthritis (in older cats,) or even a tooth or ear infection can all contribute to petting-induced aggression. No amount of behavior modification will help resolve a health issue. A simple checkup could be just the medicine your cat needs.

- *Negotiate* – Granted, nips and swats from overstimulation can be painful, but they are meant only to serve as a warning. Keep in mind, they are reactions to discomfort or pain. When in service of an Overlord, you will only get what you put in. As is always the case with felions, physical correction will only serve to elicit a negative response. Use counter conditioning by offering a reward for not biting and allowing you to pet.

- *Detective Work* – Cats don't just bite out of nowhere; there's always a trigger and a warning. But Cat Speak can often be subtle. When worshiping Your Majesty, take note of their body language and read what they are trying to tell you. Do they tense up and freeze, or are they completely relaxed during a petting session? Do their ears flatten, does their gaze follow your hand? Lip licking, tail swishing, or the skin twitching on their back can also be a good indication they feel over stimulated and it's time to stop.

- *Follow The Leader* – No matter the situation, the Overlord likes to be in control. While some can't get enough petting, others may simply enjoy your company but not be big on physical affection, especially if they are not the ones to initiate it. Learn to just appreciate your cat's unique personality, and respect their space.

- *Find The Sweet Spot* – Some cats prefer only short strokes during worship sessions. Others prefer chin or ear-scritches instead of body pets. Most felions are not fond of having their paws touched, unless this contact has been normalized from a young age. Stick to the sweet spots you know they enjoy and you'll both have a better time. When in doubt, allow Your Highness to rub against you, self-petting where and when they feel most comfortable.

- *Drain The Battery* – Keeping your cat active is a good way to avoid them becoming frustrated or bored, which can also contribute to petting induced aggression. Before you attempt to pet your Nippy Skippy, drain the battery with interactive play. Not only will you strengthen your bond, a tired, happy kitty will be less apt to bite.

- *Beat The Clock* – Once you can properly read your cat's body language, start timing how long your cat likes to be petted, but always make sure to stop before you reach their tolerance threshold. Allow some time for your cat to reset to default mode before petting again. Over time you can slowly begin to extend worship sessions as Your Majesty becomes more desensitized to your touch. However, you always want to keep one eye on the clock.

CAT TALES: *Pet, Pet, Bite!*

After being pulled from the shelter, Moon spent several weeks in boarding while the rescue tried to find this sassy gal a foster home. I wasn't certain why she had been surrendered to the shelter in the first place, but in hindsight I suspect it was likely due to instances of petting induced aggression. I would later painfully learn of this behavior firsthand.

Eventually, a vacancy opened up at Hotel Mancuso, and Moon found herself there as a VIP. The rescue's director had asked if Cathy and I would foster Moon and work with her on her social skills to make her more adoptable. We had spent the previous summer and much of the fall fostering bottle kittens. As much as I love kittens, they can be a lot of work at times, so I was more than happy to foster an adult cat.

When she first arrived, our newest guest was a bit standoffish. It wasn't until she toddled out of her carrier that I realized Moon was as round as her namesake. When I introduced myself, she offered no greeting and merely began touring her new domain, seeking an appropriate throne.

Moon had a strict hands-off policy. A very independent kitty, she often preferred to spend her hours alone. Despite the five-star service she received, Moon wasn't inclined to tip the help with so much as a head boop. Her excess weight, combined with mild Cerebellar Hypoplasia, made it difficult for Moon to get around. She was too heavy to jump, and even climbing required an Olympian effort that left her mainly relegated to the floor—something she obviously was none too thrilled about. She often waddled around the house like a grumpy Muppet.

While not a fan of affection, Moon did engage in play. She saw herself as a mighty huntress and was eager to prove her prowess against the elusive red dot. With a rigorous play schedule and portion control, her excess pounds melted over the months to follow. Soon she was able to flounce, pounce, and even climb to the window seats with little effort. Equally as important, Cathy and I were bonding with her over our daily play sessions. We were permitted to briefly pat her head as a reward. Once she was able to climb up onto the couch by herself, Moon began sitting next to me more often.

She had seen how much our other cats enjoyed human contact and eventually decided she wanted in on some snuggles and petting. She was a queen, after all, and deserved proper worship. She rubbed her cheek on my hand.

"Hey, good girl," I said, offering the usual small pat on her head.

The little pat wasn't enough. She wanted more and nuzzled my hand again.

Having always been a faithful servant, of course I was more than happy to oblige. "I knew you'd come around."

Moon had made a lot of progress since she checking in at Hotel Mancuso. Although still a bit of a chonky gal, she was no longer bursting out of her tuxedo. As much as she disliked other felions, she had reached a truce with them. And now, she was letting me pet— no, wait . . . she was biting me!

It was sudden and unexpected. One second she was loving my worship, the next she was snapping her teeth. It was a warning bite; her teeth didn't break the skin. But I'm not going lie and tell you it didn't hurt. On a bite scale of 1-10, it rated about 3 curse words, just slightly less than stepping on a Lego.

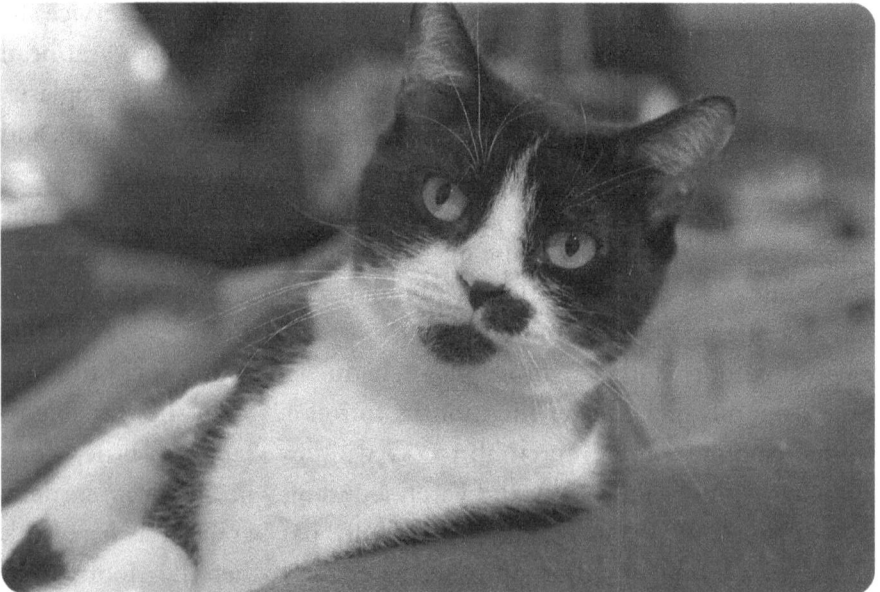

Moon: "Feeling cute. Pet me, I may bite your hand. IDK."

Moon and I looked at each other with shock.

"Hey now. That was rude."

She hissed and flopped off the couch.

"Why are you trying to play me?" I called after her as she stormed out of the room.

That was the first time it happened, but it certainly wouldn't be the last. I wasn't the only victim, either. Moon had nipped or swiped at Cathy on several occasions as well. It was a frustrating time as she was constantly sending off mixed signals. Moon would affectionately fall into me, seeking attention, but any length of petting sent her circuitry into overload. She just couldn't handle it. Pet, pet, bite. Before long Cathy and I had identified her confusing reactions as an overstimulation issue.

Once we figured out the underlying problem, we could focus on a solution. For Moon, it was all about time. Using a stopwatch, I learned that her absolute tolerance for human contact was only about twenty seconds, after which the teeth and claws came out. Pet, pet, bap!

I started with petting Moon for only twenty seconds at a time, making sure never to reach her threshold and always leave her wanting more. I would wait at least an hour before starting again. Keeping a close watch on her body language, I would gradually extend petting sessions by a few seconds as often as I could. Pet, pet, pet . . . pet, Bap! In hindsight, I realize I should have used gloves, as sometimes her claws left my hand looking like an out-of-control game of Tic Tac Toe. Within six weeks, we were almost up to one-minute intervals. Within six months, we were able to extend petting sessions by an additional two minutes.

The solution was all about time, and I don't just mean beating the clock. Not only did I have to make sure I set time aside to work on Moon's desensitization daily, but I also had to allow her the time to progress at her own rate. Granted, it was a slow process, but she wasn't going anywhere any time soon. As it turned out, after a failed adoption (through no fault of her own) Moon applied for permanent residency at The Island of Misfit Cats. Now, years later, I can pet her as much as she wants without worrying about her becoming over stimulated. Our once plumpy-grumpy independent Moon has since become a slender snuggler. 🐾

THE PROBLEM: OVERCOMING FEAR/ANXIETY

Heavy is the head that wears the crown. An anxious Overlord appears frequently stressed and afraid for no reason. But there is always a reason; it's just not always obvious. Of course, not knowing the personal history of their life before becoming such a big part of yours can make finding the trigger, and thus the solution, a bit more challenging. Anxiety could have developed from a traumatic experience, lack of proper socialization, or a history of abuse or neglect. Untreated anxiety won't get better without intervention and will likely become worse over time, with undesirable behaviors becoming more pronounced, even leading to fear based aggression.

Anxiety At Home – No two cats are exactly alike. What triggers anxiety in one cat may not have any effect on another. Determining the cause of your felion's fear can be challenging. You'll need to closely observe Your Majesty to determine the source for their fearful behavior. It may take some sleuthing to draw a conclusion, but you'll make Sherlock Holmes proud when you finally solve this mystery. Some common triggers are:

- A particular person
- A stranger
- Another pet
- A child
- Loud noises
- A particular smell or scent
- An object
- A crate/carrier

Once you know what is spooking Your Highness, you'll better be able to manage those fears by controlling exposure to the trigger. And once you have a handle on trigger avoidance, you can address the underlying problem through gradual desensitization and counterconditioning. The strategy is to first reduce fear of the trigger and eventually turn that fear into a positive association. Trust me, it's easier said than done, but well worth the effort to help Your Majesty become a truly fearless Ruler.

In order to desensitize your felion, you'll need to reintroduce the source of their anxiety, but do so in such a way that they're not totally freaked out. Determine what distance Your Majesty can be from the trigger without responding fearfully. That's your starting point. Next, what is your Overlord's favorite treat? That's your motivator. Feed your cat special treats in the presence of the person, pet, object, or sound while they remain at the safe starting distance. If your Overlord is unimpressed with the offered indulgence, you may need to up your game. Try offering bits of boiled chicken, spoons of tuna, or even small shreds of turkey meat. These sessions should be limited in time but should occur daily, so they become an anticipated part of the royal routine. Over the course of weeks, slowly move the source of anxiety closer as you continue to praise Your Majesty's bravery and offer those sweet, yummy treats. If the trigger is a sound, incrementally increase the volume on a weekly basis. It is essential that your cat shows no signs of fear or stress before you progress further. Moving too fast, too soon is bound to cause a negative reaction and can lead to an unnecessary backslide. Pay close attention to their behavior and body language for emotional cues. Heed the Stop Signs. If at any time during this process your cat shows fearful behavior, you will need to go back a step or even start over, but think of it only as a temporary setback. You're in this for the long game. Overcoming fear or anxiety is a slow process, but patience and persistence will win out in the end.

If the Overlord has an extreme fear or anxiety that you are unable to manage, you should consider intervention from a professional animal behavior specialist.

Separation Anxiety – Separation anxiety is when the Overlord becomes stressed when they are left alone in the kingdom, or in extreme cases, when you're out of sight. This condition is especially prevalent among cats with a history of abandonment or who have been repeatedly exiled and rehomed, passed from one servant to the next. An Overlord may become so afraid of losing their castle and your fealty that they begin acting anxious when they sense you're about to leave. In their distraught state, they may issue protest proclamations or exhibit some unwanted or worrisome behaviors, such as the following:

- Urinating/defecating outside the litter box (often on their servant's bed)
- Destroying/chewing things

- Hyper-attachment: seeking constant contact
- Excessive vocalization
- Constant pacing
- Excessive sleeping

- Hunger strike
- Overeating
- Lack of self-grooming
- Obsessive grooming

No servant wants their Overlord to suffer from separation anxiety, nor can we spend twenty-four hours a day worshiping The Crown, no matter how tempting that may be. Unfortunately, non-felion related obligations must be fulfilled. Let's look at some ways to normalize your temporary absence from the kingdom so it's less of a royal crisis:

- *Provide Enrichment Activities* – There are endless options for enrichment activities to keep Your Majesty busy during your absence from the castle. Music can be comforting, especially those tunes I mentioned earlier—the ones specifically designed for felions. The familiar sound of human speech on talk radio may soothe the Overlord. Some TV content and online videos are designed explicitly for felion viewing pleasure, and you can even purchase monitoring systems that allow you to toss treats and praise them remotely.

  You can also use puzzle feeders, which are toys the Overlord has to manipulate to release the food inside. Giving one to your cat before you start getting ready to leave can keep them busy, so they aren't worried about what you are doing. Working (hunting) for their food is mentally stimulating for cats. When they are left alone, such activities will keep their focus off missing you.

  Consider using an arsenal of toys designed for self-play to keep the Overlord occupied while you're out on non-felion related business. Toys should be rotated every few days and hidden when not in use in order to keep Your Highness from becoming bored with them.

- *Encourage Independence* – Encourage your cat to be independent. They should be used to spending some time away from you as a part of their usual routine. You may need to start with small increments and gradually increase your time apart. Praise them and give them treats when they choose to spend time across the room or out of sight.

- *The Silent Goodbye* – Keep your departures and returns home very low-key. This helps your cat feel like it's not a big deal when you leave the castle. Avoid making any kind of fuss over your felion ruler before exiting. Upon reentrance, resist the urge to immediately smother Your Highness with worship. Use a more cordial greeting and wait a while before a snuggle fest.

- *Another Cat* – It can be lonely at the top. Some Overlords benefit from having another felion in the castle to keep them company when you're not around. Even an emotional support animal can use emotional support.

THE PROBLEM: CAT CARRIER DRAMA

In Cat World, traveling outside the castle walls into the Great Backyard beyond is a rite of passage for all who sit upon the throne. The Great Backyard is filled with endless miles of dangerous wilderness. The only way for Your Majesty to safely traverse the perils of their expedition is to travel inside a carrier. Whether fulfilling medical obligations or escaping from the kingdom during an emergency, cat carriers are a necessity in every castle. Being enthusiasts of hidey-holes, one would think that felions would appreciate a portable cat cave. However, when it comes to enclosed spaces your cat didn't volunteer for, this mode of conveyance can feel more like a prison cell.

Needless to say, some felions hate their carriers. If the Overlord only equates the cat carrier with vet visits, the cat will instantly vanish as soon as you get out the carrier. It's like the world's most annoying magic trick. Negative association with a travel carrier will cause stress, anxiety, and all sorts of drama. They can suffer from upset stomachs or motion sickness, and then they're trapped inside with their own mess. Some cats may even experience air rage and become unruly passengers.

From Your Majesty's point of view, anxiety over carriers is quite understandable. They are an unnatural mode of transportation. The Celestial Meow gave felions four legs for a reason, and traveling on foot is by far their preferred method. Inside the carrier, your kitty has no control and no escape.

All this makes getting the Overlord into a carrier a royal pain, but it doesn't have to be.

Types of Carriers – Unless you plan to take the Overlord everywhere you go; a carrier won't need to be used very much. There are many designs and styles on the market for your cat's travel needs. While shopping for kitty's new ride, consider comfort, safety, and convenience.

- *Cardboard Carrier* – Not recommended as a permanent mode of conveyance, but cardboard carriers are better than nothing in a pinch. Most often, these transport boxes are included when you take home an Overlord from shelters or adoption centers. Of course, I've had to use them on occasion, but only if there was no alternative. Cardboard is absorbent, so urine, rain, or spilled liquids will greatly weaken structural integrity. And properly securing the box can be tricky, trust me, I've had a rescue kitty spring out like a Jack in the Box at the vet's office. Some cats will even chew through the sides. During a rescue transport of several cats from Staten Island to Barnegat, New Jersey, one of the felions made short work of her cardboard carrier. Within minutes of leaving the shelter, she chewed a hole in the side of the box and took refuge under the backseat before I made it over the Outerbridge.

- *Soft-sided Carrier* – Cats often find soft carriers cozy because of their flexible material and padding. Long shoulder straps make them easy to carry, too. Soft carriers are less bulky than hard shells, but they also happen to be less sturdy. An anxious cat can damage or tear holes in the mesh. The fabric is absorbent, which makes it more difficult to clean than its plastic counterpart, so not the best choice if kitty gets motion sickness or has an accident. Another potential con of soft carriers is that they close with zippers, snaps, or Velcro, so if you're not careful, a clever felion escape artist could pull a Houdini.

- *Backpack* – Specially designed pet backpacks are gaining popularity among felion chauffeurs. Similar to a soft carrier, the backpack's biggest advantage is that it allows you to carry Your Highness around hands free. However, depending on design, backpacks with a large viewing window can cause a cat to feel exposed and anxious.

- *Hard Shell Carrier* – Solid, dependable, and more durable than the above carriers, these are constructed of hard plastic, which also make them much easier to clean and disinfect. One possible con to hard shell carriers is that a single door only allows a front access point for your cat. If you have a fearful cat that resists going into the carrier, getting them inside could pose a challenge. Forcing a reluctant monarch through the front door could be a traumatizing experience for you both.

- *Top Loader* – Preferred by the staff of Hotel Mancuso, this is an upgrade of the hard shell carrier, with an extra door on the top for lowering a reluctant passenger inside with minimal stress. The added expense is worth the peace of mind.

Size Does Matter – At least when it comes to cat carriers, bigger is always preferable. When inside the carrier, the Overlord should be able to stand, sit, and turn around. Anything less is too small and will be uncomfortable, especially during long trips. At the same time, you don't want to use a carrier so large that Your Highness will slide around like a hockey puck during car rides; this in and of itself can cause injuries, nausea, and avoidable distress. When selecting a carrier for your kitten, choose one you think will be appropriate for their adult size.

Admit One – Unless they are kittens, all Overlords should be transported in their own separate carriers. Even if your cats usually get along, each will tolerate the stress of traveling differently. Being confined in a small space together will be unpleasant at best. At worst it could lead to a cage match, resulting in serious injury.

Pimp My Ride – Travel shouldn't feel like a prisoner transfer. The key is getting Your Majesty to claim the carrier, or at the very least, not be anxious about it. Instead of keeping it in the closet under the "open only in case emergency" glass, make the carrier a staple of your Overlord's kingdom. Pimp that ride; turn it into a limo. Leave the carrier open with comfortable bedding inside. Add their favorite toy or some catnip for enticement. Don't try to force Your Highness inside. Don't even make a big deal of it to your cat—they'll make their own decision, thank you very much. Eventually, curiosity is bound to demand an investigation of this offering. Feed your cat treats while they're inside. You can even utilize the carrier as the dining hall for royal feasts. In time, your finicky felion will develop a positive association with the carrier, and like everything else, own it. The task of cat-wrangling will be so much easier when it's time for a visit to the "V-E-T." This will save your kitty from added stress and also save your arm from protest scratches.

Royal Travel Academy – Once the Overlord is comfortable in their carrier, enroll them in the Royal Travel Academy. Through this elite training course your monarch will earn their wings and rule the sky.

- *Carry On* – Now Boarding, Zone One Passengers. Daily onboarding exercises will help your felion get used to being escorted into the carrier by a flight attendant. As a reward, have a yummy treat waiting for your felion inside the cabin.
- *Latch the Hatch* – Once your cat has mastered the embarking process, you can begin securing the door. Make sure to keep the experience as positive as possible for your cat by sprinkling some yummy treats or catnip in the carrier. Gradually extend the time the door remains shut. Do not isolate Your Majesty while they're in the carrier; your captain's voice and flight attendance will help control the cabin pressure.
- *Flight Simulator* – Practice lift off and landing drills. First, perform a safety inspection, making sure the latches are locked, the handle is sturdy, and the passenger is secure. Slowly pick the carrier up and put it back down. Carry it around the house for short flights in controlled airspace. For a stress-free flight, avoid

turbulence, and be mindful of the pitch and yaw during all flight exercises.

- *The Right Stuff* – There's no set time limit for Your Majesty to pass this travel program. Moderate your expectations. Each cat will progress at their own pace. Take the time to tailor the training course to best suit your cat's tolerance. Practice makes perfect, so keep doing all the right stuff.

First Class Ticket – Even if your Overlord is comfortable within the confines of the mobile cat cave, expeditions beyond the castle walls are still a stressful proposition. In order to help them enjoy the ride, provide the comforts of home. Keeping familiar scents inside will help to comfort your Overlord. You can even spray the bedding and carrier with a pheromone spray about thirty minutes before departure. A favorite toy could keep kitty distracted during the trip. Unless your cat is prone to a nervous stomach, consider an in-flight snack. Cover the carrier with a sheet or towel. Not only will your felion feel safer at the vet's office surrounded by strange animals, loud noises and bright lights, but a covered carrier can reduce motion sickness.

Catch The Red Eye – Some cats will always hate carriers, no matter what you do. This is especially true if they have trauma associated with carriers or travel in general. If your cat becomes overly stressed, talk to your veterinarian about prescribing anti-anxiety medication for travel. Depending on their tolerance, your felion may just need to take the edge off. It's better for the Overlord to sleep for the long haul than to be in distress during the trip. Good night, safe flight.

THE PROBLEM: THE HISS LIST

In general, Overlords find strangers tromping about their castle distressing, and even more so if one has overstayed their unwelcome. If you have a new love interest in your life, they may find themselves Enemy Number One on the royal hiss list. Your Majesty has sensed a change in the status quo, and the trespasser is upsetting the order and harmony of palace life. Even the sweetest kitty in all of Catdom can be affected by jealousy and start hissing all over your budding relationship. They view the trespasser as a time thief, hogging your attention and affection, shifting the balance of power. The Overlord may fear that their loyal servant is suffering from a crisis of faith or losing confidence that they will retain the throne.

Jealousy is born of insecurity and will present itself in different ways as the Overlord sends out proclamations of protest. Undesirable behaviors may occur, such as urinating or defecating outside of the litter box, perhaps even as a display of dominance on your partners belongings, or yours. A passive-aggressive Overlord may deny you affection or even their very presence by going into a self-imposed isolation. Possessive of their kingdom, a cat may escalate hostilities, hissing, swatting, or attacking in an effort to drive the outsider from the castle.

Thankfully, there are ways to improve the relationship between your partner and Your Highness.

Penitence and Reconciliation – Submission to an Overlord is more than just a life of humble servitude. It is a sacred union between human and felion. It's very likely that your new relationship has caused you to neglect proper worship. Reconciliation is a sacrament of healing and making peace with your felion. Recommitting to regular one-on-one time with Your Highness will help reduce feelings of jealousy and put The Crown at ease.

Spread The Gospel – Not everyone is a felion acolyte . . . yet. As a devout disciple, you have an obligation to spread the gospel. If your partner is a heathen, preach the way of the Meow. Education is the key to changing perception. Teach him or her how to decode felion body language and the importance of faithful service. More specifically, address the unique rules and laws that govern the kingdom.

Anointing of the Hissed – The felion ruler has clearly stated their disapproval of your new love interest in thought and deed. Your hisser can begin to feel more comfortable about them after a transference of scent to the hissee. As mentioned, Overlords deposit their distinctive fragrance through the blessing of head and cheek bumps; they're marking these people or objects with a pheromone that signals familiarity, security, and ownership. Present a soft cloth to your felion and collect ample blessings, then spread their scent onto your partner's belongings. Some may think anointment is an attempt to hoodwink the Overlord. However, the Great Ones are wise and not easily fooled. Anointing is meant merely as appeasement, for no aroma is more pleasing to their noses. The less Your Majesty is stressed by strange smells, the greater the chance for a change of heart.

Conversion Inversion – We all share a desire for our monarchs and partners to become BFFs, but we must not try to force a bond between them. Many servants try too hard to get the Overlord to like their sweetheart by forcing interaction, like placing the cat on his or her lap. Rookie Mistake. Even if you have anointed the person with pheromones, it is not the same as having your cat's approval. Often these bold attempts at converting kitty produce the opposite effect. It's a sure way to end up on the hiss list—the Overlord needs time to consider the outsider's petition for acceptance, and it's not looking good at the moment. Fortunately, this type of conversion inversion is reversible, and the first step is to always provide your felion with a choice. There are subtler and much more effective ways to influence their opinion.

Communal Space – Even when the Overlord is displeased with your choice of company, they still like to be around you, if only for perfunctory supervision. Don't chase your cat out of the room and close the door, as that can sow even more resentment. Instead, allow Your Majesty to come and go as they please. Permit them to conduct inspections without disruption. Make sure there are perches and hidey-holes in every room so your cat can choose a spot where they feel most comfortable in the presence of your significant other as they'll need time and space to sort their emotions. If possible, always keep a wide path clear where the cat can exit the room or get to their sandcastle without having to walk past the outsider. Your Highness may or may not choose to come out from hiding, but at least they won't be locked out.

Good Graces – One way for your partner to gain the Overlord's favor is through service. Step back from your role as head servant and allow your partner to take over daily chores. Dutifully serving royal feasts and favorite treats, as well as maintaining the cleanliness of the sandcastle, can go a long way toward their removal from the hiss list. Keep in mind, your partner should not attempt to solicit gratitude but always be open to inspection or worship when called upon.

The Same Team – To help the Overlord from feeling sidelined, your significant other can engage in playtime. These activities are a fun way to facilitate bonding. Not only will your cat burn off excess energy, but they will also be mentally stimulated, both of which will greatly improve their mood. Tired and satisfied, kitty can rest easy knowing your partner is on the same team.

Three's Company – It's unacceptable for Your Highness to be the lowest point in a love triangle. Not only is it important for each of you to spend time with your cat individually, but spending time together in cat worship will elevate Your Majesty and connect the dots.

Excommunication – If you find that your partner is unwilling to make the effort at reconciliation, there is little hope of restoring order. There will be a strain on both of your relationships. A thick cloud of unhappiness will settle over the kingdom. As tension rises and the duo battle for your heart, you may be given an ultimatum: Choose me, or the cat! In that case, consider that fact that the Overlord was right about them all along. If you ask me, the choice is easy—banish the usurper. The Celestial Meow dictates that true love is also unconditionally loving your partner's cat.

THE PROBLEM: LATE NIGHT KITTY PARTY

If your Overlord is a night owl, their late night exploits can be disruptive to your sleep. They will try to engage you in conversation, zip around like their tail is on fire, and even pounce on you for attention. Maybe you shut them out of your room, but they're on the other side of the door throwing a late night pity party. Felion renditions of heartbreak songs ring out in the dark. Nails scratch incessantly at the bedroom door, demanding attention. All with no regard for HR's promise to write you up the next time you're late. The Great Ones don't work; that's your job. They have no idea about your side gig that actually fills the castle's coffers, and even if they did, the Overlord wouldn't care. Such things are beneath them. "A cat has got to be a cat," they would tell you. "It's nothing to lose sleep over."

The likely reason your kitty is being a creeper is they are not burning enough energy during the day. If you're out or at work, they may choose to snooze the day away, waiting for your return. So, make sure to satisfy those kitty urges and reset your felion alarm clock.

No Doze – If you are at home during the day and find your sleeping beauty catching a cat-nap, gently wake them up for some activity. The less they sleep during the day, the longer they will rest at night. If you work all day, find ways to keep your cat's mind and body active during your shift.

- Hide treats around the house for them to hunt.
- Make sure they have a stimulating window view.
- Find some cat-friendly programs of birds or squirrels or fish.
- Have plenty of toys that involve self-play.
- Use a Puzzle Feeder.
- Strategically place cardboard boxes and paper bags for your cat to "discover" while exploring the kingdom.

The Runaround – Perhaps your Overlord had one too many catnaps throughout the day, and now that it is your bedtime, they are full of pep and vigor. Help your gremlin burn off excess energy by engaging them in a rigorous play session. Give them the runaround. Make your furry little hunter chase their prize, much in same the way their African cousins hunt down prey in the wild. Now that it's out of their system, you'll both sleep better.

Snack Attack – Depending how early dinner is served, the Overlord may be a bit hungry come bedtime. If you have ever had a hankering for a late night nosh, I'm sure you can empathize. Before you retire from your official duties for the evening, try a small feeding. With a full belly, the royal appetite should be satisfied until breakfast. Additionally, if your famished felion wakes you up at 2:00 am all the time, setting an automatic feeder to dispense a few treats may quell that late night snack attack and help you get a full night's rest.

No Play Zone – Keeping cat toys out of your bedroom will discourage late night playtime. Designate a play area for your midnight rambler as far away from your bedroom as possible to limit sleep interruptions. If the kingdom is small, simply put any cat toys away, particularly the noisy ones.

Winding Down – Allow at least 15-20 minutes of preparation before bedtime. Combine these tips to establish a bedtime routine. For example, after an interactive play session, pick up cat toys and put them away, or move them to an approved play zone, then provide kitty with bedtime snack. Allow the Overlord to supervise your chores as you go about getting ready to turn in. The key to building a routine is consistency and repetition. Felions have very accurate internal clocks, so be sure to turn out the lights at the same time each night. Following a nightly ritual is a great way for a Your Highness to end the day.

Off The Clock – I realize that as mere humans we serve at the pleasure of the Overlord, but a lack of proper sleep can impact quality of service. Once you're in bed, consider yourself off the clock. Ignore your felion's attention-seeking behaviors, no matter how cute or annoying, otherwise you are only allowing your cat set to establish their own nightly routine.

Having personally dealt with many of these issues firsthand over the last nine years, I know how challenging they can be. On more than one occasion someone has said to me, "You must be a cat whisperer." I'm not. Like you, I'm merely a humble felion servant. The only true attribution for my successes in breaking bad behaviors is never giving up.

FREQUENTLY ASKED QUESTIONS

"IN NINE LIFETIMES, YOU'LL NEVER KNOW AS MUCH ABOUT
YOUR CAT AS YOUR CAT KNOWS ABOUT YOU."

—MICHEL DE MONTAIGNE

WHY IS DECLAWING MY CAT A BAD IDEA?

My first cat, Sunny-Girl, was already declawed when she came to rule our little castle. As I mentioned, I didn't know diddly squat about cats back then, so at the time I thought declawing was a great solution to having claw marks on all my furniture. But that was before I learned the harsh truth about the procedure. And worse, I've seen grotesque post-surgery photos. The medical term for declawing is called an onychectomy, but no matter how you say it, it's an absolutely terrible idea. Declawing a cat isn't simply removing the nails as I had once thought; it involves amputation of the top joint of each toe. That's ten separate amputations, eighteen if all four paws are declawed. As Dr. Singh told me, for us humans it would be the equivalent of having the last knuckles of each of our fingers severed. OUCH! It sounds more like maiming to me. To put it frankly, I now find the procedure cruel and wholly unnecessary. In fact, declawing is banned in many countries around the world as it is deemed an act of animal cruelty. Although the practice is still legal in much of the United States, it is beginning to fall out of favor. New York became the first state to ban declawing in 2019 and Maryland followed suit in 2022.

Declawing is a painful surgery, putting Your Majesty at risk of developing an infection or lameness in their paws as well as other consequences that can have a permanent negative impact on their quality of life. Pain may not be relegated to only the paws; since the absence of claws will change the way they walk, declawed cats can also suffer from back pain.

This surgery may seem like an easy solution to a scratching issue, but it's more likely to cause different problems. True, you will no longer have to worry about claw marks on your couch, but declawing can lead your cat to no longer use the litter box. Since cats tend to scratch at the litter and the sides of the box, the pain from doing so can translate into a negative association with their litter box. A declawed cat is more apt to bite as they no longer have the option of using their claws as defense. Not to mention some felions have reportedly suffered a change in personality after the surgery, as the endless discomfort can make them more aggressive. In fact, these potential secondary problems—not the scratching up of personal property—are the primary cause of owners surrendering their cats to shelters. Do not declaw your cat.

SHOULD I LET MY CAT OUTSIDE?

Some humans would argue that allowing a cat outdoors gives them a better quality of life, and most cats would likely agree. After all, that is how their ancestors and ours co-existed for centuries. Felions could enter and exit the castle at their leisure. They could explore, hunt, claw trees, and enjoy all the nature the Great Backyard has to offer. However, we've slowly realized that relegating The Crown to an indoor-only rule was for their own protection. As humble servants, it is our sworn duty to put our Overlord's health and safety above all else, both of which were at risk any time they ventured into the wilderness beyond our doors.

Your Majesty should never be allowed outside of the castle unsupervised. What many would-be servants may not realize is that doing so puts their Overlord's health and life at risk. Like declawing, this in an outdated practice that can have an adverse impact on your felion's well-being and shorten their reign. Here's a list of what a Your Majesty is avoiding by being restricted to the castle walls:

- Contracting contagious diseases such as feline leukemia (FeLV), feline immunodeficiency virus (FIV), and if kitty isn't up to date on vaccinations: rabies.
- Becoming infected with parasites such as fleas, ticks, ringworm, roundworm, giardia, and ear mites, just to name a few.
- Catching viral, fungal, and bacterial infections.
- Death by motor vehicle.
- Causing a diplomatic crisis, i.e. eliminating on your neighbor's property.
- Abuse from (sub)human scumbags.
- Injuries from fights with other felions.
- Accidental poisoning from ingesting toxins.
- Being attacked by dogs or other wild animals, such as coyotes, hawks and raccoons.
- Getting stuck in a tree or on top of a pole.
- Freezing to death in the winter.
- Dying of heatstroke in the summer.
- Getting lost forever.

Keeping all this in mind, there is still a way for Your Majesty to safely enjoy the Great Backyard. Some servants escort their Overlord on outdoor adventures. When done correctly, outdoor treks will help keep your felion active and mentally stimulated, as well as serving as a great bonding experiences. As always, safety is paramount. First, you'll need to ensure that Your Majesty is up to date on all their vaccinations, and you'll likely want to speak to your vet about using preventives like flea and tick repellent and dewormer. Once that is taken care of, you can get a leash and a special harness designed for felions. Always make sure it fits snug; a loose or unsecured harness could allow them to pull a Houdini. The last thing you want is for your escape artist to disappear in the Great Backyard.

Your Majesty will probably need some time to get used to wearing a harness and being attached to you by a leash. Most likely they'll hate it and try to wriggle out. Try out the gear indoors before venturing outside, and allow them to adapt to wearing it. Start with a few minutes touring the castle and build up gradually over time. Use reinforcement like treats to create a positive association with wearing the harness. Convince the

Overlord that being tethered to you is strictly for your protection; they will begrudgingly accept the responsibility. This process could take days or weeks, so be patient. When Your Highness is comfortable walking around the castle with you, it's time to brave the outdoors. In the beginning it's a good idea to keep the trips short and limited to your own property, or somewhere in close proximity. If Your Majesty is uncomfortable or afraid, don't force them to stay outside.

Once you manage to get your cat to safely enjoy the outer rim of their domain, they're ready to conquer the unknown of the Great Backyard with you at their side. Always remember to bring food, water, and travel bowls on your adventures. Never pull or drag a monarch while on a walk, try to gently guide them instead. Use due diligence to make sure to avoid strange animals as you never know how any animal will behave towards The Crown and vice versa. Learn to read your cat's body language. If they get tired or afraid, pick them up and carry them back to the kingdom. After any excursion, make sure to thoroughly check your cat for ticks.

WHY SHOULD I SPAY/NEUTER MY CAT?

Spay/neutering your cat is the responsible thing to do. Not only is it integral to controlling overpopulation by eliminating litters of unwanted kittens, but there are also myriad health benefits for Your Majesty. Spayed and neutered cats have healthier, longer, and happier reigns than intact cats. Spaying a queen helps prevent uterine infections, uterine cancers, and mammary cancer. Snipping the royal jewels from a king eliminates the possibility of testicular cancer and lowers the risk of future prostate problems.

Unneutered felions are more likely to spray (mark their territory) in the house or act aggressively when they pick up the scent of a female in heat. And with a sense of smell fourteen times that of humans, he can pick up that scent from up to two miles away. On the other hand, "Fixed" cats are generally more relaxed. A neutered male will no longer have a sex drive and be much less likely to escape the castle in search of a one-night stand.

An unaltered queen can lure outdoor suitors to the castle during her heat cycle. To attract a mate, females will spray pheromone-laden urine and commence yowling (really loud) during their heat cycles, which can last for several months. The last thing you want is a bunch of horny Toms showing up at the palace. This could result in trial by combat on your property, spraying on your windows and doors, upsetting Your Majesty, and becoming an all-around nuisance. Whether you have an unaltered male or female, both sexes can become stressed and make life unpleasant during mating season. You and your felion will be much happier once they are spay/neutered.

Overlords and catlings from rescues and shelters are typically spay/neutered prior to their coronation. There may be occasional exceptions that preclude a felion from getting altered, such as medical conditions or advanced age. Otherwise, there's no good excuse not to have them spay/neutered.

Having been involved with rescue for years, and having worked at the Staten Island shelter, I've heard my share of lame and ignorant excuses from both potential adopters as well as cat guardians for not wanting to alter their pets. I'm sure if you speak with other rescuers, you will hear similar laughable and cringe-worthy accounts. Please don't be one of these people:

- A woman looking to surrender a litter of four-month-old kittens: "No, I didn't have my cat spayed. I wanted my daughter to witness the miracle of birth at least once." *Yeah, okay. Say that when she's a sixteen-year-old teen mom. Maybe you should teach her how to be a responsible pet owner instead.*

- Some jerk looking to rehome his cat due to urine spraying: "What? No, I didn't cut off his jewels; he won't be a male no more. He don't go outside anyway." *If you don't want to solve the problem, you're part of the problem.*

- A woman only interested in adopting unaltered females: "What do you mean you don't adopt out un-spayed cats? It's not fair to deprive them of their right to reproduce. I support PETA." I suspected this person of being a "kitten-flipper"—a backyard breeder looking to make a few bucks selling kittens. *No cat for you, go get a job!*

- Too many people: "It's too expensive." There are low-cost clinics; ask your veterinarian, local shelter or a rescue for advice and options.

WHAT EXPENSES SHOULD I EXPECT?

Initial costs will vary depending on where you and how you sign up for service. Obviously, rescues and shelters are much cheaper than getting your cat from a breeder. If you take in a stray cat or "free" kitten born in someone's home, you'll likely need to cover all the initial vet costs on your own, including spay/neuter, vaccinations, and deworming treatment.

Realistically, the admission fee into Cat World could easily run a few hundred dollars. Costs include the adoption fee and price of kingdom essentials. If you adopt from a shelter or rescue, your cat should already be altered, current on vaccinations, and have received parasitic treatments. I'd still advise a vet checkup within the first week or so after you bring them home.

"According to the ASPCA, you can plan to spend around $634 annually on your cat. This breaks down to around fifty-three dollars a month."[21] Keep in mind that this amount doesn't consider any renter's fee that may be included as part of a landlord's pet policy on your lease. Nor does it include the cost of cat-sitting or a boarding facility, should you need these services. It's a small price to pay for the honor of being owned by a cat.

When serving an Overlord, you should always have a little coin set aside in the coffers for unexpected emergencies. Keep in mind that as cats age, they often develop health issues that require ongoing treatments like medicines and/or a shift to a prescription diet. As years pass, the monthly cost of keeping Your Majesty happy and healthy will eventually see an increase. Today, more and more loyal servants are opting to get pet insurance. The cost and coverage will depend on the type of plan you choose, but it's an option worth looking into.

SHOULD I SEE A VET IF MY CAT IS NOT SICK?

You should absolutely, positively establish a relationship with a veterinarian. Ideally, Your Highness should go in for a wellness check at least once a year, even if they appear healthy and normal. Remember, Overlords are masterful at concealing health issues. This is a survival instinct carried over from the wild. Ever stoic, by the time you detect that your cat is sick, their health problems could be much worse than they let on. Annual check-ups can help you get a jump on preventing minor medical issues from becoming major problems.

WHAT SHOULD I DO IF MY CAT GETS LOST?

Your Majesty has gone missing, and you're living every servant's nightmare. On numerous occasions, I've had to help distraught felion fosters and cat servants in the community with search and rescue efforts. My first piece of advice: try not to panic. Easier said than done, I realize, but keeping a cool head and following a plan of action can make all the difference in the Overlord's safe return.

Examine the facts. Upon escape, indoor-only cats do not stray far from the castle. In an unfamiliar environment, the Overlord will revert to extreme caution as a means of self-preservation. Typically, they will seek out the first hiding spot they can find. This means they will likely remain within a radius of approximately 100 yards in any direction, narrowing your search grid for the first few days or weeks following their disappearance.

Search and recovery becomes a high stakes game of Hide-n-Seek, so you'll need to collect the facts, formulate a strategy, and recruit assistance. The sooner you can put the elements of your plan into action, the higher your chances of a happy reunion.

- Investigate for any evidence of an escape. Was a door left ajar? Is there a gaping hole in the window screen? When was the last time anyone came or went from the castle?
- Divide and conquer. If there is more than one servant, allocate one to search the outside perimeter and another to go on a safari hunt in the castle.
- Conduct a thorough search of the kingdom from top to bottom. Remember, cats are champions at hiding, so leave no throne unturned. Think of all the places you would never expect to find Your Majesty, and look there. If you think a cat could never fit in a particular space, check it anyway. Outside, search your garage, your yard, and your immediate property. Look in bushes, up in trees, or anywhere that can and can't fit a felion.

- Try to lure your missing monarch back to the castle. Cats rely on their sense of smell more than eyesight, so open your windows to get the scent of "home" wafting outdoors. Remind them of you; put a worn shirt or a familiar blanket—something that will have your scent—on your front stoop. Place their litter box on your porch or by your door. Appeal to their appetite by placing warm, smelly food, especially if they have a favorite. Try sardines, tuna, or fried chicken. (Keep it warm so the smell stays potent.)

- Expand your search grid of the Great Backyard. Grab a carrier and go on foot patrol through the neighborhood. Look under parked cars. In bushes and trees. In driveways, behind trashcans. Under porches. Request permission from the neighbors to search their backyards. Make sure you leave a photo of your cat and your contact information should there be any sightings. If you have a very social cat, they may go up to your neighbors looking for food or affection. One of my former foster cats slipped out of his new castle two days after adoption. Thankfully the big, friendly felion showed up on a doorstep several houses away a few hours later.

- If you go out to look during the day, also be sure to go out and search again in the evening, when cats become more active under the cloak of darkness. Use a flashlight to spot their reflective eyes.

- Bring a bag of treats or food, or a favorite jingle toy, anything that usually makes your cat come running over to you.

- Form a search party to cover more ground. Advise your posse not to try to chase or catch the escapee. They could scare your cat out of the area. No one should attempt to approach the Overlord. Instead, they will need to call you for backup and wait at a distance, keeping a watchful eye on the felion.

- Post "Lost Cat" flyers in your neighborhood and local businesses with your contact information and a good photo of Your Highness. Be sure to list any unique markings or features that may be not visible in the photo. For example, "last seen wearing a pink collar" or "has six toes on his rear paws."

- Check with your local shelter daily to see if any cats that fit the description of Your Majesty have recently been brought in to the facility. Remember, the person answering the phone may not even be aware that your cat was brought in unless they were at the intake desk, so politely ask them to double-check. Visit frequently, and leave photos or flyers with your contact information.

- Check with nearby vet offices to see if anyone brought in an injured or stray cat.
- Call the pet registry microchip company to report your cat missing and make sure your contact information is up to date.
- Use Social Media. You can badmouth Facebook all you want, but the one thing it is truly great for is Lost Pet Groups. When I worked at the shelter, I would take photos of the recent intakes and post them in the Lost & Found Pets Staten Island Group. I'm sure there's a community page for your area. Make a post with some photos and your contact information. This is a valuable tool that can provide you with leads and sightings. Members on these pages will often post photos from their cellphones when spotting a potentially lost pet, so make sure to check often and scroll as far back as needed.
- You may need to resort to trickery by setting up a humane trap. You can buy a spring-trap that will activate when the trip plate inside is stepped on. Some rescues or shelters might loan you one, especially if you put down a deposit. With food inside as bait, the trap will spring shut when your cat goes to eat. When setting up a trap, place a blanket or tarp over the top to make it a more appealing hidey-hole and less obviously a trap. It's also a good idea to place something inside with your scent on it. Be advised, you can end up trapping the wrong cat or possibly wildlife, such as raccoons, opossums, skunks, or foxes. Use caution when releasing them.
- Watch out for scammers! When I was a manager and main rescue contact at LLAR, I received numerous scam texts as we were trying to track down a runaway dog. There are some real lowlifes out there who will try to take advantage and prey on you. Be wary of any text you get, especially if they ask you for money.
- Above all, never ever give up hope.

ARE ANY CATS HYPOALLERGENIC?

Unfortunately, there are no known breeds of hypoallergenic cats. It is mistakenly believed that cat allergies are caused by fur, when actually people are allergic to a cat's saliva. Even if a cat doesn't lick you, they groom themselves, and the allergy causing protein in their saliva will adhere to the royal coat and spread around the kingdom, floating in the air. I've had a few allergic, would-be servants interested in service to a Sphynx because they are a hairless breed, but cat dander isn't limited to fur—it's also the shedding of dead skin cells. While hairless cats will have less dander overall, depending on your sensitivity to cat dander, you could still find yourself suffering from allergy attacks.

CAN I GIVE MY CAT MILK?

You can, but you shouldn't. Even though Your Majesty may enjoy it, cows' milk and other dairy products are bad for cats. Most felions are actually lactose intolerant, and drinking milk can cause digestive issues, not to mention a messy and extra stinky sandcastle. Milk does not actually contain any nutritional value for Your Highness, so at best it's just empty calories. There are some alternative "cat milk" products you can buy in pet stores. However, they tend to be quite fattening. If you choose to use them, do so sparingly.

SPRAY-BOTTLES: TO SQUIRT OR NOT TO SQUIRT?

Monarchs can often seem incorrigible, so dealing with unwanted felion behaviors can be frustrating even for the most loyal servant. A few squirts of water from a spray bottle can seem like an easy solution to get your adventurous Overlord to stop scratching the furniture or surfing the counter tops, but it certainly isn't the recommended method to achieve the desired result. Squirt bottles are not effective as a long-term solution. Sure, Your Highness will sprint for cover after a spritzing, but what are they really learning from this action? They are still raking their nails against the couch fabric and getting paw prints on the appliances when you're not around, so it's clear that your royal did not associate getting squirted with the unwanted behavior; the only negative association they will have made is with you.

After a single offense you may find yourself facing felion sanctions. Servants with itchy trigger fingers will henceforth be decreed as The Sprayer-Betrayer: wetter of fur and reckless maniac. A summary judgment against you can result in losing the trust of your Overlord and all the benefits and privileges that go along with it. Because of your actions, Your Majesty is now stressed and fearful, making behavior modification even more challenging than before. And if you ever have the need to use spray-on medication, *fur-get about it.* You've already set yourself at a big disadvantage.

Consider this armament only as a *Break Glass in Case of Emergency* situation. Spray bottles should only be employed in an effort to throw cold water on a heated confrontation to prevent physical harm such as during an intense showdown, a Battle Royale, or when redirecting aggression away from a person or pet. Otherwise, I encourage you to retire the spray-bottle to its holster in favor of the solutions I have outlined in the *Breaking Bad* chapter. There are plenty of other tools at your disposal which will yield positive results and not put your relationship with the Overlord at risk. Whatever the problem, don't reach for the bottle. Stock up on your most valuable assets: patience and persistence. Rethink your strategy. Now try again.

WHY IS OVER-THE-COUNTER FLEA MEDICATION DANGEROUS TO MY CAT?

If Your Majesty's rule is strictly relegated to castle life, using a monthly flea and tick preventative isn't necessary, unless you also have a canine subject residing in the kingdom. If you have a dog or escort your felion on adventures to the Great Backyard, you should consult your vet and be prescribed the appropriate preventative for Your Majesty based on the age, weight, breed, and other factors.

One of the biggest issues is inadvertent misuse of over-the-counter preventatives. Many pet owners don't know what chemicals to avoid and/or use them incorrectly, disregarding the weight requirements. Some servants have made the mistake of putting a canine flea and tick medication or product on their Overlord, but these types of preventatives are not once size fits all. Cats are much more sensitive to chemicals than dogs, and some OTC flea medication contains ingredients that can be toxic to felions. Even secondary exposure can be harmful, so it's important that you separate the Overlord for 24 hours from any dogs that were treated with a topical product. Poisoning symptoms usually occur minutes to hours after exposure and can lead to serious health risks, including seizures and death. In short, get advice from your veterinarian and be sure to carefully read the box for directions.

When I was working at Animal Care Centers, two young teens brought in an adorable orange prince named Michigan. The young duo had bathed the kitten in some type of OTC anti-flea medication. The little tabby had been having seizures due to an overdose. My coworker and I shared a look of horror. While she completed the intake paperwork, I immediately got the kitten to medical and gave him a thorough washing to prevent any more of the flea medication from being absorbed into his skin. The veterinarian had already left for the day, and vet tech on duty wasn't sure if the kitten would survive since there is no known antidote. All he could do was offer supportive care. That night, at the end of my shift, I took Michigan home with me to care for him as best I could. Miraculously, the kitten survived through the night. In the morning, his eyes were open, but he was groggy and still had some slight tremors. Over the next few days, Michigan continued to recover at Hotel Mancuso, until he was healthy enough to be taken in by Feline Rescue of Staten Island.

I'M MOVING; CAN YOU TAKE MY CAT?

I've lost track of how many times I've heard someone say, "I'm moving, and I need to rehome my cat." Moving is stressful, and searching for apartments that accept pets can be frustrating, especially if you wait until the last minute. Often when I pressed the issue, I found that a majority of those looking to surrender their cat didn't really put much thought or effort into their search. They checked out a few websites, and that was the extent of their search. *It sucks I can't bring kitty, but I'll only have a ten-minute commute to work now. I'll have access to a pool, now, bro.* Yeah, well, I hope someone pees in it. Honestly, sometimes abandoning a cat is just an excuse for lack of convenience. But I have encountered felion servants who were truly remorseful about the possible loss. One way I can tell is by how receptive they are to measures that will help them keep their Overlords on the throne. Your Majesty doesn't want to be with me or any other servant of rescue; they want to stay with you. Unless you're a total soulless heathen, that should be what you want too. So, let's look at some ways to help you take your cat with you when moving.

Dip Into the Coffers – You've already done an online search for pet friendly rentals, so what else can you do? Be ready to plead your case, and be willing to reach into your pocket. No, I'm not suggesting a bribe . . . unless you think—no, wait, I didn't just say that. Seriously, no bribes, but you can offer to pay an increased deposit or a monthly pet fee. Landlords and management companies are concerned about spending money to fix anything your cat may damage or destroy. Offering to pay a little extra may go a long way toward helping change their mind. You can also offer to get your own renter's insurance policy with a pet clause that would cover any property damages. You can try any one of these options, or sweeten the deal and offer all three. If you're able to make a deal, get it in writing.

Lobbying For Your Cat – Make sure your cat is spay/neutered (fixed cats are less prone to urine marking), get them updated on all vaccinations, and be sure to provide the landlord with a copy of those records. Perhaps you can even utilize your current vet as a reference. If you're a loyal servant, I'm sure you have a phone full of cute kitty photos and videos. Do not try to show them all to the landlord, but it can't hurt to strategically show off one or two particularly cute ones—with a clean, scratch-mark free background! This may sound like a no brainer, but avoid showing a potential landlord any videos of the Overlord being wild and adventurous. Sure, we may think their misadventures are amusing, but for those not indoctrinated into Cat World, seeing a cat dangling from the curtains will only summon visions of dollar signs from potential damage. I'm not sure if a letter from your recent landlord would help, but it couldn't hurt. If it's on official letterhead with a phone number to call for a reference, even better. Keep in mind, though, that it's easier to establish a personal connection and persuade a private landlord as opposed to a management company.

Legal Loopholes – As a rescue adoption manager, I've had quite a few adopters diagnosed with depression, PTSD, and anxiety looking to adopt a dog or cat as an Emotional Support Animal. Landlords and management companies must legally provide their tenants with a reasonable accommodation, even if the building has a no pet policy, as Emotional Support Animals are protected under the Fair Housing Act of 1968. However, you can't just say your cat is your emotional support animal; you need to provide some proof, like a verifiable letter of prescription from a psychologist or psychiatrist. Remember, your ESA letter needs to be from a licensed mental health professional, not a primary doctor or medical physician.

Unfortunately, sometimes moving is sudden and unavoidable, compounding stress, especially if you're potentially facing eviction, or at least your cat is. That doesn't mean you should simply give up hope. You can consult an attorney and have them review your lease. Not everyone has the money to spare on legal fees, though. Fortunately, there are other, less expensive options to consider.

Community Resources – When I worked at Staten Island Animal Care Centers, we had resources to assist people with keeping their pets—not just when moving, but due to a wide range of other situations as well. Check with your local shelter to see if they offer similar resources or know of free or low cost nonprofits you can contact for legal assistance. You can also reach out to rescues for assistance, they may have some recommendations. At the very least, a shelter or rescue may be able to direct you to some sites with pet friendly rentals. Also consider looking online for free/affordable legal services, assistance from tenant advocacy organizations.

WHAT IF I CAN'T KEEP MY CAT?

Ideally, you should make every effort to keep Your Majesty on the throne. We owe them that much. We made a commitment to them the day our home became Kitty Castle. To the Overlord, this oath is more sacred than a marriage vow. They have put all of their love and trust in us, which is no small thing for a felion. However, realistically, I know there are times when surrendering your cat is the only option. If you find yourself in that unfortunate position—you've sincerely considered every other possible option to no avail—then the only thing I can do is offer some guidance on how to minimize the stress of this transition on you and, more importantly, your cat.

A Matter of Time – Allow enough time to find your Overlord a new castle. Be aware that this can take several months, depending on circumstances. The longer you wait, the more stressful the situation is likely to become. Some people tend to procrastinate, not wanting to think about the prospect of giving away their friend. For others, they may be focusing on different issues, assuming that someone will take their cat on short notice. Unfortunately, last minute placement isn't always a possibility. Then what? I strongly suggest you don't wait to find out. Starting your search early will give you a much better chance of success. The situation is hard enough as it is; no reason to make your task more difficult.

Prior Vetting – Be ready to provide veterinary records to a rescue for an intake review. Ensure that your cat is current on all vaccinations. Rescues sincerely appreciate this, and it shows that you care. Offer to take Your Majesty to the vet for a wellness exam prior to surrender. The less work and money a rescue needs to put into a cat, the more likely they will be to accept them. Unfortunately, for many rescues, funds run low when donations dry up, and space in open foster homes is limited—this is how we wound up with twenty cats. A clean bill of health goes a long way. If there are any health concerns or behavior issues with your cat, be honest about them. Most rescues are willing to help a cat with issues, and being upfront about those issues will help give the organization a jumpstart on how any such problems can be addressed.

The Royal Biographer – Prepare a biography of Your Majesty. Having spent time in their service, no one knows your cat better than you. Be sure to include:

- Name, age, sex, and weight.
- Medical history/vaccination status
- The royal menu
- Preference of litter/sandcastles

- The royal activity schedule
- Personality
- Their best quality
- Quirks
- Likes and dislikes

The Overlord's bio should include high quality photos and videos. Pictures are worth a thousand words and videos are worth 29.97 frames per second. You don't need to be Steven Spielberg or Ansel Adams. Keep in mind, however, that a grainy photo of your cat sitting on a pile of dirty socks is not going to spark a whole lot of interest. Just take a few well-lit video snippets and photos of your cat being cute or funny.

Once complete, all the elements of Your Majesty's biography can be provided to the rescue and shared with their new servant. The information provided will be valuable to the recipients and your former felion ruler.

Please Be Courteous – Having been on the other end of these phone calls and emails, I know I am less inclined to go the extra mile for someone that is rude or entitled. It's not my fault you waited until a week before moving to contact me. The truth of the matter is you're not doing the rescue a favor. Don't conflate surrendering a pet with making a charitable donation. Chances are the volunteer on the other end of the phone is tired and stressed; you're likely the fifth person that week reaching out for assistance. Rescuers need your patience and cooperation. This isn't returning a TV to Best Buy. The customer isn't always right, the cat is. *Have you learned nothing from this book?*

Be Proactive – Offer to foster your cat until an adopter is found. Rescues, which are perpetually full, need you to be in partnership with them in finding a new home. Sadly, there is never a shortage of cats or kittens in need. Foster space is limited, and there could be a long wait before a home opens up. Be proactive during that time. Promote and advocate for adoption. Attend adoption events, if possible. If not, can you find a foster home? Is there a family member, or a friend that would foster your cat and be willing to cooperate with the rescue on finding permanent placement?

Quid Pro Quo – Offer to make a donation to the rescue. This is by no means a requirement, but it is a nice gesture of appreciation. Rescues rely on donations to operate and save more lives. If you need a more self-serving reason to offer a donation, rescues are charitable organizations, so your donation may be tax deductible.

Screening Process – Avoid using a "Free to Good Home" ad. If you're attempting to find Your Highness a new castle on your own, charge a nominal rehoming fee. Use due diligence interviewing applicants to weed out those not fit to serve. Not only can you encounter people with bad intentions, but people who are . . . well, to put in nicely . . . clueless, irresponsible heathens.

Care Package – Being dethroned is never easy for a royal. Send your felion off with their favorite things to help ease the transition to a new castle. Make a care package of food, thrones, toys. The Overlord will find comfort with these familiar items and scents while adapting to their new kingdom.

Gimme Shelter – Conduct some research on the local animal shelters in your area. While a shelter certainly isn't the optimal choice for your felion, it is better than the alternative. Don't abandon the Overlord, leaving them alone in the castle with no servant to care for them. Nor should your felion be tossed outdoors in the wilderness of the Great Backyard. Life on the outside is difficult. Your pampered felion is ill prepared for survival on the street. All they can expect is a short, hard life of terror before they die.

Servants who neglect or abandon their cat may be charged with a crime. The PACT Act makes animal cruelty a federal felony, punishable by up to seven years in prison and expensive fines.

As an addendum to this question, let's talk for a moment about animal shelters. In my opinion, shelters are a necessary evil. I'm aware that some fellow rescuers out there may disagree with me on this issue. However, I think it's a worthy discussion to have. By evil, I'm not implying that shelters are inherently bad places, but they are places where bad things happen to good animals. Often shelters can seem cold and emotionless, but math has no compassion, not even for adorable cats. Numbers are brutally honest. Math can't be reasoned with. It can't be bargained with. It doesn't feel pity or remorse or fear. And it absolutely will not stop . . . ever, until you are dead! Okay, so maybe I allowed my disdain of math to cloud my thinking and just quoted *The Terminator*, but for the most part, the statement holds true.

Everything costs money, and even the scroogiest Scrooge in scroogedom can stretch a dollar only so far. Look at my state as an example. Animal Care Centers of New York is an independent non-profit organization contracted by the city and overseen by the Department of Health and Mental Hygiene. Spread throughout the five boroughs of New York City, these facilities provide shelter to over 20,000 animals a year. According to its audited financial statements for fiscal year 2018, Animal Care Centers had total revenue of $21.5 million, of which $14.8 million was received from the City. That funding totaled less than $1.75 per city resident per year. ACC managed to pull in over $6 million in grants and donations that same year, with their total expenditures just over $21.1 million, $18.5 million of which was spent on the healthcare and welfare of the animals.[22]

By comparison, many smaller shelters may be operated strictly on donations and grants, with a much smaller amount from adoption and reclamation. Others may only receive local government funding to provide the bare minimum of care. Annual budgets are intended to maximize the number of animals a shelter can handle throughout the year. Unfortunately, for pets with extensive injuries or severe medical conditions, their lives are weighed against those numbers. The cost of medical services may be beyond the shelter to provide. To suppress outbreaks of disease, pets with contagious but treatable infections like ringworm or URI are euthanized. It's more cost effective to euthanize one or two animals than to treat dozens. Additionally, perfectly healthy cats are put at risk for euthanasia when shelters become overcrowded.

The shelter system is by no means perfect. Far from it. All across the United States are municipal shelters with terrible conditions. Underfunded. Understaffed. Under review. With so many pets packed into a confined space, shelters are often germ factories. I'm not about to bring up any gruesome specifics; we've all heard or read horror stories. Animal shelters should absolutely be held accountable for their shortcomings, but likewise the public needs to do a better job of supporting them and, in turn, the cats, dogs and other animals unfortunate enough to occupy the cages. Donate, volunteer, adopt, advocate, and organize. That is how we can effect change and give homeless pets the assistance they need and the outcomes they deserve.

DEALING WITH THE LOSS OF A BELOVED CAT?

We all wish our Overlord could rule forever. Although all cat lives are too short, tragically, some reigns are briefer than others. Cathy and I have had our heart broken too many times over the years. In fact, about a month into writing this guide, Hiro, our gentle old man, passed away at the age of eighteen. Given his advanced age and medical condition, his passing was not surprising, but that didn't make it any less heartrending. We stayed with him until the very end, showering him with love and kisses until he transitioned across Rainbow Bridge and became one with the Celestial Meow. Of course, we wish our time with Hiro could have been longer, but we gave him a lifetime worth of love in four years, and he returned it in kind every day. It may sound cliché, but pets truly do leave paw prints on your heart. My heart has been shattered into a million pieces, yet each time it has been made whole again by hairballs and head-boops. Maybe some would call that crazy glue? For me, I believe a cat's true love is a priceless treasure, and in that respect, Cathy and I have been emotional billionaires.

On quite a few occasions I've encountered someone that told me their cat had passed away, but they could never serve another. I understand the pain of grieving, yet I can't imagine why anyone would deny themselves the love and joy of being owned by a felion. Perhaps those people felt as if loving another kitty would be a betrayal of their dearly departed. In contrast, I've found that continuing to share your life with other cats is a great way to honor their memory.

I'm not advocating that you adopt another cat immediately or even any time soon. Everyone grieves differently. Coping with the loss of a furry family member is never easy. But I would suggest that you drain the moat around your heart and always keep the door to the castle open. Just in case. You'll be happy you did. The love bestowed upon you by Your Majesty is a wondrous gift that will carry on for as long as you share it with another felion. What better way to serve the Celestial Meow than to save another life?

I know solace can be hard to find when deep in the depths of grief, but a fellow rescuer and felion prophet shared these beautiful words of comfort with me and graciously allowed me to share them with you. May a million points of light smile down upon you. No matter what you believe, in your darkest hour, love reigns supreme.

A Million Points Of Light

In the dark of early morning
The sky's misty and it glows
You ache in your heart for me
You feel me close, I know
I wish I could have changed it
But it wasn't to be
I love you more than I can say
Don't regret for me
I'm made of a million points of light
I shine for you in moonless night
I let my soul run wild and free
No, my love, don't cry for me
We are immortal, it was just my time
A million points of light
Are now all mine
I pace through the yard, roll in grass
My kin sense me as I pass
We play for a while and I breathe
Please know I didn't want to leave
I'm here now, I'll come again
For you be comforted until then
I'm a million points of light
I run faster than I thought I might
I can ride the wind and see

All you do—I'm still me
I crossed over to watch over you
I always will
It's what I do.
Foggy night now mornings near
I purr my wisdom in your ear
As my kin take care of you
Make you smile when you're blue
Look for the magic in all that's free
For it's all a part of me
In a million points of light
Of all the mist that shields the night
I didn't leave you, this I swear
When you need me I'll be there
I move just beyond what you see
But you and I—we'll always be.

—ORANGE RUFFY, WARRIOR POET
AND MOM DEB HOFFMANN KNOWLES

Artwork by Kimbra Eberly.

Endnotes

1. Switek, Brian. "The Making of the Cat." *PBS*, November 2, 2016. https://www.pbs.org/wnet/nature/blog/the-making-of-a-cat/.
2. Mark, Joshua J. *"Herodotus On Cats In Egypt."* World History Encyclopedia 2022. https://www.worldhistory.org/article/88/herodotus-on-cats-in-egypt/.
3. Powers, Joy. *"The Feline States of America: How Cats Helped Shape The US"* July 25, 2019. https://www.wuwm.com/podcast/lake-effect-segments/2019-07-25/the-feline-states-of-america-how-cats-helped-shape-the-us.
4. Hutton, Robert. *"The Surprising Story of the Only Cat Ever to Win the Highest Honor for Animal Military Galantry."* Time, September 28, 2018. https://time.com/5396568/simon-cat-war-medal/.
5. Weitering, Hanneke. "First Cat in Space to Receive a Proper Memorial" Space.com, November 8, 2017. https://www.space.com/38702-felicette-first-space-cat-memorial-kickstarter.html.
6. Best Friends Animal Society. *"Lifesaving by the Numbers: Animal Welfare Statistics"* Accessed December 3, 2022. https://bestfriends.org/pet-care-resources/lifesaving-numbers-animal-welfare-statistics.
7. Qureshi, Adnan, Muhammad Zeeshan Memon, Gabriela Vazquez, M Fareed K Suri. *"Cat ownership and the Risk of Fatal Cardiovascular Diseases. Results from the Second National Health and Nutrition Examination Study Mortality Follow-up Study."* National Library of Medicine, PubMed Central, 2009. https://pmc.ncbi.nlm.nih.gov/articles/PMC3317329/.

8. Gee, Nancy R, Megan K Mueller, Angela L Curl. "Human-Animal Interaction and Older Adults: An Overview." National Library of Medicine, PubMed Central, August 21, 2017. https://www.ncbi. nlm.nih.gov/pmc/articles/PMC5573436/.

9. Gunter, Brianna. *"The Fifteen Most Popular Cat Breeds (by Ownership) in 2024."* Trupanion, 2024. https://www.trupanion.com/pet-blog/article/most-popular-cat-breeds.

10. inch, Kevin. *"Rescue Cat Merlin Sets New Record for Loudest Purr."* Guiness World Records, 2015. https://www.guinessworldrecords. com/news/2015/5/rescue-cat-merlin-sets-new-world-record-for-loudest-purr378630.

11. Guiness World Records. *"Most Toes on a Cat."* 2002. https://www. guinnessworldrecords.com/world-records/most-toes-on-a-cat.

12. Donnelly, Christina. *"7 Amazing Facts About Polydactyl Cats."* Spruce Pets, 2023. https://www.thesprucepets.com/polydactyl -cats-4175908.

13. ASPCA. *"Plants Toxic To Cats."* Toxic and Non-Toxic Plant List: Cats. Pet Care/Animal Poison Control. Accessed August 15, 2023. https://www.aspca.org/pet-care/animal-poison-control/cats-plant-list.

14. ASPCA. *"Plants Non-Toxic To Cats."* Toxic and Non-Toxic Plant List: Cats. Pet Care/Animal Poison Control. Accessed August 15, 2023. https://www.aspca.org/pet-care/animal-poison-control/cats-plant-list.

15. ASPCA. *"People Foods Pets Should Never Eat."* Accessed September 28, 2023. https://www.aspcapro.org/resource/people-foods-pets-should-never-eat.

16. Center for Disease Control. *"About Toxoplasmosis."* 2017. https:// www.cdc.gov/parasites/toxoplasmosis/resources/printresources/ catowners_2017.pdf.

17. Center for Disease Control. *"Symptoms of Toxoplasmosis."* January 19, 2024. https://www.cdc.gov/toxoplasmosis/symptoms/index. html.

18. Hickman, Gayle. *"How Does a Cat Brain Compare With a Human Brain? Discover the Fascinating Differences."* Petful, 2024. https:// www.petful.com/behaviors/cat-brain-compared-human-brain/.

19. Lawler, D. F. *"Neonatal and pediatric care of the puppy and kitten."* Theriogenology, vol. 70, no.3, 2008, 384–92.

20. Morici, Samantha DVM, Morrison. Barti J. DVM. *"Diabetes in Cats: Signs, Treatment and Prognosis."* PetMD, 2024. https://www. petmd.com/cat/conditions/endocrine/c_ct_diabetes_mellitus.

21. M., Heather. *"How Much Does It Cost to Have a Cat?"* ASPCA, Pet Parent Resources. https://www.aspcapetinsurance.com/resources/ cat-ownership-cost/.

22. Lander, Brad. *"Report to the Mayor and City Council on City Comp-troller Audit Operations Fiscal Year 2021."* March 1, 2022. https:// comptroller.nyc.gov/wp-content/uploads/documents/Audit Annual2021.pdf.

About the Author

WHAT STARTED AS A tribute to honor the memory of his beloved Sunny Girl turned into a consuming passion to help rescue shelter pets, especially cats. Christopher's dedication to saving cats propelled him to Assistant Director of Staten Island Hope Animal Rescue, and from 2019-2021, he was the Foster/Adoption Manager for the New York branch of Louie's Legacy, one of the country's largest foster-based animal rescues. Chris and his wife, Catherine, have fostered more than 300 cats and kittens, including those with special needs and bottle-kittens. Having taken traumatized cats into his home, Christopher has gained valuable experience helping them overcome fears and behavioral challenges. Aside from his work in animal rescue, Christopher is an award-winning screenwriter. Most recently, his screenplay *"America's Most Haunted Spooky Ghost-Hunting Adventures In The Paranormal"* was awarded Best Short Script at the 2022 Boston Horror Comedy Film Festival. Some of his other short scripts were produced by Lake Films and have won awards at festivals around the country.